THE PROPER EDGE
OF THE SKY

THE PROPER EDGE OF THE SKY

The High Plateau Country of Utah

Edward A. Geary

University of Utah Press

Salt Lake City

∞ This symbol indicates books printed on paper that meets the minimum requirements of American National Standard for Information Services—Permanence of Paper for Printed Library Materials, ANSI A39.
38–1984.

Library of Congress Cataloging-in-Publication Data

Geary, Edward A., 1937–
    The proper edge of the sky : the high plateau country of Utah /
Edward A. Geary.
        p.   cm.
    Includes bibliographical references and index.
    ISBN 0-87480-409-4
    1. Plateaus—Utah.   2. Utah—Description and travel—1981–
3. Utah—History, Local.   4. Natural history—Utah.   I. Title.
F826.G33   1992
979.2—dc20   92–24700
                                                      CIP

Contents

Introduction..1

1. A Strange and Beautiful Country...................................5

2. South of Nebo...28

3. The Mormon Corridor...39

4. The Inner Valleys 57

5. Stop and Tell Me, Red Man 84

6. Streams Ever Copious...105

7. A Wife from Sanpete County.......................................123

8. Valley at the World's End 136

9. The Backhouses of Escalante.......................................150

10. A Woman and Some Cows..177

11. The Camps..203

12. For the Strength of the Hills 245

Notes..257

Index...271

There are other places
   Which also are the world's end . . .

   —T. S. Eliot, "Little Gidding"

INTRODUCTION

T he old Kanab cowboy Rowland W. Rider, in his account of the cattle brands used on the Arizona Strip, tells how stockmen came to be identified with their brands, addressed by their associates as "Bar DR," or "Umbrella," or the like. Samuel O. Bennion's brand was **SOB**, while E. D. Wooley, who was president of the Kanab LDS stake, had as his brand **DE** and was known as "Uncle De." The Pratt brothers of Fredonia used a figure **2** lying down horizontally followed by **PP**, or in other words "Two Lazy Two P." "But," Rider says, "whenever we addressed either one of the Pratt brothers, who were big husky men, we just called them Two Lazy, we didn't put in the other two letters." Rider also describes how one brand could be changed to another by the addition of a few strokes. For example, the brand of the Winsor Cattle Company, headquartered at Pipe Spring and owned by the LDS Church, was the letter **W**. But when the federal government threatened to confiscate church property during the legal battle over polygamy, the Winsor livestock were transferred to the ownership of John W. Young. By the simple addition of a curved stroke to the first downward point of the **W** and a straight line to the second downward point, the brand was altered to **W** .[1]

These images of people taking on the identity of the things they possess, or of identities being altered by the superimposition of new elements, provide suggestive metaphors for the ways we shape and are shaped by the landscapes we inhabit. Printers sometimes prepare copy for multicolor printing by putting the matter that is to be printed in each color on a transparent overlay sheet then superimposing all of the overlays on a key plate. Military tacticians place overlays on a map in order to provide information that does not exist in the original. These, too, are metaphors for the ways in which the meanings of places are built up from the impressions of observers accumulated over time.

The idea of the landscape as a text has long been part of the American consciousness. To the seventeenth-century Puritan imagination it was sacred, revealing God's designs to the elect. To nineteenth-century travelers in the West it was often a text in Manifest Destiny, or in natural law, or in the aesthetics of the picturesque and the sublime. To one whose sense of things derives from a particular place, the shape of a particular horizon that constitutes the only proper edge of the sky, it may be highly personal, a diary, even a confession. But all texts require interpretation and tend toward ambiguity when closely scrutinized. Moreover, they always reflect the assumptions the reader brings to them. Thus, the process of reading a landscape is in large part an experiment in self-discovery, and the process of writing an exercise in self-revelation.

The High Plateaus of Utah are a group of elevated tablelands that form the boundary between the Colorado Plateau and the Great Basin. They are the water-bearers of central and southern Utah, milking the Pacific westerlies and hoarding winter snows on their broad tops for gradual release during the growing season, thereby making agriculture and community life possible in the arid valleys below. The timber and grazing lands and minerals of the High Plateaus have been the foundations of essential industries, and their great faults and monoclines, their thousands of feet of exposed sedimentary deposits, their conglomerates and tufas, their trachytes and rhyolites and andesites and basalts make them a virtual textbook of geology. They are islands of cool refreshment when the valleys wilt under the summer sun, and seasonal refuges for fishers, hunters, boaters, hikers, skiers, snowmobilers. Much of southern Utah's famous "scenery" is associated with the High Plateaus. The bright towers and canyons of Zion National Park are carved from the southern terraces of the Markagunt Plateau. Cedar Breaks and Bryce Canyon are amphitheatres eroded into the pink cliffs of the Markagunt and the Paunsagunt. Capitol Reef National Park takes its name from the Waterpocket Fold, which emerges from beneath the Thousand Lake Plateau and runs south and east along the base of the Aquarius. Despite the loftiness of their summits, the dominant visual character of the High Plateaus is horizontal rather than vertical, an effect of the level strata and the long mural walls that lead the gaze into the blue distance. It is a country of long views, a spacious country, yet the horizon, however distant, is always clearly defined, the ridgelines providing a proper edge to the immensity of the sky.

The geological record in the High Plateaus region extends all the way back to the Precambrian. The archaeological record includes the fascinating rock art of the Anasazi and Fremont cultures. The literary and historical record covers little more than a century and a half, but over

2

that period this distinctive landscape has shaped a cultural region unlike any other in the West. The pages that follow are neither guidebook, nor travel narrative, nor natural history, nor social history, nor literary history, nor personal essay, though they incorporate elements from all of these genres. They represent an effort to see and know a richly varied land through my own experience and the overlaid impressions of others who have dwelt in or visited or written of the High Plateau region.

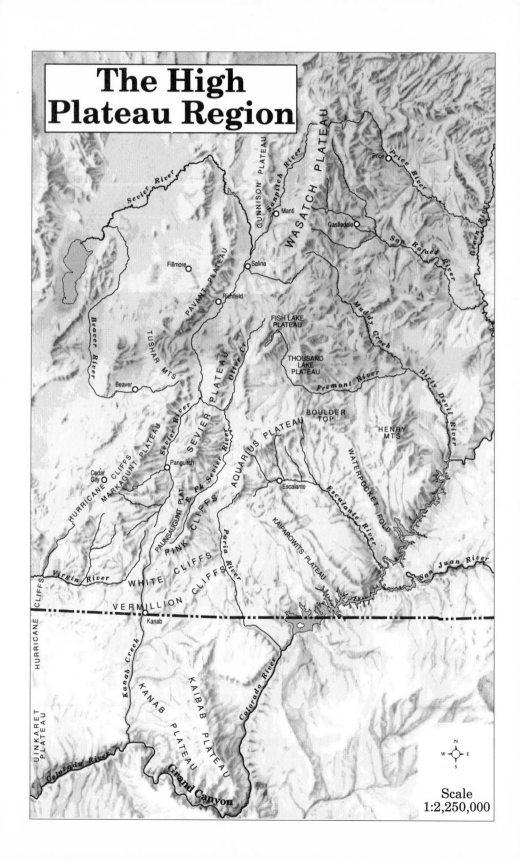

The High Plateau Region

Scale
1:2,250,000

1

A STRANGE AND
BEAUTIFUL COUNTRY

On August 8, 1988, a backhoe operator working on the reconstruction of a reservoir dam at the nine-thousand-foot level on
the Wasatch Plateau in south-central Utah uncovered some
large bones, much too big for an elk or a cow. Further probing brought
to light a massive skull and long, curving tusks—clearly the remains of
no creature that currently inhabits the region.

John Nielson, the contractor on the project for the Huntington-
Cleveland Irrigation Company, has admitted to experiencing mixed
feelings when he first viewed the elephant-like skeleton. Construction
on public land requires extensive and time-consuming reviews and is
subject to numerous regulations that tend to be regarded as bureaucratic
obstructionism by people who live under the dominion of the two major
federal landlords in the West, the Forest Service and the Bureau of Land
Management. At this elevation the snow cover typically lasts into June
and can return before October. By August, the brief construction season
is nearing an end, and Nielson was working on a tight timetable. Also a
farmer and stockholder in the irrigation company, he was well aware of
the vital importance of water storage to the arid region. A work stop-
page of even a few days might prevent completion of the dam in time
for the 1989 irrigation season. Notwithstanding these concerns, Nielson
followed prescribed procedures and dispatched a message to the headquarters of the Manti-LaSal National Forest in Price. Forest officials in
turn notified Utah State Paleontologist David Gillette, and construction work was halted for a preliminary investigation.

It soon became apparent that this was a find of unusual importance.
The skeleton was almost complete and so well preserved that the bones
still retained some flexibility. Most significantly, however, the creature
was not a mastodon, as had first been assumed since mastodon remains
have been found in the area, but a Columbian mammoth, a species not
previously thought to have lived at high elevations.

From a contractor's perspective the antiquities laws and Forest Ser-

Huntington Reservoir, Wasatch Plateau. Photo by the author.

vice regulations seem strongly tilted in favor of environmental and scientific values, but the view is quite different to those whose job it is to protect such interests. The regulations allowed Gillette only a few days to conduct an exploratory dig and recover the bones. Quickly assembling a team of professionals and amateurs—including volunteers from the Castle Valley chapter of the State Archaeological Society, who had previously worked with state officials on digs in the area—Gillette removed the mammoth skeleton, together with soil samples from various levels of the pit.

Word of the discovery spread rapidly among the towns that lie at the base of the plateau, and the residents, who have a proprietary regard for "their" mountains, flocked to the site, only a few yards from State Highway 31. Reports in the Salt Lake City press brought visitors from other regions as well, and considerable efforts were required to handle the spectators.

Under these circumstances it was nearly impossible to conduct as thorough a study as might be desired, and subsequent events indicated that the recovery project was indeed compromised in some degree. Several days after construction work resumed on the dam, a local resident turned over to authorities part of the skull of an extinct short-faced bear that had reportedly been found in the same pit as the mammoth. After a rainstorm in early September, a watchman at the construction site picked up a three-inch projectile point in the area where the mammoth skeleton had been found. Concerned at the possibility of further delays, he kept his find secret for several weeks. Then he brought it to Dr. J. Eldon Dorman, a Price physician and antiquities buff who served as curator of archaeology at the College of Eastern Utah Prehistoric Museum. Dorman turned the projectile point over to Utah State Archaeologist David Madsen, who subjected it to various tests and analyses, leading to an identification as a possible "Pryor stemmed point" dating to approximately 9,500 years ago.[1] Still, the available evidence was too sketchy to determine whether humans or predatory animals had anything to do with the mammoth's demise.

Scarcely was the skeleton—now dubbed the "Huntington Mammoth" by virtue of its discovery at Huntington Reservoir—out of the ground before a competition arose among nearby towns to be selected as a permanent repository for the treasure. Because the remains were discovered on federal land, the Smithsonian Institution has official custody, but it is customary to permit the display of such specimens in museums near the site where they were found. The Huntington Reservoir is located in Sanpete County, and the nearest town is Fairview, which has converted an old school building into a museum. However, the waters impounded by the reservoir flow into Emery County, which was preparing to begin construction of the Museum of the San Rafael in Castle Dale. The headquarters of the Manti-LaSal National Forest are in Price, where the College of Eastern Utah operates a museum specializing in prehistoric items. All of these institutions immediately claimed the skeleton. After some consideration, the College of Eastern Utah Museum was selected on the condition that it obtain full accreditation within a specified period. In the meantime, the skeleton was housed at the State Museum of Natural History, on the campus of the University of Utah in Salt Lake City, where casts are being prepared to supply replicas to other interested museums. In fact, the skeleton is far too fragile ever to be placed on public exhibition, and the museum that gains eventual custody will be obligated to provide costly atmospheric-controlled storage for the actual bones while displaying only a replica.

The unusual completeness and state of preservation of the skeleton have made possible some studies of considerable interest. The mammoth was a male, about sixty years old, and in poor physical condition. Gillette secured the assistance of Robert H. Horne, a Salt Lake City orthopedic surgeon, in making a series of X-rays and CAT-scan photographs of the bones. These show the animal to have been severely crippled by arthritis. Routine movement must have been extremely painful, especially with the added burden of a pair of ten-foot tusks. There are also indications of malnutrition, which may reflect a lack of suitable feed or simply an inability to forage effectively.[2] In its weakened state and with restricted mobility, the creature would have been easy prey—or an inviting target for hunters. Or the mammoth, old, weak, and in great pain, may have simply blundered into a bog and lacked the strength to extricate itself.

What was a Columbian mammoth doing at such a high elevation? Mastodons, the other elephant-like species that inhabited North America during the most recent ice age, were browsing animals, eating shrubs and willows. The deep winter snows of the high plateau were not a threat to their survival. But mammoths, more closely related to modern Asian elephants, were grazers, creatures of the grasslands, and it has been assumed that they were restricted to lower elevations. It is conceivable, in light of the incontrovertible presence of at least one member of the species above nine thousand feet, they might have migrated with the seasons, feeding in the mountain meadows during the summer and moving to the lower valleys in the winter. Gillette maintains, however, that mammoths were not physically suited for travel up and down steep mountain slopes.[3]

Carbon-dating techniques applied to materials excavated from the pit indicate that they are between 12,500 and 9,500 years old. The later date is especially intriguing to Gillette, since it would mean that this mammoth lived two thousand years after the species is commonly thought to have become extinct. He thinks it possible that a small population could have found an ecological niche in the central Utah mountains, isolated from others of their kind, and thereby have survived the extinction of the remainder of the species. Gillette says, "We could be looking at fifteen hundred to two thousand years of survival in a refuge habitat. That could be significant."[4]

There is something fitting about such a discovery in such a location. The High Plateaus of Utah are full of wonders. Wallace Stegner once characterized them as "those remarkable mountains that are not mountains at all but greatly elevated rolling plains."[5] Climatological and ecological islands, the High Plateaus continue to serve as refuge habitats for many species of plants and animals, and the wanderer among their lush groves and secret canyons would scarcely be surprised to come upon a still-living mammoth grazing in a water meadow, happily unaware of its own extinction.

Horseshoe Mountain, Wasatch Plateau. Photo by the author.

The ascent leads us among rugged hills, almost mountainous in size, strewn with black bowlders, along precipitous ledges, and by the sides of canons. Long detours must be made to escape the chasms and to avoid the taluses of fallen blocks; deep ravines must be crossed, projecting crags doubled, and lofty battlements scaled before the summit is reached. When the broad platform is gained the story of "Jack and the beanstalk," the finding of a strange and beautiful country somewhere up in the region of the clouds, no longer seems incongruous. Yesterday we were toiling over a burning soil, where nothing grows save the ashy-colored sage, the prickly pear, and a few cedars that writhe and contort their stunted limbs under a scorching sun. To-day we are among forests of rare beauty and luxuriance; the air is moist and cool, the grasses are green and rank, and hosts of flowers deck the turf like the hues of a Persian carpet. The forest opens in wide parks and winding avenues, which the fancy can easily people with fays and woodland nymphs. On either side the sylvan walls look impenetrable, and for the most part so thickly is the ground strewn with fallen trees, that any attempt to enter is as serious a matter as forcing an *abattis*. The tall spruces (*Abies subalpina*) stand so close together, that even if the dead-wood were not there a passage would be almost impossible. Their slender trunks, as

9

Christian Otteson farm and Gentry Mountain, Wasatch Plateau, 1983. Photo by the author.

straight as lances, reach upward a hundred feet, ending in barbed points, and the contours of the foliage are as symmetrical and uniform as if every tree had been clipped for a lordly garden.[6]

Clarence E. Dutton, the author of the first detailed study of the High Plateau region, here describes his encounter with the Aquarius Plateau; the passage serves, however, to characterize the High Plateaus as a group in relation to their surroundings. To ascend any of these massive tablelands from the semi-arid valleys is to enter a world strange, beautiful, and indispensable. The Wasatch Plateau, home of the Huntington Mammoth, is the northernmost member of the group, beginning at the same forty-degree latitude and about fifteen miles east of Mount Nebo, the southernmost peak of the Wasatch Range. It is the largest of the High Plateaus in surface area, extending almost eighty miles from north to south and varying in width from fifteen to twenty-five miles. The west front is formed by a monoclinal fold rising at a steep angle to an almost continuous summit ridge that runs the entire length of the table. This lofty upwarp presents an effective barrier to the storm-laden westerlies and, combined with a large high-elevation surface area, makes the plateau a good waterbearer. The Wasatch Plateau's east front is an erosional wall of sheer cliffs and steep talus slopes, one of the

Manti before the turn of the century. G. E. Anderson photo, courtesy Utah State Historical Society.

great escarpments in the plateau country. There are numerous north-south trending faults on the plateau, several of which have formed grabens, or rift valleys. The largest of these are Pleasant Valley in the north, Joe's Valley near the middle of the plateau, and Gunnison Valley in the south.

The lower northern portion of the plateau drains into Thistle and Soldier creeks, tributaries of the Spanish Fork in the Utah Lake drainage system. From the skyline ridge, numerous steep canyons run westward to feed the Sanpitch River, a tributary of the Sevier. East of the ridge, in some places only a few yards wide, the land typically drops off abruptly for several hundred feet into short canyons, some of them glacial cirques, that drain into the longitudinal rift valleys. Deep canyons then carry the accumulated streamflow from these valleys through the eastern ridge of the plateau toward an eventual union with the Green and Colorado rivers. Gunnison Valley forms the headwaters of Salina Creek, which flows into the Sevier. Fully three-quarters of the plateau's surface drains to the east. The west slope receives the heaviest precipitation, but much of the snow is drifted by the prevailing winds to sheltered hollows east of the skyline ridge, where snowbanks can accumulate to a depth of fifty feet or more.

As surely as a canyon from the Wasatch Plateau opens upon the valley floor, so surely will one find a farm, a village, or a town. Each of these small islands of civilization is nourished, as by a silver umbilical thread, from snows that accumulate in the nearby highlands.[7]

European settlement in the region of the High Plateaus began in the fall of 1849 when Brigham Young sent a party of colonists to the site of Manti, on an alluvial fan at the western base of the Wasatch Plateau. From this mother colony, settlers ventured forth to occupy the irrigable land on other creeks in Sanpete Valley. Ephraim, Spring City, and Mount Pleasant were settled during the first three years, abandoned more than once during the Indian troubles of the 1850s, and firmly reestablished by the end of the decade.[8] Soon there were villages up and down the valley: Fairview on Cottonwood Creek, Moroni on the benchlands above the Sanpitch River, Gunnison near the confluence of the Sanpitch and the Sevier, and Fountain Green, Wales, and Fayette at the base of the Gunnison Plateau on the west side of the valley.

These early settlers depended on the Wasatch Plateau for irrigation water, timber to build their homes, and fish and game to supplement their pioneer diets. During the first two decades, however, the human impact on the mountain landscape was relatively light. Accessible stands of Douglas fir (better known locally as "red pine") were stripped from the lower slopes, but livestock grazing was largely confined to the valley floor and the foothills.

Mormon settlement policy in the nineteenth century had two main thrusts. One was to build an egalitarian society by a cooperative development of land and water to enable as many families as possible to subsist upon the produce of their own farms. The other was to generate the human and material resources to occupy new lands, thereby extending control over a larger area. Both of these processes were apparent in Sanpete Valley. Arable land surrounding the villages was initially divided into small individual "inheritances," some less than five acres in size. Albert Antrei recounts the case of James Van Nostrand, who was awarded twenty acres of land upon being called to settle Moroni in 1859. With the arrival of new colonists, Van Nostrand's "inheritance" was split, then split again and again, leaving him with only two and a half acres.[9]

This attempt to stretch land and water resources further and further had lasting effects. An 1890 U.S. Department of Agriculture report noted that because of repeated subdivision of water rights in Sanpete County, "The water supply is scanty even for one-half the land." As a result, the report said, "in dry seasons all suffer together, and at other times there is barely enough water for all, and they do not receive sufficient returns to insure prosperity or contentment."[10] By that time, the pioneer period had ended, and consolidation of land and water into larger and more economically viable holdings was already well under way. As late as 1925, however, sixty percent of the farmers in Ephraim owned less than fifty acres, and only twenty percent owned more than seventy-five acres, and this typically in small, scattered plots.[11]

With a continuing influx of new residents, largely from Mormon missionary work in Scandinavia, the population of Sanpete Valley soon reached the saturation point for its original agrarian economy. The limited availability of land and water for these new arrivals, and for the younger generation as it came of age, served as a stimulus to the second thrust of Mormon settlement, encouraging those who wished to improve their economic condition to migrate to new regions. The tide of settlement spread up the Sevier Valley in the 1860s, and by the late 1870s colonies were being planted east of the Wasatch Plateau.

Besides out-migration, another response to the scarcity of arable land was a shift in the economic base toward livestock raising. The vast expanse of the High Plateaus must have seemed an inexhaustible summer pasture, and Sanpete Valley was ideally situated in a natural "drift" between the Wasatch Plateau and the winter range in the western Utah valleys. Sanpete farmers increasingly turned to the grazing lands to supplement the limited income from their farms, until within a few years farming had become supplemental to the livestock industry.

While the local herds were expanding, western Utah cattlemen such as the Bennion, Whitmore, and Swasey families also entered the region. The first ventures were not always profitable. In 1875, for example, the Bennions moved two thousand head of cattle from overstocked ranges in the West Desert to the Fish Lake Plateau, leaving them in the care of fifteen-year-old Israel Bennion and sixteen-year-old Tom Simpers. Young Bennion and Simpers were entirely on their own for three years, spending the summers at Fish Lake and wintering in Castle Valley, where they established a camp on Ferron Creek and spent much of their time visiting other camps and swapping tales with older cowboys. The two boys branded about seven hundred calves each year, but when their elders came to round up the herd in the fall of 1878, they could find only seventeen hundred head.[12]

On the other hand, when brothers Orange and Wellington Seely took the cattle and sheep of the Mount Pleasant United Order to winter in Castle Valley in 1875, they were so favorably impressed by the grazing prospects and the undeveloped land and water that they took up homesteads in the valley and later led the first colonizing party to the site of Castle Dale in 1877.[13]

Richard H. Jackson has argued that settlers were encouraged to enter what he calls "Utah's harsh lands" by a systematic mythologizing of the initial settlement along the Wasatch Front. During the 1860s and 1870s, Jackson claims, Mormon church leaders' descriptions of the Salt Lake Valley at the time of its settlement "increased its aridity and desolateness in direct correlation to the harshness of the area they were then encouraging settlers to occupy," thereby suggesting that the same transformation of the desert into a garden could be achieved in the new settlements.[14]

No doubt this vision of "making the desert blossom as the rose" was a powerful influence, as was the sense of religious obligation faithful Mormons felt to fulfill a settlement "mission." But economic opportunism also played a role in peopling the regions east of the High Plateaus. By the late 1870s, the second generation was coming of age in Sanpete Valley, only to discover the arable land already occupied. Some prominent families, the Seelys among them, were systematically planting their sons on homesteads in newly opened areas with a view to building the clan. Young couples less well connected saw the new settlements as their best chance to have a place of their own. John Wesley Powell's *Report on the Lands of the Arid Region* presented a more positive view than earlier surveys had done of eastern Utah's agricultural potential, estimating some "200 square miles of arable land, generally of good quality," in the basin of the San Rafael River.[15] (In fact, the report greatly overestimated the water supply. The flow of the San Rafael was measured at 1,676 cubic feet per second in July 1876, which must have been a season of exceptional runoff. The same report estimated a flow of only 1,825 cubic feet per second from the entire drainage of the Duchesne River, a stream several times larger than the San Rafael.)

As the Castle Valley settlements grew, their livestock joined the Sanpete herds on the summer range of the Wasatch Plateau. Cattle dominated the range until about 1880, but during the next twenty years they were replaced by sheep, especially in Sanpete County. Cattle were less vulnerable to predators and required less care, but sheep multiplied more rapidly and provided two cash crops instead of one. Moreover, the extensive subalpine zone on the plateau top was better adapted to grazing sheep than cattle. An ambitious and opportunistic young man,

adept at protecting his animals and finding good range, could start with nothing and by herding for others "on shares" build a substantial herd of his own within a few years. For example, John H. Seely leased the Mount Pleasant cooperative herd in 1885, contracting to provide each owner with two pounds of wool per head and eight lambs per hundred head of mixed sheep each year. At the end of three years, when he gave up the lease, Seely had built his own herd to 3,800 head.[16] John K. Madsen began herding sheep at age thirteen for ten dollars a month. Nine years later, he was earning thirty dollars a month and taking part of his wages in old ewes. He eventually became one of the most prosperous sheepmen in Utah, his Mount Pleasant Rambouillet Farm a major producer of purebred breeding stock.[17]

Thus by means of "nickels from a sheep's back," Sanpete Valley attained a measure of prosperity previously unknown and still traceable in the fine houses built in Ephraim and Mount Pleasant and Fairview between 1890 and 1910.[18] Fountain Green, originally a starve-acre village in the northwest corner of the valley with only a limited supply of spring water for irrigation, at one period boasted the highest per-capita income in Utah from the profits of the "Jericho Pool," named for the shearing pens on the winter range in Tintic Valley.[19]

Science has said that running water purifies itself in running seven miles, but during the spring high waters and summer rains, the filth from sheep camps comes down for a distance of 25 or 30 miles, and when we dip up a bucket of water from our town ditches to drink or cook our food in, and find sheep droppings in it, as we often do, all of the science on earth can not make us believe that it is pure water.[20]

The prosperity brought by the sheep boom came at a high ecological price, as suggested in part by this petition drafted by residents of Huntington, Lawrence, Cleveland, and Desert Lake, Emery County, in 1903 and sent to the commissioner of the General Land Office. During the nineteenth century, the rangelands were virtually unregulated, available to the first or most aggressive taker. The grasses and forbs that must have seemed inexhaustible to the first herders were being seriously overgrazed by the 1880s, and the damage was intensified by the practice of setting brushfires in the fall to reduce the shrub cover and make it easier for the sheep to move around the following year. In addition to the rapidly growing herds based in Sanpete and Castle valleys, "tramp

Tollgate, Cottonwood (Fairview) Canyon, Wasatch Plateau, before 1900. G. E. Anderson photo, courtesy LDS Church Archives.

herds" from other regions were brought to the Wasatch Plateau each summer. Some of these were driven west from Colorado during the fall and winter, grazed the eastern foothills in the spring, and moved onto the plateau top from June to September. Others were shipped from as far away as Oregon to Manti by rail, drifted northward on the plateau through the summer, then shipped from Colton in the fall.[21] Just before the turn of the century, sheep populations peaked at somewhere between eight hundred thousand and a million head on the Wasatch Plateau each summer,[22] in addition to probably more than twenty thousand cattle and several hundred horses.

These numbers were far in excess of the range's carrying capacity. Albert Antrei, who came to Sanpete County to work for the Forest Service in 1936, has collected a most telling group of personal reminiscences of the Wasatch Plateau before and after overgrazing. For example, Lauritz Neilsen claimed in a 1953 statement that in the mid-1880s the grass on Bluebell Flat in Ephraim Canyon was tall enough to hide the grazing sheep and that "there were no steep, raw banks dropping into the creek. It was possible to drive across the creek in many places with team and wagon." A few years later, he remembered "looking through the aspen and there was not a green leaf or sprig of any kind as high as the sheep could reach and the ground was absolutely bare. They ate everything that was green."[23] A Forest Service official named R. V. R. Reynolds, writing in 1911, reported that "between 1888 and 1905 the Wasatch Range from Thistle to Salina was a vast dust bed, grazed, trampled, and burned." This account, according to Lincoln Ellison, "is substantiated by old Sanpete residents, who tell of being able to count the herds of sheep on the mountain by the dust clouds they could see from the valley."[24]

With the watershed vegetation destroyed, gullies formed on the steep mountain slopes, streams became roily throughout the year, and the runoff from summer cloudbursts tore through the canyons. The "Sanpete Chronology" included in W. H. Lever's 1898 history makes no mention of flooding before 1889, when on August 16, "Floods in Manti and the southern part of Sanpete caused much damage, and a boy was killed at Mayfield."[25] Lauritz Nielsen remembered the ravines in Ephraim Canyon as dating from this year.[26] Serious floods hit Manti again in July 1890 and at least a dozen times thereafter. Ephraim Creek flooded eleven times between 1887 and 1938, as did Cottonwood Creek that runs through Orangeville and Castle Dale. There were nine floods on Price River between 1917 and 1931.[27] Manti and Mount Pleasant, which had been built straddling creeks that were quite innocuous at the time of their founding, were especially vulnerable to flood damage. L. R. Anderson, elected as mayor of Manti in 1900 on a "no more floods" platform, petitioned for the establishment of a national forest to protect the Manti Creek watershed, and the Manti National Forest was established by executive order of President Theodore Roosevelt on May 29, 1903.[28] Over the next few years, the forest boundaries were extended to include other Sanpete Valley watersheds and eventually took in most of the plateau top.

The science of forestry—especially as it pertained to the conditions of southern Utah—scarcely existed at the time, and early forest supervisors and rangers, such as A. W. Jensen, Parley Christiansen, David Williams, Beauregard Kenner, and J. W. Humphrey, had to learn their craft on the job. During the summers, they spent almost all of their time in the field, living in ranger stations and patrolling their districts on horseback. For the most part, they were local men with family ties to the stockmen, yet they soon became aware of the need for radical changes in the management of the high plateau terrain. One of the first measures adopted was to remove sheep entirely from the critical watershed areas on the west side of the plateau. In addition, a system of grazing permits was established in place of the free-for-all scramble for range that had prevailed until this time. But there was continual conflict between the forest officials' sense of the needs of the damaged range and the stockmen's desire to preserve their herds. Albert Potter, a range specialist from Arizona sent in to inspect the area of the proposed forest in 1902, recommended a reduction of sheep on the forest to 125,000 head, a proposal that brought vigorous protests from the sheepmen. A. W. Jensen, the first supervisor of the forest, wryly recalled, "This number was later raised, following a meeting in Manti City Hall."[29] In fact, 250,000 sheep were allowed on the range in 1904, double the Potter recommendation, with a gradual reduction to 190,000 by 1906.[30]

While sheep were removed from the steep western slopes of the plateau, they continued to be permitted in excess numbers on the east-running watersheds. Because most of the sheep were owned by Sanpete interests and the ongoing watershed damage affected Castle Valley residents, this practice led to conflict between the two valleys. While the Sanpete stockmen were protesting the proposed reduction in livestock numbers, farmers in Castle Valley were petitioning to have the cuts made effective—provided that they be granted at least one-third of the permits. Huntington attorney William Howard complained in a letter to the editor of the *Emery County Progress* that "most of the sheepmen are like corporations; they have no souls when something stands between them and what they want despite the rights of other people."[31] The *Progress* reported in October, 1903, that Hyrum Christensen, herding sheep belonging to the Manti Co-op, had been convicted of "befouling the waters of Ferron creek and reservoir" and fined fifty dollars.[32]

The tampering with the natural ecology of the Wasatch Plateau has not been limited to the introduction of domestic livestock. Game-management policies tilted toward hunting interests have resulted in deer populations far beyond the numbers found on the plateau when the first European settlers came to the region. Stockmen and hunters alike have supported the eradication of predators, leading to a population explosion of voles, marmots, and other rodents whose burrows honeycomb the hillsides.

The restoration of the Wasatch Plateau has been a slow and difficult process, still not completed after ninety years. Even after the livestock numbers were reduced, the denuded lands continued to spill mud and boulders into the valley with each summer storm. The most devastating floods in Sanpete history occurred in 1909, and the flood basins at the mouths of the canyons even yet have their uses. A significant chapter in the restoration process was the establishment of the Utah Experiment Station (later renamed the Great Basin Experiment Station) in Ephraim Canyon in 1912, which brought the first true range scientists into the region. Albert Antrei rightly claims that such "Spearmint Station" men as Arthur W. Sampson, A. Perry Plummer, and plant ecologist Lincoln Ellison deserve the title of pioneer as much as the first Sanpete settlers in 1849.[33] Ellison, for example, set out in the early 1950s to try to determine what the original vegetation of the Wasatch Plateau had been before the onset of grazing. In their own way, however, the early, untrained rangers had been asking the same questions. In addition to planting hundreds of thousands of trees on deforested areas of the plateau, J. W. Humphrey and his associates were responsible for the small log enclosures that can still be seen here and there on the plateau, designed to gauge the impact of grazing.

Today there are only about thirty thousand sheep and five thousand head of cattle on national forest lands on the Wasatch Plateau. Gullied hillsides and lost topsoil require ages rather than years to heal, and the plateau will never be exactly as it was before the introduction of domestic livestock—indeed, there is no way to know the exact mix of flora and fauna a hundred and fifty years ago. But nature has amazing restorative powers. The bare hillsides that I can remember in the 1950s are bare no longer. While the grass is not as tall as early reports claimed, it grows abundantly now on most of the plateau, slowing the advance of sagebrush on the drier slopes. Vigorous stands of young quaking aspen, Engelmann spruce, and subalpine fir now supplement the aging mature groves. (During the worst overgrazing, almost all saplings were destroyed, leaving a scarcity of middle-aged forest.) There is a rich understory of shrubbery in the aspen groves, dogwood, service berry, elderberry, and few places in the West can match the Wasatch Plateau in the abundance and variety of its wildflowers.

The names attached to the land suggest the range of activities that have been conducted over the last century and a half. Dairy Fork, Dairy Canyon, Dairy Point, Andrew Dairy Creek, and less transparently Rilda Canyon and Nuck Woodward Canyon allude to the mountain dairies that represented one of the earliest incursions of grazing stock onto the High Plateaus. Typically a pool of cows from various village owners would be taken to the high country in the summer, where the cool climate and abundant forage stimulated milk production. In most instances mountain dairies were operated by women and children while the men tended the valley cropland. Children herded the animals during the day and assisted with the milking morning and night, while the women and older girls made butter and cheese. The icy mountain streams and the mild days and chilly nights of the High Plateau summer helped keep the produce fresh until it could be shipped to market in Salt Lake City or the mining camps.[34]

Pole Canyon, Slab Pile Spring, Tie Fork, Sawmill Canyon, Shingle Creek, Mill Fork, Meetinghouse Canyon, Stump Flat, Loggers Fork, Eccles Canyon, and Academy Mill Reservoir all reflect the timber harvested from the Wasatch Plateau, though its spruce-fir forests have been less valuable for this purpose than the extensive stands of ponderosa pine on the more southerly plateaus. Coal Canyon, Coal Hollow, Boardinghouse Canyon, Finn Canyon, and Winter Quarters Ridge are reminders that most of the coal mined in Utah has come from either the Wasatch Plateau or the adjacent Tavaputs Plateau.

The grazing industry is memorialized by a multitude of place names, including Sheep Flat, Cow Fork, Trail Canyon, Bull Hollow, Cowboy Creek, Wild Horse Ridge, Wild Cattle Hollow, and Horse Heaven. The names of early stockmen also dot the land: Candland Mountain, Gentry Mountain, Nelson Mountain, McHaddon Flat, Miller's Flat, Star Point, Bennion Ridge, Swasey Ridge, Biddlecome Hollow, Seeley Creek, Singleton Creek, Pete McElprang Canyon, Ray Grange Hole, and many more. Such intriguing names as Sweat Canyon, Bacon Rind Canyon, and Coffee Pot Spring were likely attached to the land by the cowboys and sheepherders who labored there.

Powerhouse Ridge commemorates the development of small hydroelectric generating plants on several of the creeks in the early years of this century, while Electric Lake, one of the newest names on the plateau, refers to a large storage reservoir that supplies the coal-fired steam turbines of the Utah Power and Light Company's Huntington Plant. Fish Creek and Buck Basin remind us that humans have turned to the High Plateaus from time immemorial for fish and game, while names such as Baseball Spring and Old Folks Flat reflect additional dimensions of the Wasatch Plateau as a community recreation ground. Indeed, with the easy penetrability of the rolling tabletop by roads, the numerous trout streams and reservoirs, and the nearness of the Wasatch Plateau to the burgeoning population of the Wasatch Front, recreation seekers have grown in numbers as grazing livestock have diminished, so that recreation is second in importance only to the watershed itself among the uses of the plateau today.

The Wasatch Plateau begins rather unimpressively at the point where Thistle Creek and Soldier Creek join to form the Spanish Fork. The busy railroad town of Thistle once occupied the junction of the three canyons. Here helper engines were attached to eastbound Denver and Rio Grande Western trains for the pull up to Soldier Summit. The Marysvale branch line also connected with the main line here. The advent of diesel-electric engines, eliminating the need for helpers, and the consolidation of the railroad's divisions had already turned Thistle to practically a ghost town when, in the wet spring of 1983, an immense landslide blocked the Spanish Fork just below the town, creating a temporary lake that covered what was left of the town with fifty feet of mud and water.

All that remains now are a few ruined houses, most of them uprooted from their foundations, some buried to their eaves, and the walls of the red rock schoolhouse. The Marysvale rail line was abandoned after the flood, but Thistle is still a highway junction where U.S. 89 connects with U.S. 6. Highway 89 follows the western base of the Wasatch Plateau up Thistle Creek then over the divide south of Indianola and through the Sanpete and Sevier valleys to Salina. Highway 6 traces the eastern margin up Soldier Creek to the pass at Soldier Summit, then passes through a series of open parks that divide the Wasatch Plateau from the Tavaputs, then descends Price Canyon, emerging from the cliffs at Helper. At Price, State Highway 10 branches off to complete the route through Castle Valley.

Three sometimes-passable dirt roads provide access to the northern portion of the Wasatch Plateau. From Thistle, the Lake Fork road runs into the plateau for about eight miles, where it meets the roads from Dairy Fork and Little Clear Creek. This part of the plateau is characterized by relatively open canyons and rounded hills rising to between eight and nine thousand feet in elevation. Much of the terrain belongs to either the oakbrush or the pinyon-juniper vegetation zone, depending on the amount of precipitation, but there are some groves of quaking aspen and Englemann spruce on the higher slopes. The canyon streams are lined with narrowleaf cottonwood, squawbush, chokecherries, and water birch, with an occasional clump of bigtooth maple. An unused road leads steeply up from the ranching hamlet of Birdseye to the hilltop where "Birdseye marble" (actually a hard, fine-grained, richly colored limestone) was quarried during the early years of the century.

Road access to the higher reaches of the Wasatch Plateau begins at Tucker, where the Utah Department of Transportation has developed a shady roadside rest area on the site of a railroad town that preceded Thistle as a connecting point for helper engines. Three branches of Soldier Creek merge at Tucker. Highway 6 and the D&RGW main line follow the East Fork to Soldier Summit. A good dirt road leads some distance up the South Fork, following the abandoned route of the Utah and Pleasant Valley Railroad. This road deteriorates in the upper reaches of the canyon but is sometimes passable over the ridge and into Pleasant Valley. But the route to the top of the world leads from Tucker up Clear Creek Canyon, where it forms the northern access to the Skyline Drive.

Originally built in the 1930s by the Civilian Conservation Corps, Skyline Drive is surely one of the most remarkable roads in a region of scenic routes. It winds along the ridge for more than seventy miles, much of the way at elevations above ten thousand feet, affording spectacular vistas at every turn. The eighteen-mile section from the head of Clear Creek Canyon to the junction with State Highway 31 has recently been upgraded with a good gravel base and is safe for travel anytime from June to September. From this stretch of road the traveler can enjoy panoramic views of the rolling plateau top, open grassy hillsides interspersed with shimmering groves of quaking aspen and dark patches of spruce-fir forest. To the west, steep, densely wooded canyons cut through the monocline, dropping in three or four miles to the valley floor: Thistle Creek, North Sanpitch, South Sanpitch, Little Pine, Crooked Creek, Dry Creek, Oak Creek. To the east, longer and more gently sloping canyons, Bear Canyon, Fish Creek, Silver Creek, descend into the Pleasant Valley graben where their waters are impounded in Scofield Reservoir, the largest and most popular body of water on the plateau.

The single paved road across the Wasatch Plateau, State Highway 31, leaves U.S. 89 at Fairview and ascends the monocline by way of a steep dugway up Cottonwood Canyon to its junction with the Skyline Drive on the summit ridge. At this point, the pavement divides, with the left branch crossing Gooseberry Valley, then running through Flat Canyon, Upper Huntington Canyon, and over Trough Springs Ridge to the coal mines of Pleasant Valley. The right branch follows the Skyline Drive route south for four miles, then turns east, dropping down to Huntington Reservoir, continuing past Cleveland Reservoir, and coming into Huntington Canyon just below Electric Lake. Huntington Canyon is the longest canyon in the Wasatch Plateau, slicing diagonally through the table for thirty miles, descending gradually from subalpine water meadows through the blue spruce zone and on to the cottonwoods of the lower canyon and the dry pinyon-cedar woodlands at the canyon mouth, where the massive towers of the Huntington Power Plant rise from a bench south of the creek.

The paved stretch along Skyline Drive runs in places on hogsback ridges barely wider than the road. Here there are wonderful views of the checkerboard Sanpete Valley towns lying far below, encircled by a patchwork quilt of irrigated farmland. On the other side of the road the land falls off for a thousand feet to the floor of Gooseberry Valley, where Fairview Lakes reflect the blue sky. Farther to the east the scene is distinctly plateaulike. Rolling uplands and valleys stretch away to the limits of vision, with here and there a glimpse of the higher peaks of the Tavaputs Plateau. To the north, the peaks of the Wasatch Range are well in view at a distance of fifty or sixty miles. Because the plateau gradually declines toward the north, these peaks appear to be considerably higher than the plateau top, but in fact the Wasatch Plateau has four times more terrain above ten thousand feet than the entire Wasatch Range. For those who like to look close as well as far, a fifty-yard stretch of roadside slope in midsummer can display the blooms of green gentian, scarlet gillia, purple lupine, California corn lily, wild geranium, wild delphinium, wild sweet pea, alpine sunflower, coneflower, woodland star, forget-me-not, bluebells, charlock, hyssop, blue penstemon, and in the shade of the aspens the delicate columbine.

Where Highway 31 turns east, the Skyline Drive reverts to unimproved dirt, rock, and mud. Only the bold and well-equipped should attempt the next stretch, and then only in dry weather. It is possible to continue the journey southward on better roads by following Highway 31 to the Miller's Flat–Joe's Valley turnoff, half a mile below Huntington Reservoir. A graveled road follows the rift valleys through Miller's Flat and Scad Valley and across the divide into Upper Joe's Valley. A rougher road then descends the slope to Lower Joe's Valley, its reservoir second only to Scofield as a recreation destination on the Wasatch Plateau. From Joe's Valley a rough but usually passable road ascends Seely Creek to link up with the Skyline Drive above Ephraim.

Indeed, the traveler on the Wasatch Plateau has plenty of roads to choose from, even though most of them are unimproved. Almost every canyon has a road that ties into the network of dirt tracks crisscrossing the platform, leading to small reservoirs, to the ruins of holding pens made of aspen logs, to heaps of bleached slabs and decayed sawdust that mark abandoned mills, or to sheep camp garbage piles strewn with rusty condensed-milk cans, or to no apparent destination at all. And the roads are still used, sometimes in surprising ways. You can be bouncing along a rutted track, wondering what madness led you to such an impossible spot, and suddenly come upon a huge motor home parked beside a stream at the edge of an aspen grove, its generator chugging contentedly away and a television antenna protruding from the roof.

You won't find many motor homes on the central portion of the Skyline Drive, but for those willing to risk the journey the rewards can be great. The stretch between Highway 31 and the Joe's Valley–Ephraim road is the highest and most spectacular portion of the entire route. The road winds along the ridge at elevations ranging from 10,500 to 10,800 feet, offering the sensation of looking down upon red-tailed hawks and golden eagles as they ride the summer thermals. From some points it is possible on (increasingly rare) clear days to see both the Snake Range on the Nevada border and the LaSal Mountains on the Colorado border, a view spanning the entire width of Utah.

East of the ridge, glacier-carved basins drop off for five hundred feet before leveling out to become Lake, Rolfson, Staker, Jordan, Potter's, Bacon Rind, Bulger, and Reeder canyons. Castle Valley farmers built small reservoirs in several of these canyons during the early years of the twentieth century to hold the runoff from the deep snowbanks that accumulate under the ridge. In some places, glacial moraines already provided partial dams that required only modest additions by team and scraper to form impoundments.[35]

Small reservoirs were also constructed in suitable locations on the Sanpete side of the divide. The steep west-running canyons, however, have few good reservoir sites, and none comparable to Scofield, Joe's Valley, or Electric Lake. The narrowness of the skyline ridge and the depth of the snowbanks at the head of the east-running canyons early suggested to some enterprising Sanpeters the possibility of diverting water from the east slopes to the west. Their diversion works can be seen at several points along the Skyline Drive, in the form of collection ditches that channel water to tunnels running through the ridge to the head of Manti, Ephraim, Oak Creek, Twin Creek, and Cottonwood canyons. These projects have long been a sore point between water users on the east and west sides of the plateau. The diversions were facilitated by the fact that the political boundaries do not correspond to the drainage basins. Sanpete County extends well to the east of the skyline ridge, taking in most of the productive watershed. In addition, the headquarters of the Manti National Forest were in Ephraim until the merger of the Manti and LaSal forests in 1950, and Sanpete interests had a disproportionate influence on forest policies.

The water users east of the plateau maintain that there is no surplus in their watersheds and point out that Sanpete Valley has substantial reserves of undeveloped groundwater, unlike Castle Valley, which must depend entirely on mountain runoff. In earlier years there were a few incidents of vigilante action in which collection ditches were dynamited. For the most part, however, the controversies have quieted in recent decades. The area from which the existing diversion systems can collect water is not large, and government-sponsored storage projects on the Price and San Rafael drainages have given more stability to the water supply there.

The exception to this de facto truce is the Gooseberry Project, dear to the hearts of Sanpeters but anathema to Carbon County. Gooseberry Valley, on the upper watershed of the Price River, is the only place where a large storage project with trans-basin diversion is feasible. At the turn of the century, Sanpete irrigation interests constructed the Mammoth Reservoir at Gooseberry Narrows, but the poorly engineered dam washed out during the first season. However, Sanpete water users maintained their claim to Gooseberry water, and the diversion tunnel was enlarged in the early 1960s in anticipation of the building of a large reservoir. To this point, however, Carbon County water users have managed to keep the dispute over water rights tied up in the courts.[36]

A little south of the Oak Creek Canyon road that leads down to Spring City, Skyline Drive winds around the base of the two highest peaks on the Wasatch Plateau, North Tent (11,230 feet) and South Tent (11,285 feet). These peaks are about the same elevation as Lone Peak and Twin Peaks, the highest points on the eastern skyline of the Salt Lake Valley, and only about five hundred feet lower than Mount Timpanogos and Mount Nebo. But while it requires an arduous hike over many miles of steep trails to climb the alpine peaks of the Wasatch Front, the summit of South Tent, because it rests atop a ten-thousand-foot platform, is only a half-hour's walk from Skyline Drive. Nothing more clearly indicates the essential character of High Plateau terrain than this contrast.

Just beyond South Tent, the road swings west and follows the rim of perhaps the most distinctive formation in the west wall of the Wasatch Plateau. Variously called the Horseshoe, the Queen's Throne, and the Bishop's Armchair, this great glacier-carved scallop appears virtually inaccessible from the valley floor. But again, because the Wasatch Plateau is a great table, you can without effort stand at the 10,500-foot rim and gaze down upon a dizzying convergence of canyons. On the other side of the road lies the broad Horseshoe Flat, a gently rolling alpine meadow that was once a favorite site for the Sanpete-Emery "reunion," held annually until well into this century. Here several hundred people would come by wagon at an appointed time in July or August, leaving the heat and dust of the valleys to pitch their tents and spend several days visiting friends and relatives from the other side of the mountain. There were races and rodeos in the daytime and dances at night on wooden platforms built close to great bonfires to ward off the mountain chill.

From the Ephraim–Joe's Valley road to the Twelve Mile Creek road, Skyline Drive once again has a gravel base. The ridgeline is quite open here, with few overshadowing hills, and therefore the sense of elevation is more tangible than in some places that are actually higher. Manti Canyon, midway along this stretch, is probably the best place to view the upturned formations of the great monocline. Manti Canyon is also the site of the largest landslide to occur in the plateau region in historic times. In June 1974, an entire square mile of the mountain began to move, rupturing the city water line and threatening to block Manti Creek before it stopped.

South of Joe's Valley, the character of the Wasatch Plateau's eastern drainage alters. Instead of the longitudinal rift valleys and deep canyons of the Price, Huntington, and Cottonwood Creek systems, the Ferron Creek drainage basin is a broad amphitheatre that begins at the skyline ridge and gradually converges upon a pass through the east wall of the plateau. The Muddy Creek basin is similar though on a smaller scale and with a deeper and narrower gorge at its east end. From the Skyline Drive, these long downslope vistas make an interesting contrast to the steep western canyons, and there are also fine views of the San Rafael Swell and beyond it the peaks of the Henry Mountains.

Shortly before the Skyline Drive reaches the Twelve Mile Canyon junction, a road drops down on the east to Ferron Reservoir, perhaps the most picturesque of the Wasatch Plateau's lakes. Built on a glacial moraine early in the century to provide water storage for downstream farmers, "Ferron Res" is a small impoundment that looks like a natural lake, situated in a dramatic cirque and surrounded by alpine spruce-fir woods. With the completion of Millsite Reservoir at the canyon's mouth, the small storage capacity of the old reservoir was no longer needed, and therefore the water is now held at a constant level and the lake is used for recreational purposes only. Recreation was an important function, however, from the very beginning. Ferron native Lowry Nelson recalls in his memoirs a time when "almost the whole community, except those left to attend to the irrigation and to do the chores, hitched teams to covered wagons and went to the reservoir for a week or ten days."[37]

These community excursions were not restricted to Ferron. Every town and village at the base of the Wasatch Plateau once had a favorite spot—Flat Canyon, Philadelphia Flat, the Forks, Upper Joe's—where the residents would go for refuge from the valley heat between the first and second cuttings of hay. While the mass community outings are a thing of the past, many families still hold their reunions at the same sites every year.

South of Twelve Mile Canyon, Skyline Drive deteriorates once more, though it is still worth traveling for the views of Emerald Lake and the back side of Musinea, the whitecapped peak, best known locally as Mary's or Molly's Nipple, that dominates the prospect of the Wasatch Plateau from the Sevier Valley. Skyline Drive leaves the skyline ridge near Blue Lake and curves down the upper end of Gunnison Valley, another north-south trending graben that separates the main body of the Wasatch Plateau from the western promontory crowned by Musinea. The road gradually improves as it follows Salina Creek down to a final junction with Interstate 70.

Just before Skyline Drive begins its long, curving descent, a rutted track branches off to the left. If you follow this track past Henningson and Julius Flat reservoirs, it leads to the top of the thick cap of hard Flagstaff limestone that crowns the southern part of the table. From this point, the final great view from the Wasatch Plateau opens out into the very heart of the High Plateau region. Directly to the south across the saddle of Salina Pass the imposing peaks of the Fishlake Plateau rise to meet the gaze. Far to the southwest, the great bald domes of the Tushar appear, while to the southeast you can see, as Clarence Dutton saw it a hundred and twenty years ago, "the long, straight crest-line" of the Aquarius, "stretched across the sky like the threshold of another world."[38]

Another world, indeed, this "strange and beautiful country somewhere up in the region of the clouds."

2

SOUTH OF NEBO

W allace Stegner described Utah as having "a spine like a Stegosaurus."[1] The "Wasatch Line," considered by geologists "the most prominent geographic and geologic feature of Utah," is an extensive fault zone running from north to south and dividing the state into "distinctly different western and eastern provinces."[2] Along the northern portion of this line, the Wasatch Range forms the western outlier of the Rocky Mountain system. The Wasatch Mountains have an alpine character, with lofty peaks rising abruptly from the terraces of ancient Lake Bonneville. South of Mount Nebo, the landscape changes. In place of alpine mountain chains, three rows of broad-backed plateaus mark the course of the fault zone. The western row, which forms an extension of the Wasatch Range, includes the Gunnison Plateau, the Pahvant, the Tushar, and the Markagunt, culminating in the dramatic Kolob Terraces that look down upon Zion Canyon. The eastern range begins with the Wasatch Plateau and continues south through the Fish Lake, Thousand Lake, Awapa, and Aquarius plateaus. These two rows spread farther apart toward the south, and a middle range comprising the Sevier and Paunsagunt plateaus occupies the space between them. These are the High Plateaus of Utah.

The course of the Wasatch Line has made north-south travel relatively easy but raised difficult barriers in the path of those going east or west. The earliest historic travelers in the region, the Dominguez-Escalante party in 1776, made a wide circle around the High Plateaus, going north through Colorado then west through the Uinta Basin and crossing the Wasatch Range by way of Strawberry Valley, Diamond Fork, and Spanish Fork. From Utah Valley, they traced the western base of Mount Nebo and the Gunnison Plateau, anticipating the general route of Interstate 15 as far as present-day Holden before swinging farther west in search of a route across the Great Basin to California. Only after the casting of lots on October 11 did the party abandon the hope of reaching Monterey and turn their attention to the difficult problem of finding a way back to Santa Fe. They swung south of the Markagunt Plateau and struggled across the canyons and fault scarps of the Arizona Strip, only to get boxed in by the cliffs at the mouth of the Paria River. By the time they had found a way out of the place they named San Benito Sal-sipuedes—"get out if you can!"—and across the Colorado River, they had probably seen all they wanted to see of the High Plateau region.

The fifty years following the Dominguez-Escalante expedition saw the development of an active trade in horses, furs, and Indian slaves be-tween New Mexico and a wide region including northern and eastern Utah. However, the trappers and traders, like the Spanish padres who preceded them, tended to skirt the High Plateaus in favor of easier and more rewarding routes. The Green River crossing below the mouth of Gray Canyon, about six miles north of the town of Green River, and the route through northern Castle Valley and across Soldier Summit to Utah Valley most likely came into use during this period.

The next recorded entry into the High Plateau region was made by the trapper and explorer Jedediah Smith in 1826. After the trappers' rendezvous that summer at the bend of the Bear River, Smith with a party of about fifteen set out on the "Southwest Expedition" that would make them the first Americans to reach California by an overland route. In a letter to his former partner William H. Ashley at the conclu-sion of this journey, Smith indicated that he had followed a "general course" running southwest and west from the Salt Lake Valley until he reached the Sevier River, which he named the Ashley. Then, he said, he "passed over a range of mountains running S.E. and N.W. and struck a river running S.W. which I called Adams river, in compliment to our president."[3] This statement led many historians, including Smith's biog-rapher Dale L. Morgan, to assume that the party followed the route of Dominguez and Escalante along the western base of Mount Nebo and the Gunnison Plateau to the Sevier crossing near the present site of Yuba Dam.[4] The assumption was that Smith then followed the Sevier upstream and reached the Virgin (Adams) River either by crossing the western range of high plateaus or by going over Long Valley Divide, south of Panguitch, and down the East Fork of the Virgin.

Then in 1967 a detailed narrative of the journey turned up in St. Louis, prepared from Smith's notes by his scribe Samuel Parkman.[5] This account indicates that the Smith party did not proceed directly to the Sevier from Utah Valley. Instead they went into the mountains, proba-bly by way of Spanish Fork Canyon, to meet a Ute chief named Con-marrowap, whose band was harvesting serviceberries. The exact route is not clear, but three days were required to reach Conmarrowap's camp, which probably put the party on or near the Wasatch Plateau. George R. Brooks suggests that the Utes were camped in Soldier Creek Canyon somewhere near Tucker, and that upon leaving them Smith's party followed the present route of the Denver and Rio Grande Railway and U.S. Highway 6, up the East Fork of Soldier Creek to Soldier Summit, and then down the Price River to Castle Valley.[6]

Smith, however, reported that upon leaving the Ute encampment they found the country "extremely rough until ascending a considerable Mt we kept on the top of a ridge running Eastwardly."[7] This description does not fit well with the terrain between Tucker and Soldier Summit, which, as John C. Fremont reported in 1844 and as the traveler on U.S. 6 can easily see today, is "an open and easy pass."[8] From the summit ridge, the party traveled "a few miles" to "a valley and a Creek about 20 yds wide running North East." The Price River and its tributary the White, which a traveler would come upon soon after crossing Soldier Summit, both run southeast.

To be sure, the directions given in Smith's narrative are often incorrect—as, for example, when the account later says the party traveled up the Sevier River "nearly N W," an obvious impossibility.[9] But even so, there is a possible route that fits the details of the narrative better than the Soldier Summit route. If we assume that Smith went up the South Fork of Soldier Creek after leaving the Indian camp, the directions given make more sense. The South Fork is a narrower and more rugged canyon than the East Fork, and it culminates in a ridge that curves to the east around the rim of the Dry Valley graben. From here, a descent of about four miles into Pleasant Valley leads to Fish Creek, the major tributary of the Price River, which matches the size of the stream Smith describes and which does run northeast to its junction with the Price.

From this point, the Smith account says,

I then moved on South having a high range of mountains on the West and crossing a good many small streams running east into a large valley the valley of the Colorado. But having learned that the valley was verry barren and Rocky I did not venture into it. The country is here extremely rough little appearance of Indians and game quite scarce a few Mt. Sheep and Antelope. after traveling in this direction 2 days the country looked so unpromising that I determined to strike westward to a low place in the Mountain and cross over.[10]

Brooks assumes that the party traveled down Price Canyon then followed the base of the Wasatch Plateau through Castle Valley to Ivie

Creek Canyon, the eastern gateway to Salina Pass. This would make a distance of about ninety miles—considerable territory to cover in two days! But it would not have been necessary for Smith to go this far. Even though Salina Pass offers the only crossing point under eight thousand feet, that would not have been a crucial consideration for a mounted party traveling in August. Moreover, it does not appear any lower or easier than other canyons as viewed from the valley floor. There is some evidence that the Utes used a trail through Rock Canyon as a summer access route to Castle Valley because there was no creek to negotiate.[11] It is about sixty miles from the head of Price Canyon to Rock Canyon, still a difficult two-day trek but not impossible.

The Smith party may have traveled southward through the plateau-top graben valleys rather than descend into Castle Valley. Such a route would be consistent with the report of crossing "a good many small streams." The numerous streams of the plateau top are consolidated into only a few creeks before they pass through the eastern wall of the plateau. The ten-thousand-foot skyline ridge west of the grabens would still match the description of "a high range of mountains." The statement that Smith "did not venture into" Castle Valley is somewhat ambiguous. It could mean, as Brooks seems to assume, that he followed a course close to the base of the Wasatch Plateau—though the rugged pediment benches make it difficult to travel without venturing some distance into the valley. Utah Highway 10, which runs from Price to Ivie Creek Canyon, generally follows a course of least resistance about midway between the base of the Wasatch Plateau and the first reefs of the San Rafael Swell. But "I did not venture" could mean exactly what it says—that he didn't go into Castle Valley at all, but perhaps "learned" of its barrenness by surveying it from the plateau top, as Clarence E. Dutton would do fifty years later. From the plateau-top valleys, there are a few relatively low places in the skyline ridge, including the 9,200-foot pass where Highway 31 crosses today. Two days' journey would be ample time to reach this pass from Pleasant Valley, even with a side trip to the top of Castle Valley Ridge to survey the country to the east. Working against this route, however, are Smith's observations that the country had little game and looked "unpromising" to beaver hunters. The small streams on the Wasatch Plateau provide excellent beaver habitat.

Once Smith reached the Sevier, he apparently followed it upstream to the mouth of Marysvale Canyon then turned west into Clear Creek Canyon and crossed the divide between the Pahvant and Tushar plateaus to the site of Cove Fort, where Interstate 70 runs today. After a couple of days spent in following west-running streams to where they petered out in the desert, the Smith party turned south along the western base of the High Plateaus, passed through Beaver Valley, Little Salt Lake Valley, and Cedar Valley, then dropped down Ash Creek Canyon to the Virgin River, which they followed to its confluence with the Colorado. The expedition's further route took them south to the Mojave Indian country and then west across the Mojave Desert to the Los Angeles Basin.

Thus the trail that Fathers Dominguez and Escalante had hoped to establish from New Mexico to California a half-century earlier was completed by the mountain men. The first recorded journey over the entire route of what came to be known as the Spanish Trail began in September 1830, when a party of trappers led by William Wolfskill set out from Taos. Except for Wolfskill's ledger, the surviving accounts of this expedition were all written several years after the fact. The most detailed narrative is that of George C. Yount, written down by an Episcopal clergyman named Orange Clark sometime around 1855. This account provides a good example not only of early responses to the region of the High Plateaus but also of the power of received notions in the interpretation of a landscape.

Evidently, the party entered Utah south of the LaSal Mountains, forded the Colorado near present-day Moab and the Green a few miles north of Green River, cut across the northern slopes of the San Rafael Swell into Castle Valley, and entered the High Plateaus at Salina Pass, in the saddle between the Wasatch and Fish Lake plateaus. The trappers found the region between the Green River and the Wasatch Plateau to be "the most desolate & forlorn dell in the world—Every thing about it was repulsive & supremely awful—Unanimously they resolved to abandon so dreary a region, & rather than sojourn there, forego the acquisition of any benefit in the world." But two days' journey brought them to a place they called Pleasant Valley (perhaps the Gunnison Valley graben on the headwaters of Salina Creek), with "Sweet water, luxurient grass, & beautiful timber":

> On leaving this garden of nature, the party realized the forlorn condition of the first human pair, when expelled & driven out from Eden—Their spirits drooped and their hearts sank within them—As they pursued their journey, all around them was soon wild wintry waste—The party encountered deep snows and solitary gloom—very little timber, interspersed with scattered clumps of dwarfish cedars & Juniper Bushes, & rugged, icebound streams—Nature's verdure all departed.[12]

Like subsequent travelers, the Wolfskill party probably avoided the virtually impassable Salina Creek gorge by ascending Yogo Creek and crossing another summit, actually higher than Salina Pass, and entered the Sevier Valley by way of Lost Creek. Instead of following Jedediah Smith's route up Clear Creek Canyon, Wolfskill apparently continued south along the Sevier and led the party onto the highlands of the Markagunt Plateau, "where they encountered the most terrible snowstorm they had ever experienced," continuing for several days:

> After the storm subsided and the weather had softened, Yount & Wolfskil ascended a lofty Peak of the mountains for observation—In the whole range of human view, in every direction, nothing could be discerned, in the least degree encouraging, but only mountains, piled on mountains, all capped with cheerless snow, in long and continuous succession, till they seemed to mingle with the blue vault of heaven and fade away in the distance.[13]

Eventually, they made their way across the High Plateaus and descended into the Virgin River Valley, which Yount described as

> another of those enchanting vallies—There the earth was bare of snow, & the evergreens waved in gentleness & calm serenity—The Elk, deer and antelope, driven from the mountains, by the snow & piercing cold, were basking, with their frolicsome fawns, unawere & unintimidated by the sight of man—They would flock around like domestic sheep or goats, & would almost feed from the hand—Flocks of their young of every age & size, would bound & glide gracefully from hillock to hillock, & approach like lambs, in the farmer's farmyard—There, at evening, our adventurers encamped in a perfect Elysium.[14]

There is no neutral middle ground in the Yount-Clark narrative. The reading of the landscape appears to owe more to the biblical dichotomy of wilderness and promised land than it does to any probabilities of southern Utah geography and climatic conditions during the months of November and December.

Wolfskill and Yount never returned to New Mexico, but instead became prominent Anglo pioneers in California. The general path they had traversed came to be known as the Old Spanish Trail, rightly described as "the longest, crookedest, most arduous pack mule route in the history of

America."[15] In addition to the Wolfskill route through Sevier Valley, an alternative trail came into use that crossed the Fish Lake Plateau then proceeded through Grass Valley and the East Fork Canyon to rejoin the Wolfskill trail near the present site of Circleville.[16] The reunited trail crossed the western range of High Plateaus by way of Bear Valley and Red Creek Canyon, emerging at the site of Paragonah, then followed the base of the Markagunt Plateau to Cedar Valley before swinging west and passing over the rim of the basin at Mountain Meadows.

From 1830 to 1850, the Spanish Trail was the main trade route between New Mexico and California. Horses multiplied so rapidly in the coastal valleys that the supply far outran the local market. Indeed, the animals became a positive nuisance, trampling cropland and luring away the working stock of the ranchos. A horse worth a hundred dollars in Santa Fe and perhaps twice that much at a trappers' rendezvous could be purchased in California for two woollen blankets. California mules, bigger and more rugged than those bred in the States, cost more but were in high demand for the freight teams that plied the Santa Fe Trail.

The merchants of Santa Fe and Taos quickly recognized and seized an opportunity. New Mexico had plenty of sheep and a native weaving industry, and woollens were relatively light and easy to pack. Each October, a caravan would set out from the New Mexico settlements with as many as two hundred men and several hundred pack animals, on a journey that typically required two months to complete. The object of their timing was to cross the high passes before they were blocked by snow and reach the Mojave Desert after the summer heat. They then spent the winter months assembling several thousand head of horses and mules for the spring drive to New Mexico, which usually began in late April.[17]

It didn't take long for such astute adventurers as Bill Williams and Pegleg Smith (put out of their trapper's trade by the collapse of the fur market in 1840) and the Ute Chief Wakara to realize that horses could be acquired more cheaply by raiding than by trading. The lightly guarded ranchos were an easy target, and Mexican authorities would rarely follow the raiders into the Mojave. When a party did pursue the thieves after the great raid of 1840, they were ambushed in the desert and robbed of their own mounts.[18]

While the animals were cheaply acquired, losses were heavy during the long Mojave *jornadas*, with as far as seventy miles between waterholes and feed entirely inadequate for such large herds. Later travelers reported that the route of the Spanish Trail was littered with bones. Mountain Meadows—then known as Las Vegas de Santa Clara—was vitally important as a recruiting place after the desert ordeal, and the caravans would often remain there for two or three weeks to allow their stock to feed on the abundant grass.

John C. Frémont followed the Spanish Trail across the Mojave on returning from his first expedition to California in 1844. He was not favorably impressed by the Virgin River Valley, that "perfect Elysium" of the Yount-Clark account. Frémont called the Virgin "the most dreary river I have ever seen."[19] On the other hand, he was delighted by Mountain Meadows, "rich in bunch grass, and fresh with numerous springs of clear water, all refreshing and delightful to look upon," and by the alluvial plains at the boundary of the High Plateaus and the Great Basin, which he described as "a region of great pastoral promise, abounding with fine streams; the rich bunch grass—soil that would produce wheat, and indigenous flax—growing as if it had been sown."[20]

The famous mountain man and guide Kit Carson, who was a member of the 1844 Frémont party, crossed the High Plateaus in 1847 and again in 1848 carrying military dispatches. On the 1848 trip, when the dispatches included the first news of the gold discovery at Sutter's Mill, he was accompanied by Lieutenant George D. Brewerton, who later published an account of the journey. The party followed the branch of the Spanish Trail that crossed the Fish Lake Plateau, and Brewerton's is probably the first published description of Fish Lake:

> We encamped one evening upon a beautiful little lake situated in a hollow among the mountains, but at so great an elevation that it was, even in summer, surrounded by snow, and partially covered with ice. There we were again visited by the Eutaw Indians, who, as usual, behaved in a very friendly manner. Our provisions had now become so scanty that it was necessary to add to our stock by purchasing what we could from the Indians. From the party who here visited us, we managed to obtain a portion of a Rocky-Mountain sheep, or "big-horn," as it is often called; and, upon Kit's asking for fish, one of the Indians departed, but in a few minutes returned with a fine trout, which we bought for a couple of charges of powder. Our bargain had hardly been placed upon the fire when we discovered that the fish had been killed with an arrow-wound in the back. While we were wondering at this novel mode of taking trout, two of our men came into camp with as many fish as they could carry, and told us that they had caught as many more, but left them upon the banks of the lake. It seemed that in wandering about, they had discovered a little stream, a tributary to the lake, but quite shallow; this stream they represented as swarming with fish, so that they had gone in and killed them with sticks.

By sunrise next morning we were not only settled in our new camp, but up to our knees in the icy water in pursuit of its frightened tenants . . . such a slaughter of the finny tribe I have rarely seen. For my own part, with an old bayonet fastened to a stick, I caught five dozen—and a twinge of rheumatism, which reminds me of the circumstances even now.[21]

The California Gold Rush brought some additional traffic across the Spanish Trail but also led to its eclipse as a major route as better roads were developed along the Humboldt and Gila rivers. The western portion of the trail, however, was incorporated into the "Mormon Corridor" between Salt Lake City and Southern California.

Brigham Young is known to have been influenced by Frémont's report in deciding to settle in the Salt Lake Valley. It seems likely that Frémont's positive though brief description of southern Utah's agricultural potential was one factor in the early decision to extend Mormon settlement southward rather than to the north. Another influence was the advice of mountain man Jim Bridger (given, in the view of Richard H. Jackson, with a design of putting "as much distance as possible between the Mormon settlements" and his own territory) that "the country is . . . better the farther south one goes until the desert is reached, which is upwards of two hundred miles south of Utah Lake."[22] The Southern Exploring Expedition sent out by Brigham Young in 1849 seemed to confirm Bridger's claims. Its leader, Parley P. Pratt, estimated that the natural resources of the Little Salt Lake Valley "were capable of sustaining and employing from 50,000 to 100,000 inhabitants."[23] Pratt was equally generous in his assessment of the Pahvant Valley, declaring its agricultural potential "probably more than sufficient to sustain the present population of Rhode Island."[24]

Where the agricultural prospects seemed unpromising, the Mormon explorers expressed little interest in the scenic qualities of the landscape. Surveying the Virgin River Valley from a campsite near Pintura (where Interstate 15 now descends the Black Ridge, and probably near the point where the Wolfskill party entered into "Elysium") and seeing "no signs of water or fertility," Pratt found the view both unappealing and unsettling: "a wide expanse of chaotic matter presented itself, huge hills, sandy deserts, cheerless, grassless plains, perpendicular rocks, loose barren clay, dissolving beds of sandstone . . . lying in unconceiveable confusion."[25]

While the 1850s and '60s saw the founding of settlements along the Mormon Corridor and in the Sanpete and Sevier valleys, much of the plateau region remained undeveloped and only superficially explored. In

1853, the search for a central railway route brought the ill-fated expedition led by Captain John W. Gunnison into the region, the first party to bring wagons across the High Plateaus from east to west. Gunnison's route ran along the base of the Book Cliffs, a few miles north of the present route of Interstate 70, to the Green River crossing. Instead of following the Spanish Trail across the San Rafael Swell, Gunnison in search of a better road swung north into the Price River Valley, rejoining the Spanish Trail near the present site of Castle Dale. After crossing Salina Pass, he followed the Sevier River downstream to the marshes below the present village of Deseret, where he and six of his men were massacred by Pahvant Indians on October 26.

The official report of the expedition was compiled after Gunnison's death by his assistant, Lieutenant E. G. Beckwith, whose comments on the country reveal mixed feelings. On the one hand, his responsibilities as an economic geographer demanded a hardheaded assessment of the region's apparent resources, which he summed up in these terms: "Unless this interior country possesses undiscovered mineral wealth of great value, it can contribute but the merest trifle towards the maintenance of a railroad through it, after it shall have been constructed."[26] On the other hand, though he was repelled by the barrenness of the landscape, he enjoyed the long views that are characteristic of the plateau region and found the rock formations intriguing. Describing the area that is now Arches National Park, he wrote:

> The Mountain on Grand river is very broken, and during the day presented many beautiful rocks standing high above the adjacent ledges and ridges. From one position a majestic shaft stood out clear against the sky; and chimney rocks were almost hourly presented as we rode along, with piles occasionally resembling ruins of immense churches and dwellings, and one or two low eminences, resembling the ruins of mighty cities of adobe buildings.[27]

In the cliffs at the Green River crossing, Beckwith saw "the appearance of an unfinished fortification, on a scale which is pleasing to the imagination, and contrasts the works of man strongly with those of nature." This recourse to architectural analogy was common among nineteenth-century travelers in the plateau country and perhaps represented an unconscious attempt to humanize a landscape they found forbidding and uninhabitable.

John C. Frémont thought he should have been put in charge of the central Pacific railway survey instead of Gunnison. When he failed to get the appointment, he hurriedly fitted up a private expedition that crossed the region during the hard winter of 1854. So desperate were the party's circumstances that no detailed record was kept of their route through the High Plateaus. Frémont claimed in a letter written from Parowan to his father-in-law, Senator Thomas H. Benton of Missouri, that he had saved "nearly a parallel of latitude" over the Gunnison route.[28] It seems likely that he crossed the Green River near the mouth of the San Rafael River, then attempted to follow the San Rafael through the rugged reef that marks the eastern boundary of the San Rafael Swell. Stopped by the impassable Black Box, the party followed the reef south until they could find a negotiable pass.[29] It was once assumed that they traveled up the Fremont River—hence its name in the explorer's honor—but that is by no means certain. In preparation for their desperate final push toward the southern Utah settlements, they evidently cached much of their equipment in northern Rabbit Valley, near the present village of Fremont.[30] But one would expect that if they had come into Rabbit Valley by way of the Fremont River they would have made directly west on the present route of Highway 24 across the Awapa Plateau, rather than following the river north toward the higher Fish Lake Plateau. A route through northern Rabbit Valley suggests that they might have crossed the San Rafael Swell by way of Muddy Creek and then have come over Hogan Pass, on the present route of Highway 72. In any event, once they reached Grass Valley they presumably followed the eastern branch of the Spanish Trail to the main fork of the Sevier River. Instead of taking the Spanish Trail route through Bear Valley, however, Frémont crossed the western range of the High Plateaus a few miles farther north, through Dog Valley.

The paths these early explorers broke by difficult labor are now the routes of the main highways that traverse the region. Interstate 15 follows the Mormon Corridor along the alluvial plains where the High Plateaus meet the Great Basin. U.S. 89 runs beside the Sevier River in the interior valleys between the western and the middle range of plateaus. Interstate 70 roughly traces the Spanish Trail route through Salina Pass and the Jedediah Smith route over Clear Creek Pass. U.S. 6 from Green River to Wellington and Utah Highway 10 from Price to Emery approximate the Gunnison Trail, as does a portion of Highway 28 from Gunnison to Levan. The Fish Lake branch of the Old Spanish Trail can be followed from the lake to Circle Valley by way of Highways 25 and 62, though its probable route across the Fish Lake Plateau remains an unpaved track. To follow any of these routes is to experience the dramatic unfolding of the High Plateau landscape.

3

THE MORMON CORRIDOR

T he traveler going south on Interstate 15 first encounters the High Plateaus near the town of Nephi but may not be aware of the changing form of the highlands. At first sight, the Gunnison Plateau appears to be an extension of Mount Nebo, cut off from the main mass by Salt Creek Canyon. The difference in structure soon becomes apparent, however, if one travels up Salt Creek on Utah Highway 132. While Nebo soars up to its 11,900-foot peak and back down again within a horizontal distance of two or three miles, the northwestern cliffs of the Gunnison Plateau settle into a tabular platform that curves east and south past Fountain Green to form the western horizon of Sanpete Valley, descending gradually toward the south until it breaks into low hills near the town of Gunnison. With a platform averaging about eight thousand feet in elevation, the Gunnison is the lowest of the High Plateaus. Like the Wasatch Plateau, it was heavily overgrazed during the last decades of the nineteenth century. Because of its lower elevation and attendant lower precipitation, its recovery has been less complete. Still, the plateau top has the characteristic groves of quaking aspen and spruce/fir interspersed with grass and brushlands.

Even from the west side, the tabular character of the Gunnison Plateau becomes apparent by the time one reaches the village of Levan, situated at the mouths of the twin canyons of Pigeon and Chicken creeks. Interstate 15 follows the west side of Juab Valley, bypassing Levan, which is worth a visit as one of the better surviving examples of the traditional Mormon farm village, with its substantial brick houses on the corners of the blocks and barns and corrals on the town lots.

Speeding down the Interstate, probably intent on reaching Las Vegas or Los Angeles, or perhaps St. George, the modern traveler can have little idea of the more deliberate experience of wagon or pack-train travel along the Mormon Corridor. A fine account of such a journey on this route was published in 1874 by Elizabeth Wood Kane, the wife of Colonel Thomas L. Kane. An influential friend of the Mormons since he first met them as a band of outcasts on the Iowa prairies in 1846, chief arranger of the government relief effort known as the Mormon Battalion, and mediator in the Utah War of 1857–58, Colonel Kane was probably the most respected "Gentile" in Mormondom. The Kane family accompanied Brigham Young on his annual trip from Salt Lake City to St. George in late 1872, and Mrs. Kane wrote perceptively, if somewhat warily, of the landscape. She remarked how the snowcapped peaks of Mount Nebo remained visible day after day as the party traveled south. At the Sevier crossing, which was near the present site of Yuba Dam, she noted "a few huts, partly burrowed into the hillside," and a shanty saloon established to serve the teamsters from the Pioche mines. She described Scipio, still recovering from the depredations of the Black Hawk War, as "the poorest and newest of the settlements we stopped at" and lamented, "[W]hat can atone for the absence of trees in a landscape?"[1]

Today Scipio, nestled in its basin valley with no natural outlet, is embowered in trees, suggesting that its early residents felt the same need as Mrs. Kane. The village enjoyed a season of prosperity around the turn of the century, when it served as a home base for ranching operations extending from the High Plateaus to the West Desert, and its best houses date from that period. Despite the loss of several important structures in recent years, it remains a good example of the traditional Mormon village.

Upon leaving Scipio, Interstate 15, like its predecessor roads, climbs a saddle that connects the Canyon Range to the Pahvant Plateau. The Canyon Range is typical of Great Basin mountains, alpine in character with peaks reaching above nine thousand feet but with a relatively small extent of high terrain. The Pahvant, which stretches some forty miles from Scipio to Cove Fort, is a hybrid. Like the Gunnison Plateau, it presents on its western face the appearance of a Basin range, though a tabular platform is visible above the village of Kanosh. Its plateau character is obvious if viewed from U.S. Highway 50, which follows its northern and eastern front from Scipio to Salina. The Pahvant is also among the less lofty of the High Plateaus, with a platform averaging between 8,000 and 8,500 feet in elevation and higher ridges reaching a little above 10,000 feet. While it, too, has been extensively grazed, the relatively little additional elevation makes its upland forests and meadows distinctly more lush than those of the Gunnison.

Father Escalante described the Pahvant Valley as "a vast plain surrounded by sierras." His route took him through the western part of the valley, among the cinder cones and lava flows of geologically recent volcanic activity, and he found the valley "in most places . . . very short of pasturage and although two rivers enter it . . . we saw no place whatever suitable for settlement."[2] We have seen how favorably impressed Parley P. Pratt was in 1849 by the alluvial plains and subirrigated meadows near the base of the Pahvant Plateau. Several travelers on their way to the California goldfields that same year also commented on the agricultural promise of the Pahvant Valley and on the extensive Indian remains near Chalk Creek on the present site of Fillmore. Sheldon Young described "the ruins of an ancient city . . . five miles in extent" and declared, "This is the most pleasant valley that we have passed through."[3] Addison Pratt judged that Chalk Creek "would sustain a small settlement" (a more modest estimate than Parley P. Pratt's claim that the valley could support the entire population of Rhode Island) and wrote of "low praries [sic] covered with immense quantities of grass."[4]

Traveling the same route some twenty-three years later, Elizabeth Wood Kane found "a plain . . . grassy enough to be entitled to be called ranch-ground, but wasting away into the Sevier Desert pure and simple." The settlement of Cedar Springs (now Holden) "was buried in fruit trees." She recounts her impressions of Fillmore, which by virtue of its central location had served as the Utah territorial capital for a brief period during the 1850s:

> The place was on a rising ground above the plain, and was backed by peaked mountains. I remember that I was shown the great, red building as we passed it; I remember driving through an orchard that clothed two hillsides, sloping to a rivulet, with three neat cottages embowered among the trees, the homes of Bishop Collister.[5]

The settlements along the Mormon Corridor, while determined primarily by the availability of irrigation water, also served as travelers' stops. Under average conditions, it was an easy day's journey from Nephi to Chicken Creek (Levan), a somewhat longer trip from Chicken Creek to Scipio, and another day's travel from Scipio to Fillmore. However, from Kanosh, twelve miles south of Fillmore, to Beaver there was a stretch of almost fifty miles without a stream large enough to support a village. This was too great a distance to cover in a day. During the Indian troubles of the 1860s, Brigham Young directed Ira N. Hinckley to erect a fortified way station on Cove Creek.

Elizabeth Wood Kane visited Cove Fort on a cold December day, and she found the volcanic rubble-strewn landscape "a dreary region." The frigid barrenness of the surroundings served to highlight the comforts of the fort, where the Kanes were given a "nicely furnished" room with "a magnificent pitch-pine fire blazing on the hearth." All in all, she found it a place of strong contrasts:

> We supped in the telegraph office, where the ticking of the instrument insisted on being heard as we all knelt down for prayers.—Prayers after the patriarchal Hebrew manner; a shot-proof fort; an electric battery clicking the latest New York news; armed men; unarmed women with little children; a meal served with dainty precision in a refectory walled with rough-hewn stone: this medley of antichronisms is Mormon all over.[6]

Cove Fort, recently restored to something like its original appearance, is a mile or so off the present course of the highway. Near this point Interstate 70 joins Interstate 15 after climbing over the ridge connecting the Pahvant Plateau to the Tushar.

The Tushar is not a true plateau in structure but instead the remnant of an ancient volcanic center. Its geologic strata are highly convoluted, and it represents probably the greatest concentration of metallic minerals in the High Plateaus region, including gold, silver, lead, zinc, uranium, and aluminum, in addition to commercially exploited deposits of potassium and sulfur.[7] It has the broad uplands characteristic of a plateau in the form of a massive dome with an elevation of about ten thousand feet. On top of this, however, are set dramatic peaks including Mount Belnap, Mount Delano, and Baldy, all reaching above twelve thousand feet.

Solomon Nunes Carvalho reported an interesting experience in the area of the Tushar in his *Incidents of Travel and Adventure in the Far West*. Carvalho came west with Frémont's 1853–54 expedition as the party's official artist and daguerreotypist. His strength was so exhausted by the winter struggle across the High Plateaus that he chose to remain behind in Parowan when Frémont pushed on to California. After a two-week period of recuperation, he caught a ride to Salt Lake City with Bishop Henry Lunt of Cedar City, who was going to April conference. A religious Sephardic Jew, Carvalho was interested in and sympathetic toward Mormon beliefs and folkways (except polygamy) and apparently developed a wide acquaintance during his two months in Salt Lake City, boarding with Apostle E. T. Benson and painting portraits of such notables as Brigham Young, Daniel H. Wells, and Wilford Woodruff. His six chapters on Salt Lake City are the best early travel account.

Carvalho left the city on May 6, in company with Brigham Young and a large party going to visit the southern settlements. The first destination was Chicken Creek, where Young held a peace conference with Wakara and other Ute leaders in an effort to settle the so-called "Walker

War." After the conference, Wakara accompanied the party on its southward journey. They evidently camped at Cove Creek, and Wakara told the party of a "vinegar lake" located about two miles off their route. Going to the place, Carvalho discovered a mineralized lake bed:

> We with great caution commenced to walk over this surface, and discovered that it undulated with the weight of our bodies. I felt as if walking on thin ice, which bent, without breaking beneath my weight. As we approached the centre, we heard a roaring, which our Indian said was caused from "big fire below." I put my ear close to the earth, and was almost sure it proceeded from the escape of either gas or the passage of water. With a pickaxe, brought for exploring purposes, an orifice about a foot in diameter was dug. The axe was suddenly driven through, when a yellow, muddy liquid gushed forth in a continued stream. I tasted the liquid, when to my surprise, it was a strong acid, which immediately set my teeth on edge.[8]

Carvalho's "vinegar lake" apparently occupied the site now known as Sulphurdale, which can be reached by a side road from Cove Fort. Here, sulfur-laden springs emerge from the northwestern base of the Tushar and run in yellow streams. Heaps of sulfur remain from earlier mining operations, and the hollow is now the site of a geothermal electric generating plant, driven by superheated steam drawn from deep wells.

Beaver City, pleasantly situated in a meadow valley on the largest stream that flows from the Tushar, was for two or three decades the most important town in southern Utah. In 1869, it became the seat of the Second Judicial Court of the Territory of Utah. In the early 1870s, the discovery of rich mineral deposits in the San Francisco Mountains to the west brought miners to the region. An army post named Fort Cameron was established at the mouth of Beaver Canyon in 1873 at the request of Judge C. M. Hawley, who complained that the court was unable to take action against the perpetrators of the Mountain Meadows Massacre:

> This district is settled almost entirely by Mormons, there being only about two hundred Gentiles in the district. From the time of said massacre, there has been a rising feeling in the minds of the Gentiles and a few loyal Mormons against the principal leaders and perpetrators of that deed. At every session of the Court, this question has been brought up by the Grand Jury, or rather by individuals thereof, and yet the U.S. Attorney and the Jury have not dared to introduce the subject to be investigated. . . .

There are several indictments now in the hands of the U.S. Marshal, to execute upon felons which, he reports, he is unable to execute. Beaver City, where I hold my court, is two hundred and twenty miles south of Salt Lake. It is beautifully situated, well watered and healthy, and besides it is the diverging point leaving to Pioche, a hundred and twenty miles west, and to St. George, one hundred and ten miles south, and it is about one hundred miles southeast to Knob [Kanab], the Gibraltar of Church felons, where there are one hundred and twenty men thoroughly armed, and where the leaders of said massacre have taken refuge.[9]

While Fort Cameron was established for the purpose of securing federal control over the Mormon population of southern Utah, Beaver City Mormons enjoyed an economic boost from the contracts to build the fort and from supplying the 250 soldiers stationed there. The post also made available to local residents the only hospital in southern Utah. Moreover, according to a local history,

With the arrival of the officers and families, social functions became the order of the day, and this routine of life continued for over a period of ten years. Many a soldier began to pay marked attention to the young ladies of the town and when the time of their enlistment expired, they married and established themselves in our midst as private citizens.[10]

Fort Cameron remained in operation for only ten years. After its abandonment, the land and buildings were acquired by the LDS Church and became the campus of Murdock Academy, a boarding school that drew students from throughout southern Utah from 1898 to 1922. When the school closed, the stone buildings were dismantled and their materials used in other structures. Today only one low barracks remains to mark the site.

Though it is no longer the judicial and educational center of the region, Beaver remains one of the best examples of a southern Utah town on a generous scale. During the period of prosperity in the 1870s and '80s, when Fort Cameron was occupied and a sizeable woollen mill provided employment, local craftsmen Thomas Frazer and Alexander Boyter (who, incidentally, was one of the Fort Cameron soldiers who settled down in Beaver) erected several dozen solidly built houses of black basalt and pink tuff quarried from the nearby hills.[11] These structures together with the well-preserved Beaver County Courthouse (1882) and later brick houses, all built on spacious lots with ample garden room, provide a continuing sense of a firmly established human presence in the landscape.

There is no easy approach to the Tushar. The one paved road, Utah Highway 153, enters Beaver Canyon near the site of Fort Cameron and climbs four thousand feet in about a dozen miles, passing between the vertical black cliffs of Box Canyon, up a steep dugway, and through extensive groves of mountain mahogany before reaching the upper platform. So great is the fall of Beaver River that it supplies four separate hydroelectric plants. The abruptness of the uplift at the edge of the Great Basin makes the Tushar a region of heavy snowfall, and nowhere in the plateau region are the forests more dense, the meadows more lush. Elk Meadows Ski Resort has been established here to take advantage of the extraordinary snow depth, drawing much of its clientele from Las Vegas. Just before you reach Elk Meadows, a rugged road, now incorporated into the extensive network of all-terrain vehicle routes called the Paiute Trail, winds north among the high Tushar peaks, passing between Mount Delano and Mount Belnap and offering breathtaking views into the deep canyons that drain toward the east. But be warned—I found the road blocked by snowdrifts in the middle of July.

Beyond Elk Meadows, the Big Flat covers several thousand acres of the high table, an extensive, rolling expanse of groves and meadows where elk can frequently be seen feeding. Here too is the lovely Puffer Lake, a favorite recreation spot from the earliest days. I have heard an old man from northern Utah reminisce fondly of the summer following his high school graduation, when he and a friend set out in a Model T Ford to see the world. By the time they reached Puffer Lake, he had seen enough to know that this was where he wanted to stay, and though it turned out to be only a couple of months of camping on the shore and living on trout it still represented, sixty years later, the most idyllic season of his life.

From Beaver Valley, Interstate 15 crosses a pass to Little Salt Lake Valley. The Tushar drops off at its southern end into broken hills and valleys that extend for several miles before the Markagunt Plateau begins its gradual rise. It was in this gap between the Tushar and the Markagunt that the Old Spanish Trail crossed the western range of High Plateaus. Little Creek Peak, at 10,142 feet, and Bear Peak, at 9,551 feet, provided early explorers with excellent lookout points from which to survey the southern Utah landscape.

Elizabeth Wood Kane, weary of the long winter journey, found her introduction to the Little Salt Lake Valley unsettling. The caravan made a midday stop at Buckhorn Springs in the dry northern section of the valley—now the site of a rest area on Interstate 15—where she saw "No garden, no trees, nothing but rock and sand to look at till our eyes rested on the mountains in the distance. The house stood on a slight elevation above the plain, and was inhabited by an aged pair who were wearing out the evening of their days in comfortless desolation." Her eastern-bred sensibilities were offended not only by the barrenness of the landscape but by "violent effects of color":

> There is no home-like scenery in Utah; a scene-painter's nightmare would be tame to nature's productions here with rocks and sand. The afternoon was wearing on to the sunset when we came to a blood-red land,—cliffs, soil, and a crumbling old adobe fort, all red. Beside it a rushing stream dashed up wavelets of turbid red. Then came three or four red adobe houses, and some stacks of the brilliant straw-colored hay, with freshly-opened green hearts. The dreary wind howled and whistled among the walls and palings, and shook our carriages when we halted for a few minutes. Thankfulness overpowered me that, wherever else my lot in life might be cast, it was to be neither at Buckhorn Springs nor Red Creek Village!"[12]

Red Creek Village is now known as Paragonah (pronounced, southern Utah style, Para*goo*na), and from the Interstate appears in summertime as a vivid green grove against the red backdrop of the Hurricane Cliffs, the great fault scarp that forms the west face of the Markagunt Plateau. The Markagunt rises gradually from north to south, reaching high-plateau elevation at Parowan, four miles south of Paragonah.

Mrs. Kane liked Parowan much better than Paragonah. The travelers were greeted by the town's brass band on their arrival, and the Kanes were put up at the comfortable home of William H. Dame, "low-roofed but wide-spreading." She writes, "The principal houses surround the court-house square, and are shaded generously by double rows of cotton-wood trees. These grow so fast that although planted only twenty-one years ago, in the infancy of the settlement, they give the town quite a middle-aged look, their branches already over-arching the streets."[13]

Parowan stands in the same relation to southern Utah as Manti does to central Utah. It is the mother community, founded at the end of 1850, from which other towns were settled. However, in this instance the eldest daughter, Cedar City, has far outstripped the parent in size and importance. Its location near the coal veins of Coal Creek Canyon and the iron ore deposits to the west made Cedar City the site of the first attempt to manufacture iron in southern Utah. While these efforts were unsuccessful, they stimulated an expectation of growth that was very much in the air when Solomon Nunes Carvalho visited the town in 1854. By then, Cedar City was already larger than Parowan, and Carvalho declared that it was "destined to become a great place of business."[14]

46

In fact, after the iron industry fizzled, Cedar City remained about the same size as Parowan for the next fifty years. The two towns had comparable supplies of water and arable land, and similar access to the Markagunt Plateau and the West Desert grazing lands. Near the turn of the century, however, Cedar City was chosen as the site of the southern branch of the State Normal School, which after several changes in name and mission is now known as Southern Utah University. While the manufacture of iron was never commercially successful in southern Utah, the ore deposits were exploited from the 1920s onward to feed the steel mills of Utah Valley, Colorado, and Southern California. Also in the 1920s, Cedar City became the terminus of a spur line from the Los Angeles and Salt Lake Railroad in the Union Pacific system, and the headquarters of the Utah Parks Company, the U.P. subsidiary that managed the lodges at Zion and Bryce canyons, Cedar Breaks, and the north rim of the Grand Canyon. Tourists would arrive at Cedar City on the U.P., stay a night at the El Escalante Hotel, then be hauled from one park to the next in rugged motor buses. These and other stimuli to development made Cedar City the unchallenged metropolis of southern Utah until the 1970s, when the attractions of Utah's one small corner of the Sun Belt sent the population of St. George soaring.

Parowan, in the meantime, retains the character of a traditional Mormon town. Elizabeth Wood Kane would probably recognize the place if she could revisit it today. Several pioneer adobes, including the Dame house, still stand, in addition to the old rock meetinghouse. The cottonwoods that once lined the streets have largely been replaced by slower growing shade trees, but these in their turn have matured until their limbs reach high and spread wide. If Parowan appeared middle-aged in 1872, it is now an old town, but one that wears its years well and continues to breed an intense loyalty in those who grew up there. The most populous section of town is the cemetery, where former residents who for perhaps fifty years or more have made their homes and careers elsewhere return to be buried in their native soil.

Mrs. Kane used the occasion of her visit to Parowan to comment on the egalitarian character of Mormon village society, noting that,

> in the southern Mormon settlements, at least, there is no distinction made between mistress and servant. The younger "sisters" think it no degradation to go to live in the houses of the married ones and help them with their work, and when work is over, they sit down to meals or "go to parties" together. I am not speaking of the rougher sort alone. I have met a wealthy bishop's daughter at a dance, dressed in white muslin, who has

opened the door for me next morning with arms fresh from the wash-tub, when I went to call upon her mistress.

She notes, however, that "Such girls sometimes marry their masters. A nice possibility for the wife hiring 'help' to keep before her eyes!"[15]

She also makes a shrewd assessment of Brigham Young's leadership style as manifest in his readiness to listen to everyone who comes to call on him in each town he visits:

> At these informal audiences, reports, complaints, and petitions were made; and I think I gathered more of the actual working of Mormonism by listening to them than from any other source. They talked away to Brigham Young about every conceivable matter, from the fluxing of an ore to the advantages of a Navajo bit, and expected him to remember every child in every cotter's family. And he really seemed to do so, and to be at home, and be rightfully deemed infallible on every subject. I think he must make fewer mistakes than most popes, from his being in such constant intercourse with his people. I noticed that he never seemed uninterested, but gave an unforced attention to the person addressing him, which suggested a mind free from care. I used to fancy that he wasted a great deal of power in this way; but I soon saw that he was accumulating it.[16]

On the road to Cedar City, Mrs. Kane was shown the abandoned iron works and reflected upon the hardship caused by the settlement of marginal lands and the insistence on "home industry" by which

> the manufacturers and consumers are expected to show their faith in Providence by flying in the face of Adam Smith. It would have been ludicrous, if it had not been pathetic, to hear the exhortations to saints who had been told off to Southern settlements where the desert had failed to blossom as the rose, and the torrid sun had disordered their livers.[17]

State highways lead from both Parowan and Cedar City through strikingly beautiful canyons to the lofty platform of the Markagunt. As is typical of the High Plateaus, the uplands are crisscrossed by roads, including one that leads to the 11,307-foot summit of Brian Head, surely one of the highest points in North America accessible to automobiles.

The plateau ranges in width from about a dozen miles at the north end to more than thirty miles along its southern rim. It extends for about forty miles on a north-south axis, though as Clarence Dutton observed long ago it is difficult to fix a northern boundary. There is little sense of elevation on the northern portion of the table, which seems to be merely an uneven plain at the base of Little Creek and Bear peaks. While, as Dutton remarked, "the country is rough with hills and rocky valleys . . . these inequalities upon so vast an expanse as the back of the Markagunt are as mere ripples or waves upon the bosom of a great lake."

Clarence E. Dutton has been described by Wallace Stegner as "the first literary tourist in a country where tourist travel has become the number one business."[18] Dutton was a Yale graduate, class of 1860, educated for the ministry, winner of the Yale Literary Prize, and by his own claim "omnibiblical."[19] In the nineteenth-century polymath tradition, he educated himself as a geologist through his reading, his career in the Army Ordnance Corps, his association with some of the best minds of the time in the Washington Philosophical Society, and his work in the field. When he joined John Wesley Powell's survey in 1875, he brought a fine analytical mind, a ready wit, and a sensibility conditioned by romantic landscape aesthetics, yielding a division of the world of beauty between the "picturesque" and the "sublime" and a tendency to associate high thoughts with high places. These qualities and tendencies are apparent in Dutton's two classic studies of the High Plateau region, *Report on the Geology of the High Plateaus of Utah* (1880) and *Tertiary History of the Grand Cañon District* (1882). Dutton found traveling on the northern Markagunt

> a pleasure excursion, but not remarkably instructive to the geologist. The explorer will enjoy the luscious camps beneath the shade of century-old pines, beside sparkling streams of the purest water, and will see with pleasure the keen relish with which the animals devour the luxuriant wild grass. Nature is here in her gentle mood, neither wild nor inanimate, neither grand nor trivial, but genial, temperate, and mildly suggestive.[20]

Most of the High Plateaus have at least one traditional resort where people from the neighboring valleys have gone for many years to fish, boat, ski, or simply enjoy the delights of the forests and meadows. The Markagunt has several, old and new. The oldest is undoubtedly Panguitch Lake, which was a favorite summering place for the Paiutes long before the arrival of Europeans in the region. With the resettlement of Panguitch after the Black Hawk War, the moderate 8,500-foot elevation of the lake basin made it a favored location for mountain dairies, and several ranches were established in the surrounding meadows during the mid-1870s. By the end of the decade, the lake had developed into a resort for the miners from Silver Reef, with a racetrack, saloons, and gambling halls. By the 1890s there was a large dance pavilion, a covered grandstand for the racetrack, rows of stables for the racehorses brought to the area from throughout Utah and Nevada, and numerous lodges and hotels surrounding the lake. Panguitch Lake was even on the summer circuit of several professional theatrical companies.

The coming of Utah statehood in 1896 threw a damper on some activities at the lake, as betting on horseraces was outlawed and fish and game laws were passed regulating the taking of fish from the state's waters. Panguitch Lake was a natural fishery of exceptional quality, and visitors to the resort "feasted on fish three times a day."[21] By the turn of the century, the stock of native trout was becoming exhausted, and chubs began to appear in large numbers. Because chubs became numerous about the time the state Fish and Game Commission was established, the local people accused the state officials of having planted them. Two members of the Fish and Game Commission were named Walker and Sharp, and to this day chubs are known in southern Utah as "Sharpwalkers."[22]

Navajo Lake, more than a thousand feet higher than Panguitch Lake, is somewhat smaller but lovely in its narrow wooded basin. Impounded by a lava flow, Navajo Lake has no surface outlet but drains through sinkholes, part of its waters finding their way to Cascade Falls and the Virgin River, and part flowing to the Sevier drainage by way of Duck Creek Spring. The Brian Head ski area is the largest mountain resort in southern Utah, while nearby Cedar Breaks National Monument, though not developed for extended visits, provides tourists with striking views of the same wildly eroded Pink Cliffs formation found at Bryce Canyon, but here a thousand feet higher in elevation. Together with neighboring Pine Valley Mountain, the Markagunt constitutes the closest extensive high mountain area to the burgeoning population of Las Vegas. Much of the plateau surface is privately owned, having been acquired by local ranchers before the establishment of the Dixie National Forest, and in recent years Las Vegans have been buying vacation property at a rate that alarms some southern Utah residents.

Markagunt supposedly means "highland of trees" in Paiute.[23] If so, the plateau is well named, for its forests are extensive. The ponderosa-pine zone is much wider here than it is in the northern plateaus, and supplies most of the commercial harvest. The Markagunt is also the most important water source in southern Utah. The southern terraces supply most of the streamflow in the Virgin River, while Asay and Mammoth creeks, which drain the long, gentle, east-running slopes, are the major headwaters of the Sevier. In addition to the lakes and streams and forests, the most notable feature of the plateau's surface is the extensive and geologically recent basalt flows. A basalt field south of Panguitch Lake appears, as Dutton puts it, "so recent and so fresh in its aspect that we wonder why there is no record or tradition of its eruption"[24]—though in fact it could easily be two thousand years old.

While there is little sense of elevation on the northern and eastern portions of the Markagunt, the southern rim more than compensates for any deficiency. Here the earth drops off in broad terraces to the Virgin River Valley almost seven thousand feet below, the greatest vertical distance in the High Plateaus region. Dutton, who had an unerring instinct for the most spectacular viewpoints, writes:

> From the southwest salient of the Markagunt we behold one of those sublime spectacles which characterize the loftiest standpoints of the Plateau Province. Even to the mere tourist there are few panoramas so broad and grand; but to the geologist there comes with all the visible grandeur a deep significance. The radius of vision is from 80 to 100 miles. We stand upon the great cliff of Tertiary beds which meanders to the eastward till lost in the distance, sculptured into strange and even startling forms, and lit up with colors so rich and glowing that they awaken enthusiasm in the most apathetic. . . . Standing among evergreens, knee-deep in succulent grass and a wealth of Alpine blossoms, fanned by chill, moist breezes, we look over terraces decked with towers and temples and gashed with cañons to the desert which stretches away beyond the southern horizon, blank, lifeless, and glowing with torrid heat.[25]

By the time he visited the Markagunt, Dutton had spent probably three summers among the High Plateaus, learning to read the distinctive landscape. While he had found that because of the exposed strata, "Nature here is more easily read than elsewhere,"[26] he also characterized the immense cliffs and canyons of the Plateau Country as

> a great innovation in modern ideas of scenery, and in our conception of the grandeur, beauty, and power of nature. As with all great innovations it is not to be comprehended in a day or a week, nor even in a month. It must be dwelt upon and studied, and the study must comprise the slow acquisitions of the meaning and spirit of that marvellous scenery which characterizes the Plateau Country, and of which the great chasm [the Grand Canyon] is the superlative manifestation. The study and slow mastery of the influences of that class of scenery and its full appreciation is a special culture, requiring time, patience, and long familiarity for its consummation.[27]

One of the challenges in coming to terms with the plateau landscape, for Dutton as for Elizabeth Wood Kane, was that its colors are derived from an unfamiliar palette:

> The gentle tints of an eastern landscape, the rich blue of distant mountains, the green of vernal and summer vegetation, the subdued colors of hillside and meadow, all are wanting here, and in their place we behold belts of fierce staring red, yellow, and toned white, which are intensified rather than alleviated by alternating belts of dark iron gray.[28]

By the end of her southward journey, Mrs. Kane was beginning to grow accustomed to a landscape formed on a different scale and painted in different colors from her native Pennsylvania, as is apparent in her description of the Kolob Canyons:

> The air was so clear that every object stood out in stereoscopic relief. The view was perpetually changing as our horses brought us abreast of openings in the gray mountain-wall on our left, revealing glimpses of a crowded world of red and yellow crags and peaks beyond. More golden sunshine seemed to rest on them than fell on us outside. For me to say that they were unnaturally vivid in color and harsh in their contrasts, would only signify that I was used to the gentle outlines and soft hues of Nature at home. Moses led his people forty years through such scenery as this.[29]

Interstate 15 crosses the rim of the basin not far from the route Mrs. Kane followed and permits brief views into these bright canyons for the traveler sufficiently alert to catch them. Near this point once stood Fort Harmony, established in 1852 by John D. Lee, mercilessly buffeted by the winds that sweep through the pass, and finally destroyed in 1862 by a rainstorm that lasted for twenty-eight days and literally melted the settlement's adobe walls. Two of Lee's children were killed when their dwelling collapsed. Rather than rebuilding, the settlers relocated to more sheltered sites at New Harmony, in a cove of the Pine Valley Mountain to the west, and at Kanarraville, nestled up against the Hurricane Cliffs to the east.

The motorist speeding down the Interstate can have little sense of the dread felt by earlier travelers of the rocky, twisting road through Ash Creek Canyon. Mrs. Kane tells of "winding down a narrow road painfully excavated along the side of what I now see to be a chasm, sheer down which I can look hundreds of feet—and I much prefer not looking!"[30] From the less hazardous road below Pintura (then known as Bellevue), she could admire the distant prospect of the Zion Canyon region:

Far off in the east rose a chain of lofty mountains, their sides striped with party-colored bands, terrace on terrace, to what seemed a great city; its golden buildings crowning the summit. Behind its palaces the white towers of a cathedral appeared. The glowing colors were heightened by the snowy covering of still more distant peaks; some so remote as to be only faintly visible against the iridescent sky. The sun was now shining upon them in full splendor.

At the same time, she found "something saddening in that distant view of great courts and domes, empty and silent, with no human history or legend attached to them."[31]

While Mrs. Kane's Mormon hosts were eager to make her appreciate the wild and vivid beauty, even they had required time, and probably a deliberate effort, to learn to read this landscape in a positive way. George A. Smith, one of the great promoters of southern Utah colonization, was still somewhat taken aback on his visit to the Virgin River settlements in 1857: "It is rather rough; but I could not but admire its extreme beauty; and I think, if the Lord had got up all the rough, rocky, and the broken fragments of the earth in one, he might have dropped it here." Smith reported that the soil in which the settlers were trying to grow cotton "is nothing but the red sand of the Sahara," then added a comment on the climate: "The country seemed very hot to me; otherwise I enjoyed the visit very well. But the brethren insisted that it was a very cool spell while I was there."[32]

For the settlers "called" to what Juanita Brooks (herself deeply tied to the Virgin River Valley) termed "the ragged edge" of Mormon Country,[33] the prospects often seemed bleak. Sometimes, however, the very hardship could provoke a wry humor, as in George Hicks's song about his move from the Salt Lake Valley to "Utah's Dixie," which reportedly scandalized the audience at its first performance at a Twenty-fourth of July celebration in St. George:

Oh, once I lived in Cottonwood and owned a little farm,
But I was called to Dixie, which did me much alarm;
To raise the cane and cotton, I right away must go;
But the reason why they called on me, I'm sure I do not
     know.

I yoked old Jim and Bolly up all for to make a start,
To leave my house and garden, it almost broke my heart.
We moved along quite slowly and often looked behind,
For the sand and rocks of Dixie kept running through my
     mind.

53

At length we reached the Black Ridge where I broke my wagon
    down,
I could not find a carpenter so far from any town,
So with a clumsy cedar pole I fixed an awkward slide;
My wagon pulled so heavy then that Betsy could not ride.

While Betsy was a'walking, I told her to take care,
When all upon a sudden she struck a prickly pear.
Then she began to blubber out as loud as she could bawl,
"If I was back in Cottonwood, I would not come at all!"

. . . .

Next we got to Washington, where we stayed a little while
To see if April showers would make the verdure smile.
But, oh, I was mistaken and so I went away,
For the red hills of November looked just the same in May.

I feel so weak and hungry now, there's nothing here to cheer
Except prophetic sermons which we very often hear.
They will hand them out by dozens and prove them by the
    book—
I'd rather have some roasting ears to stay at home and cook.

. . . .

My wagon's sold for sorghum seed to make a little bread;
And poor old Jim and Bolly long ago are dead.
There's only me and Betsy left to hoe the cotton-tree;
May Heaven help the Dixie-ite wherever he may be![34]

There are two routes around the southern base of the Markagunt
Plateau. One is State Highway 15, which goes up the Virgin River to
the mouth of Zion Canyon, then climbs a slickrock slope and enters the
famous windowed Zion Tunnel, eventually reaching the East Fork of the
Virgin and an intersection with U.S. 89 at Mount Carmel Junction.
This is one of the most scenic roads in a region of scenic roads, passing
through the one-time farming villages, now tourist stops, of Virgin,
Rockville, and Springdale. At the bottom of Zion Canyon, which was
carved by the North Fork of the Virgin, the elevation is about three
thousand feet, and there are views of the Kolob Terrace at ten thousand
feet. As massive and overpowering as the gorges and towers are here,
however, there is a yet more striking viewpoint.

   The other route around the Markagunt is State Highway 17, which
climbs the face of the Hurricane Cliffs east of the town of Hurricane
and follows the Vermillion Cliffs to Kanab. About midway between the

Hurricane Cliffs and the stateline towns of Hildale and Colorado City, a dirt road leaves the highway and winds northeast through the hills, entering the Virgin River Valley near Rockville. The road approximates the route taken by Clarence E. Dutton.

While Dutton was not the first to appreciate the spectacular landforms of Zion Canyon, his description of them in *Tertiary History* surpasses all earlier ones. In the autumn of 1880, Dutton and W. H. Holmes climbed to what is now known as Dutton's Notch on the flanks of Smithsonian Butte. From this vantage point, Dutton caught his first full sight of Zion Canyon, "a scene never to be forgotten. In coming time it will, I believe, take rank with a very small number of spectacles each of which will, in its own way, be regarded as the most exquisite of its kind which the world discloses":

> From right to left across the further foreground of the picture stretches the inner cañon of the Virgen, about 700 feet in depth, and here of considerable width. . . . Across the cañon, and rather more than a mile and a half beyond it, stands the central and commanding object of the picture, the western temple, rising 4,000 feet above the river. Its glorious summit was the object we had seen an hour before, and now the matchless beauty and majesty of its vast mass is all before us. Yet it is only the central object of a mighty throng of structures wrought up to the same exalted style, and filling up the entire panorama. Right opposite us are the two principal forks of the Virgen, the Parunuweap coming from the right or east, and the Muku'ntuweap or Little Zion Valley, descending towards us from the north. The Parunuweap is seen emerging on the extreme right through a stupendous gateway and chasm in the Triassic terrace, nearly 3,000 feet in depth. The further wall of this cañon, at the opening of the gateway, quickly swings northward at a right angle and becomes the eastern wall of Little Zion Valley. As it sweeps down the Parunuweap it breaks into great pediments, covered all over with the richest carving. The effect is much like that which the architect of the Milan Cathedral appears to have designed, though here it is vividly suggested rather than fully realized—as an artist painting in the "broad style" suggests many things without actually drawing them. . . . The flank of the wall receding up the Mukuntuweap is for a mile or two similarly decorated, but soon breaks into new forms much more impressive and wonderful. A row of towers half a mile high is quarried out of the palisade, and stands well advanced from its face. . . . Just behind them, rising a thousand feet higher, is the eastern temple, crowned with a cylindric dome of white sandstone. . . .

Nothing can exceed the wondrous beauty of Little Zion Valley, which separates the two temples and their respective groups of towers. Nor are

these the only sublime structures which look down into its depths, for similar ones are seen on either hand along its receding vista until a turn in the
course carries the valley out of sight. In its proportions it is about equal to
Yo Semite, but in the nobility and beauty of the sculptures there is no
comparison. It is Hyperion to a satyr. No wonder the fierce Mormon
zealot, who named it, was reminded of the Great Zion, on which his fervid
thoughts were bent—"of houses not built with hands, eternal in the heav-
ens."[35]

This passage, written more than five years after Dutton's first introduction to the region of the high plateaus, illustrates the full development
of his sensitivity to the western landscape.

4

THE INNER VALLEYS

J ohn Wesley Powell called the Markagunt and Paunsagunt the Terrace Plateaus. Viewed from the south, they are probably the most spectacular uplifts in the plateau region. From the broad plain of the Arizona Strip, a "Grand Staircase" (another term coined by Powell) rises in bold steps: first the Brown Cliffs of the Shinarump formation, then the Vermillion Cliffs (Chinle and Wingate formations), the White Cliffs (Navajo Sandstone), the Gray Cliffs (Cretaceous), and at the upper rim the brilliantly tinted Tertiary limestone formation of the Pink Cliffs. Attempting to convey a visual sense of these terraces to readers unfamiliar with the plateau landscape, Powell offered this simple analogy:

> Place a book before you on a table with its front edge toward you, rest another book on the back of this, place a third on the back of the second, and in like manner a fourth on the third. Now the leaves of the books dip from you and the cut edges stand in tiny escarpments facing you. So the rock-formed leaves of these books of geology have the escarpment edges turned southward, while each book itself dips northward, and the crest of each plateau book is the summit of a line of cliffs.[1]

The town of Kanab is picturesquely situated in a cove carved in the Vermillion Cliffs by Kanab Creek on its course from its headwaters on the southwestern slopes of the Paunsagunt Plateau to its confluence with the Colorado in the heart of the Grand Canyon. It is difficult to imagine that this tourist-oriented town, in surroundings familiar to the viewers of classic Western movies of the 1940s and '50s, was the notorious "Knob," the "Gibraltar of [Mormon] felons," of Judge Hawley's 1873 letter requesting an army presence in southern Utah. In fact, though some men implicated in the Mountain Meadows Massacre did relocate to Kanab and the surrounding area at the end of the 1860s, it was far from being a rip-roaring frontier town.

On his second trip down the Green and Colorado rivers in 1871,

Powell pulled out of the river at the mouth of the Paria and made his headquarters in Kanab for the winter. Frederick S. Dellenbaugh, a young member of Powell's party, provides the following description of the settlement as it was then:

> The village, which had been started only a year or two, was laid out in the characteristic Mormon style with wide streets and regular lots fenced by wattling willows between stakes. Irrigating ditches ran down each side of every street and from them the water, derived from a creek that came down the canyon back of the town, could be led to any of the lots, each of which was about one quarter of an acre. . . . Fruit trees, shade trees, and vines had been planted and were already beginning to promise near results, while corn, potatoes, etc., gave fine crops. . . . Altogether there were about 100 families in the village. The houses that had been built outside the fort were quite substantially constructed, some of adobe or sun-dried brick. The entire settlement had a thrifty air, as is the case with the Mormons. Not a grog-shop, or gambling saloon, or dance-hall was to be seen; quite in contrast with the usual disgraceful accompaniments of the ordinary frontier towns.[2]

The chief early access route to Kanab followed the base of the Vermillion Cliffs from St. George by way of Short Creek and Moccasin Springs. Because this route was used by young couples from Kanab and from the Mormon settlements in Arizona to go the St. George temple to be married, it came to be known as the Honeymoon Trail. There was a rough road leading north from Kanab across the Navajo Sandstone reefs to Long Valley, on the East Fork of the Virgin, but because of this route's difficulty the main northern access road swung several miles east along the Vermillion Cliffs to Johnson Canyon, a flat-bottomed valley that leads up to the Gray Cliffs terrace at the base of the Paunsagunt. The road divided near the head of Johnson Canyon, with one branch of the road leading northeast to Skutumpah and the other, more used branch turning west through what was then known as Upper Kanab (now Alton) and over a low pass to the Sevier.

This was the route my great-grandfather, Edward Long Geary, and his family took in the spring of 1881 on their way from northern Utah to the Mormon colonies on the Little Colorado River in Arizona. They came through here again the following fall, having decided Arizona was not for them. On this occasion, seeing some beehives near their camp in Johnson Canyon, my great-grandfather went to the ranch house to inquire whether he could purchase some honey. Because he had no container, he also bought a glass pitcher from the ranch wife. My grandfather, who was five years old at the time, never forgot the taste of that honey. The pitcher stood among other treasured knickknacks in the glass china cupboard, and I heard retold on many occasions of my childhood the story of the trip through Johnson Canyon and the pitcher full of honey.

Though my grandmother was evidently unaware of it (otherwise she would certainly have told me), Johnson Canyon took its name from her relatives. In 1871 brothers Joel Hills, Joseph Ellis, Benjamin Franklin, and William Derby Johnson brought their families to what was previously known as Spring Canyon and established what they ambitiously called Johnson City. The large family of Ezekiel and Julia Hills Johnson had joined the LDS Church in the early days in Kirtland, Ohio, all except the father, who was regarded as something of a reprobate. Joel Hills, the eldest son and author of a favorite Mormon hymn, "High on the Mountain Top," moved from Johnson Canyon to the Upper Sevier Valley and founded a village named Hillsdale (not to be confused with Hildale on the Utah-Arizona border). Nothing now remains of this settlement, which was located just south of the turnoff to Bryce Canyon National Park, except a few ranch outbuildings. Another son, Benjamin Franklin Johnson, had been among the first settlers of Springville and Santaquin (then known as Summit Creek) before coming to Johnson Canyon, and later helped to settle Mesa, Arizona. Yet another son, George Washington Johnson, my great-great-grandfather, had a claim to be considered as the founder of Fountain Green, since he surveyed the first blocks of the townsite. Though he planned at one time to join his brothers at Johnson City, he never completed the move. Johnson daughters married Shermans, Babbitts, Bartons, and LeBarons, and had numerous progeny. All in all, it is a huge clan that still claims to be the biggest of all Mormon families. Johnson descendants have generously peopled not only mainline Mormondom but also several fundamentalist cults in southern Utah and Arizona. I have rarely been in a group of more than twenty Utahns without finding at least one other person with Johnson antecedents.

Today the connecting link between Kanab and the north is U.S. 89, which follows Kanab Creek north for a few miles then crosses over the divide into Long Valley, meeting State Highway 9 at Mount Carmel Junction. Long Valley has a pleasantly bucolic air, with deep-shaded villages and their crazy-quilt fields strung along the East Fork of the Virgin between the enclosing walls of the Markagunt Plateau and Glendale Bench. The largest village, Orderville, was once the site of the most successful Mormon experiment in communal living, lasting from the mid-1870s until the late 1880s.

The United Order, a theocratic cooperative system designed to unify the people in a common cause and eliminate extremes of wealth and poverty, was attempted in numerous Mormon communities during the 1870s for varying periods of time and with varying degrees of success. Only in Orderville was there sufficient dedication, sufficient isolation, and sufficient undeveloped resources to enable it to prosper. The initial attempt to institute the United Order in Long Valley occurred at Mount Carmel, but when some residents resisted pooling their resources the more zealous ones moved a couple of miles up the river and founded a new community entirely dedicated to the Order. And dedicated is the right word. Each family had its own small cabin inside the stockade, but privacy and individual choice went little further than that. The entire village awoke to a bugler's call at five o'clock in the morning, breakfasted together in the communal dining hall, then separated to their assigned tasks, meeting again for the noon and evening meals.

The economic goal of the Order was self-sufficiency. They sawed their own timber, wove their own wool, made their own plain clothing, tanned their own leather, and cobbled their own thick shoes. They had a blacksmith shop, of course, and also a furniture shop and a soap factory. As Wallace Stegner writes in "Arcadian Village,"

> It is difficult to find anything that the Orderville brethren were compelled to buy, aside from arms, ammunition, and a minimum of machinery. In the town itself, or on the farms and ranches the Order acquired in the canyons, out on the Arizona desert, and down in the semi-tropical lower valley of the Virgin, practically every necessity was grown or manufactured. The orchard and vegetable garden, just outside the square, produced peaches, apricots, grapes, currants, gooseberries, garden truck, watermelons. From the hillsides came timber and firewood, and up the valley a few miles was a coal mine. Down near Washington, on the "Cotton Farm," they grew cotton that was ultimately processed in their own mill. At Moccasin Springs, between the Vermilion Cliffs and the Grand Canyon, there were great fields of sugar cane and the simple machinery and vats for making molasses. Sugar they could not manage, but what they could not manage they did without. Molasses, poured over crumbed-up bread, satisfied the sweet-tooth of the children. Candy could be made from the green skimmings of the cane. Peaches and other fruit could be boiled down in molasses for preserves.[3]

The original members of the Order all received an equal share in its capital stock in return for whatever assets they had to contribute. Every man

John Wilson's boys, about 1905. G. E. Anderson photo, courtesy Brigham Young University photo archives.

in the community, no matter how skilled or unskilled, productive or unproductive, received the same wage of a dollar and fifty cents a day. Women earned seventy-five cents and children lesser amounts depending on age and gender. But no wages were paid in cash. They merely represented credit on the books against which the cost of board and supplies was debited. Any surplus or deficit at the year's end was simply wiped off the ledger, and everybody started afresh. While some members probably consumed more than they produced, the Order as a whole accumulated a large surplus, which was used not to improve the rather bare-bones living standard, but to expand the Order's land and livestock holdings.

Among the several factors that led to the United Order's eventual demise, one was clearly a flaw in the planning. No provision was made for young men to "buy into" the Order when they came of age and began their own families. They could, of course, continue to work for subsistence wages, but they had no share in the cooperative's growing wealth. With the opening of the mines at Silver Reef, just across the Markagunt Plateau, and the availability of jobs that paid cash wages, many of the younger generation abandoned the community. Another factor was resentment in neighboring communities at the Order's economic expansion. A third likely factor was that people simply got tired of the plain living. As Stegner puts it,

One of the most important things that Orderville forgot . . . was that the perfect society may starve, may freeze, may be chased and outlawed, may do almost any number of things almost permanently, but only for a very short time, during the very height of its initial enthusiasm, may it dispense with ornament. . . . Fashion, as much as anything else, killed Arcadia.[4]

Perhaps because of this very absence of conspicuous consumption, scarcely anything remains in Orderville except the name itself to suggest its distinctive origins.

From Orderville, the highway runs past Glendale and the turnoff to Alton then climbs to Long Valley Divide. Here, at an elevation of about 7,600 feet, a wooded ridge connects the Markagunt to the Paunsagunt Plateau and forms the divide between the Virgin and the Sevier watersheds. Here, too, Utah Highway 14 offers a pleasant route across the broad back of the Markagunt to Cedar City. In contrast to its fault-scarp western wall and dramatic southern terraces, the eastern slope of the Markagunt is gentle. Because the Sevier River Valley rises at a rate only a little lower than the plateau highlands, both the Markagunt and the Paunsagunt appear to be rather low platforms from this vantage point.

On February 16, 1873, only a couple of months after Elizabeth Wood Kane's outbound journey along the Mormon Corridor, Frederick Dellenbaugh left Kanab for Salt Lake City by way of the inner valleys of the High Plateaus. Dellenbaugh's account is a reminiscence of youthful adventure, written almost forty years after the events it narrates, and a romantic distance colors its reading of the land. With immense zest, he describes spending the night in a haystack at Glendale—"I never slept more comfortably in my life"—and waking in the morning to find "a heaviness on top of us we knew meant snow. We were covered by a full foot of it, soft and dry."[5] In the same spirit, he tells of getting lost in a blizzard near Long Valley Divide and being forced to make camp under a pine tree:

> Our pack contained enough food for supper; breakfast would have to take care of itself. We also had some grain, which we fed to the hungry animals and tied them under the cedars, where they were protected in a measure from the sharp wind though they were standing in deep snow. For ourselves we cut twigs from the green cedars and made a thick mattress on the snow with them. Our blankets on top of these made a bed fit for a king.

Isaac Wagstaff residence and post office, Angle, Grass Valley, 1896. G. E. Anderson photo, courtesy Brigham Young University photo archives.

The storm cleared entirely; a brilliant moon shone over all, causing the falling frost in the air to scintillate like diamonds.[6]

The Upper Sevier Valley is still cold and clear in the winter, and not too warm even in the summer. At an elevation of between 6,500 and 7,000 feet, the growing season is short, and the land is mostly devoted to hay and pasture. The little village of Hatch always strikes me as rather exposed and vulnerable to the elements. Panguitch seems to have a firmer grip on the earth. Here, as in Parowan and Beaver, there are many fine houses and public buildings from the nineteenth and early twentieth centuries. The Southern Utah Equitable is probably the best surviving example in Utah of the old-fashioned general store.

From Panguitch, the highway runs northward between the descending table of the Markagunt and the rising platform of the Sevier Plateau. State Highway 20, running west from the ghost town of Orton to connect with Interstate 15 at the north end of the Little Salt Lake Valley, traces a section of the Old Spanish Trail in its crossing of the west range of High Plateaus. A few miles farther north, where the Tushar begins its rise, an immense lava flow once blocked the course of the Sevier, and the highway follows the river through the narrow channel it has carved.

Where the valley begins to open up once again, near the Garfield-

Piute county line, you can see across the fields to the west the house where Robert LeRoy Parker—better known to Western legend as Butch Cassidy—lived as a boy. The villages of Circleville, Junction, and Kingston occupy Circle Valley, some six miles in diameter, situated at the point where the East Fork has cut a gorge through the Sevier Plateau to join the main South Fork of the Sevier.

The middle range of High Plateaus, the Sevier and the Paunsagunt, are uplifted fault blocks along the Sevier Fault, which forms their western wall and continues south into the Grand Canyon region. The Paunsagunt has no peaks worth mentioning but is entirely tabular, reaching its 9,200-foot summit at the rim of the Pink Cliffs. The Paunsagunt and the Sevier join at a high transverse valley once known as Panguitch Hayfield, now called Emery Valley, site of the Bryce Canyon Airport. The Sevier Plateau rises gradually northward to 11,000-foot Mount Dutton, dips down to the East Fork Gorge, then rises again, reaching its highest point at 11,226-foot Monroe Peak. From this summit, a steep ramp drops off into low broken hills near Glenwood. Like its western neighbor the Tushar, the Sevier Plateau is mainly composed of volcanic materials accumulated over a long series of eruptive periods. It is a relatively narrow uplift, seventy miles long and varying between ten and fifteen miles wide, and is distinctly tabular, though, as Dutton pointed out,

> there are many stretches along its western front which appear quite like a common mountain range. Profound gorges, V–shaped, heading far back in its mass, have cut the table from summit to base and open through magnificent gateways into the valley. The residual masses between these gorges present their gable-ends to the spectator, who cannot see what is behind them, and they look exactly like so many individual mountains, while in reality they are merely pediments carved by erosion out of a gigantic palisade.[7]

These massive pediments occur for the most part in the northern portion of the plateau, near the town of Monroe. Farther south, as Dutton observed, "long stretches of the western front are unbroken and present to the valley of the Sevier a wall of vast proportions."[8]

Dutton's work in the High Plateaus region was concentrated on the areas accessible from the inner valleys. In addition to pioneering the geology of the region, he developed a kind of plateau landscape aesthetics, noting, for example, how "the absence of Alpine forms and the predominance of the long and slightly-inclined profiles of the plateau type rob these great masses of their grandeur and beauty; for they produce an optical deception which carries the horizon up near their summits, while in reality it is far below." Because "every object is molded upon a grand scale," careful discrimination is needed to read the landforms accurately: "it is only by long study and familiarity that the huge proportions are realized."[9] The walls of Circle Valley provided him with materials for speculations on the theory of mountain sublimity:

> On the east rises the long palisade of the Sevier Plateau 4,300 feet above the river; on the west the wall of the Southern Tushar, which opposite the valley is 4,200 feet above it and from 5,000 to 6,000 feet above it in its northern and southern extensions. The Tushar shows rugged peaks and domes planted upon a colossal wall; the Sevier Plateau shows a blank wall without the peaks. Very grand and majestic are these mural fronts, stretching away into the dim distance calm, stern, and restful. Yet they fail to impress the beholder with a full realization of their magnitude. This is true of mountains in general, but pre-eminently so of great cliffs. If one-third of the stuff in the Sevier Plateau, east of Circle Valley, had been used to build a range of lively mountains, they would have seemed grander and possessed what no palisade can ever possess—beauty and animation. It is otherwise with the Tushar. There the great wall has magnified the mountains by giving them a noble sub-structure on which to stand, and the mountains have magnified the wall by giving it something to support.[10]

North of Circle Valley, the Sevier and Tushar masses draw closer together, eventually confining the Sevier River to the narrow Marysvale Canyon. The town of Marysvale is situated in a hollow at the base of the Tushar just upstream from this canyon. According to Josiah F. Gibbs, the name of the site was originally Merry Vale, so called because an exploring party led by George A. Smith camped there in 1856 and amused themselves with a "stag dance."[11] Like its neighbors Circleville, Kingston, and Junction, Marysvale began in the mid-1860s as a Mormon farm village, but in 1868 precious metals were discovered in the Tushar, and the village was "taken over" (to adopt the words of the Daughters of Utah Pioneers marker in the middle of town) by miners. Mines sprang into existence almost overnight in canyons that still bear such names as Gold Gulch, California Gulch, Bullion Canyon, Crystal Basin, Revenue Gulch, Surprise Gulch, and Alunite Ridge. By 1872 Bullion City boasted of fifty buildings and a population of several hundred.

The Marysvale district experienced the boom-and-bust cycles typical of a mining economy. While some rich pockets were discovered, the crazy geology of the Tushar made it difficult to follow the ore-bearing veins. Nevertheless, several million dollars worth of gold, silver, lead, and zinc came out of the deep canyons west of Marysvale—at a period when a million dollars meant something. The deposits of alunite at the base of the Tushar and Sevier plateaus have been mined from time to time for their potash and sulfur values, though their nineteen percent alumina content cannot compete with foreign bauxite ores as a source of aluminum. In the mid-twentieth century, Marysvale's uranium mines helped fuel the beginnings of the Atomic Age—and left its residents with one of the world's highest cancer rates.

Because of its mines, Marysvale became the terminus of a branch line of the Denver and Rio Grande Railway and thereby a shipping point for cattle and wool and a supply station for ranches and villages across a wide stretch of southern Utah. Nethella Griffin Woolsey's history of Escalante relates how "going with the wool" to Marysvale was an eagerly sought privilege among the town's children.[12] Despite this commercial activity, however, Marysvale never attained a very large population. With the fading away of the mines and the disappearance of the railroad, it has become once again what it started out to be, a quiet Mormon farm village. Yet there are differences. The streets are too narrow, the blocks and town lots too small, the ghostly business district too large in relation to the residential areas.

North of Marysvale, beyond the deep gorge of Beaver Creek, is Gold Mountain. Here, on June 22, 1891, a man named Newton Hill located the Annie Laurie deposit on a steep slope at the 9,500-foot level.[13] This discovery brought the usual rush of prospectors, and soon the Blue Bird, Grasshopper, Hastings, and other mines dotted the slopes of Mill Creek Canyon, while the Sevier, Holland, and Deer Park mines were developed across the ridge in the next canyon to the west. In 1900, the Annie Laurie mine was purchased by an eastern syndicate led by Peter L. Kimberly, whose name would be given to the town growing around the mines.[14] The Kimberly syndicate erected a mill designed to process two hundred tons of ore per day. While the mines near Marysvale produced mainly silver, lead, and zinc, Kimberly was a gold district. This metal captured the popular imagination and probably contributed to the local legends in Piute and Sevier counties that portray Kimberly as a quintessential boomtown.

In fact, Kimberly was neither very big nor very wild as mining towns go. While some accounts claim as many as five thousand people inhabited the town at its peak, Dean Herring offers a more reasonable estimate of 1,200 during the summers and fewer in the winters, when many families returned to their homes in the valley. The Annie Laurie company erected a group of eighteen frame cottages in "Upper Kimberly," near the mine, and about fifty others at three clusters in "Lower Kimberly," where the mill and the business district were located. Midway between the two sections, the "Lodge" occupied a fine view site. It was a large stone and frame structure built to accommodate important visitors and later used as the manager's residence. The Lodge may well have been the first house in central and southern Utah to have two bathrooms, one on each floor. In addition to the more permanent housing, Lower Kimberly also had a tent village in a meadow by the creek, and many miners lived in cabins or shanties scattered over the mountainside. The business district in 1908 consisted of "three general stores, three livery stables, two hotels, three barber shops, two large boarding houses (plus several small ones), a school house, a doctor's office, a post office, an opera house, a dairy, a laundry, three saloons, a butcher shop and several specialty shops."[15]

A mining camp with only three saloons obviously does not rank very high on a scale of wildness. Ed Tilton, whose father, Fred Tilton, managed the mine properties for more than twenty years after the 1908 bankruptcy, responds to legends of brothels in Kimberly in these terms:

> The only "whore house" that existed at Kimberly, according to every old timer I talked to, consisted of 2 girls imported from Price, Utah. Business at Kimberly was so slow that the "pimp" who brought them returned the girls in a week. . . . 90% of the men at Kimberly were Mormons from the small valley towns. Most had their wives with them at Kimberly. These are not conditions under which "whores" prosper.

Tilton adds, "It may make for good reading, to make Kimberly out as a Hell Raising, Rip Snorting Mining Camp like Cripple Creek or Ely, Nevada, but the logic refutes the 'bad man' picture. . . . Kimberly was too small and not rich enough to get the drifters . . . and the 'boys' were too close to home to 'cut up' much."[16]

Nevertheless, Kimberly represented a distinct novelty in south-central Utah. Josephine Pace, whose father, Charles Skougaard, operated the largest hotel, recalled that "the town attracted many young blades with stiff straw hats, good manners, and eastern accents. The pretty girls from Elsinore and Richfield had a ball." She also remembered being permitted to spy on the "very elegant" parties held at the Lodge when she was a child:

> From my vantage point, belly boost at the top of the stairs, I could see it all—the ladies in their dresses, with demitrains which they would hold just

James Thompson family, Elsinore, 1904. G. E. Anderson photo, courtesy Utah State Historical Society.

high enough to show the lovely petticoats under them. . . . One of the gentlemen passed a tray of tiny glasses filled with wine which the ladies sipped as slowly as I would eat my Sunday ice cream.[17]

The Gates of Monroe, Sevier Plateau. G. E. Anderson photo, courtesy Utah State Historical Society.

Peter Kimberly died in 1905, and the mining company was taken over by a British company. The new managers adopted faulty mining practices in an attempt to increase production. This combined with diminishing ore values and the expense of operating a mill that used an obsolete process resulted in the bankruptcy of the Annie Laurie Mining Company in 1908, after less than a decade of full production. Like many other mining towns, Kimberly continued with a kind of posthumous existence after its real economic life had ended. The Salt Lake Hardware Company and Fred Tilton, owner of a general store in Kimberly, as the largest creditors took possession of the mine and kept up a limited production until 1938, with Tilton as general manager for most of that period. The mill was dismantled in 1943, and the remaining structures were demolished in the early 1950s.

Today the traveler must look carefully to find evidences of the town at all. What was once the business district is now only a wide terrace beside the road. In Upper Kimberly, a single cottage remains standing, its roof sagging towards collapse. The mill's concrete foundations can be seen across the canyon from the road. Near it, a steel-clad building of more recent date shows that the hope of extracting wealth from the Tushar has not yet died. Only a fireplace, a couple of retaining walls, and a pile of debris remain of the Lodge, though the site still offers a fine view. Portions of the tramline from the mine to the mill can be traced down the mountainside, and those who probe through the thick growth of manzanita will discover rotting logs and boards and the remains of rock foundations in many places. The "cyanide dam" where the remnants of the leaching process were dumped is either too toxic or too sterile to support plant growth and makes a blotch on an otherwise lush green north-slope landscape. Photographs from the turn of the century show the mountainside denuded, as the mill required a huge supply of wood for its process of roasting the ore. But nature has made almost a full recovery, and the subalpine forest looks much as it must have done when Newton Hill first discovered the Annie Laurie vein.

From Marysvale Canyon, the Sevier River flows into the wide plain of Sevier Valley, with its deep alluvial soil and numerous towns and villages set amid rich fields. Here Highway 89 meets Interstate 70 at the mouth of Clear Creek Canyon. The Interstate then follows the benchlands of the Pahvant Plateau along the western edge of the valley, offering an unfolding panorama of the High Plateaus. The eastern escarpment of the Pahvant is dry, sparsely covered with brush and scrub woodlands of juniper and pinyon. Across the valley the great amphitheater of Monroe Canyon breaks the high blue wall of the Sevier Plateau. As we travel north, and the Sevier Plateau slopes down to the gypsum hills near Sigurd, glimpses appear of the black volcanic table of Fish Lake

Sevier LDS Stake Tabernacle, Richfield. Photo courtesy Sevier County Historical Society.

Plateau farther east, while to the north Musinea Peak marks the beginning of the Wasatch Plateau, which reveals its sedimentary structure in massive white cliffs of Flagstaff limestone that tilt upward in a monoclinal fold, then become horizontal at the top.

At the midpoint of Sevier Valley lies the commercial center of Richfield, a pleasant and well-kept town with few visible remnants of its history. Richfield is now a Main Street town, with a business section stretching for a mile or so and newer developments concentrated near the north and south entrances to the Interstate. Like other nineteenth-century Mormon towns, however, it once focused on a town square, site of the original Fort Omni established in 1865. On this square, west of Main Street, were built the schoolhouses, while the Sevier County Courthouse, erected in 1892 and demolished in the 1970s, stood on the east side of the street. The dominant structure, however, was the ill-starred Sevier Stake Tabernacle, probably the largest church hall ever erected in central or southern Utah.

In the nineteenth century any Mormon town with pretensions of importance had to have a tabernacle, and fine examples of the genre survive in St. George, Loa, Provo, Heber City, Vernal, Bountiful, Brigham City, and Logan. The Richfield Tabernacle was substantially larger than any of these. The proposal to erect such a building was first put forward by Joseph A. Young, Brigham Young's son and first president of the Sevier LDS Stake, in 1875, only five years after the town's resettlement following the Black Hawk War. Despite the sudden death of Joseph Young in August of that year, the work of quarrying and shaping the stone began, and walls were partially constructed before the foundations were discovered to be inadequate.

In 1888, a new site was chosen a few feet away from the original spot, and construction began again from a design by Niels M. Skougaard, a Danish-born local builder.[18] The work continued intermittently for ten years, with periods of inactivity when funds ran short. Finally, in October 1898, the structure was complete except for minor finish work when it caught fire and burned to the ground, leaving only the shell of the stone walls. This great loss (there was no insurance), combined with the earlier problems and the suspicious origins of the fire, evidently led some residents to believe that the project was foredoomed. A report published in the Salt Lake City *Deseret News* declared,

> Last Wednesday there was an exceptionally large eagle flew into this city from the mountains east. It soared around and found the building and finally alighted upon the topmost spire of the main tower. It remained there and would not be molested despite the stone throwing by a large crowd which had assembled at the scene of the strange freak.
>
> An old woman of the town, who claims to be a foreseer, gave it out that the matter was an omen that the building would be destroyed by fire

inside of three days. The time of her prophecy would have expired yesterday at about 8 o'clock, when the building was a total wreck.[19]

The loss of twenty years' labor might well have made the residents of Richfield abandon the dream of a tabernacle. It served instead to increase their determination. An intensive fund drive was launched, reconstruction was begun, and the building was dedicated by LDS Church President Lorenzo Snow the following summer. The *Deseret News* of July 15, 1899, carried a picture of the tabernacle on the front page, together with the headline, "Phoenix-like It Has Arisen."

It was a remarkable edifice. The style was more or less Gothic Revival, but with nineteenth-century exuberance it incorporated many other motifs as well, from Greek pediments to onion domes. It could hold four thousand people, twice the population of Richfield at the time. The tower was 187 feet high, making it in all likelihood the tallest building in Utah outside of Salt Lake City. It dominated the townscape much as medieval cathedrals dominated the towns clustered at their base. It ought to have been a building to weather the ages, gathering the patina of time on its stones and the foot-worn grooves of generations in its steps. But such was not to be. On November 13, 1901, a strong earthquake rolled across southern Utah, cracking walls and toppling chimneys in dozens of towns. A report from Richfield stated that "a great deal of plastering was shaken from the tabernacle."[20] Perhaps the earthquake was the cause of the building's deeper structural problems, or perhaps the soil of the site, which had already failed under the first attempt to build there, was too unstable to support the immense weight of the building. Perhaps the construction or the design itself was faulty. In any case, disquieting signs of weakness had appeared by 1906 and grew until 1914, when a large chunk of the ceiling fell during a meeting. The building was then condemned for public use.

For nine more years the tabernacle stood, an imposing but empty hulk, vandalized and boarded up. By the time demolition began in 1923, the local newspaper, the *Richfield Reaper*, was referring to it as "the old eye sore"[21]—only twenty-four years after its long-desired completion had been greeted with joyous celebration. But the final irony was yet to come. When the demolition crews began their work, they discovered that the "unsafe" building was so solidly constructed that it could hardly be dismantled. The *Reaper* reported,

> Several people, in view of the solid construction, went even so far as to
> suggest that the foundation be reinforced, a new roof put on the building

73

and the tabernacle to be put to use again. . . . After thorough deliberation, however, a conclusion was reached that reconstructing the old tabernacle would be nearly just as expensive as building a new one, and then the stake would have a tabernacle only that would be inadequate to the needs of the church as well as community.[22]

So the walls were dynamited, the property sold, allowing commercial development for the first time on the town square, and a new stake building erected on a less valuable site two blocks to the west. The newer building is utterly devoid of distinction, but it has now served the community for more than half a century, three times the useful life of its remarkable but doomed predecessor.

At Salina, twenty miles from Richfield, Highway 89 leaves the Interstate and continues north toward Sanpete Valley. Interstate 70 turns east and begins the longest stretch without services on the entire interstate highway system, a hundred and eight miles to Green River. Traversing the narrow gorge of Salina Creek, the road climbs the saddle between the Wasatch and Fish Lake plateaus to the only pass under 8,000 feet in a 150 north-south miles. This was the route of the Old Spanish Trail and of the Gunnison railroad survey.

At the beginning of the 1880s, Colonel William Palmer, the impresario of the Denver and Rio Grande, always long on grandiose plans but short on capital, set out to develop this route. Palmer's original intention—as reflected in the name of his railroad—had been to construct a north-south line connecting Denver with El Paso by way of the Rio Grande Valley. When the better-financed Santa Fe won the race to the Southwest, Palmer redirected his aim toward California and started laying track westward from the Colorado mining camps. At the same time, he set crews to building a roadbed—still visible in places—up Salina Canyon, while yet other crews worked on the Buckhorn Flat east of Castle Dale, roughly following the route of the Old Spanish Trail. The apparent intention was to take the line into Sevier Valley and then build one branch going north to Salt Lake City and another going southwest to Los Angeles. When funds ran short, Palmer lowered his sights and adopted Salt Lake and Ogden as a western terminus. Instead of completing the Spanish Trail route, the Rio Grande built along the northern edge of Castle Valley and over Soldier Summit. While the unfinished roadbed represented a total loss for the railroad company, the wages paid to the construction crews—largely made up of local farmers with their teams and scrapers—contributed substantially to building up the new Castle Valley settlements. Not until the era of the Interstate

Highway System was the dream of a central passage through the high plateaus realized with the construction of Interstate 70 as the most direct route between Denver and Southern California.

In his *Geology of the High Plateaus*, Clarence Dutton says little about the Mormon villages that were strung along the valleys at the base of the High Plateaus and that must have served as supply bases for his fieldwork. When he refers to the settlements at all, they are merely geographical reference points. There is, however, one notable exception. Dutton began his fieldwork in the summer of 1875 in the region of the Fish Lake Plateau, and the village of Salina would presumably have served as the most convenient supply station.[23] Perhaps he had a bad experience with the residents and took his revenge in an unflattering portrait of the community. Or perhaps the biblical associations of the nearby salt deposits reflected in the town's name proved irresistible to someone of Dutton's literary turn of mind:

> Fourteen miles south of Gunnison is the little Mormon village Salina, a wretched hamlet, whose inhabitants earn a scanty subsistence by lixiviating salt from the red clay which underlies the Tertiary beds in the vicinity. Around and beyond this village is a dismal array of bad lands of great extent, presenting a striking picture of desolation and the wreck of strata, while beyond and above them rise the northern volcanic sheets of the Sevier Plateau. The lava, the desolation, and the salt strongly suggest recollections of Sodom and Gomorrah.[24]

The salt hills still provide a background for Salina, which is today a pleasant town of shady streets and well-maintained homes. While the village no doubt had some rough edges in 1873—only four years after its resettlement following the Black Hawk War—it is hard to imagine it as being any more "wretched" than numerous other settlements in the region.

This, however, was not to be Dutton's last word on Mormon village life. In 1888, during the protracted debate over Utah statehood, he published an article entitled "Church and State in Utah" in which he criticizes others who have written on the Mormon question because they "have gained their knowledge of the subject at Salt Lake City, among the ruling class, and have seen little of the real Mormondom in its true strongholds, the village communities."[25] "The people of Utah are unfit for statehood," he declares, not primarily because of polygamy, which Dutton terms "the smallest part of the Mormon question," but because the Mormon "hierarchy" is "about as far removed from the republican form guaranteed by the Constitution as it is possible to conceive."[26] He goes on to say, "The erection of a State of the Union whose population consisted of Turks or Afghans, would not be a worse blunder or fraught with more dangerous consequences than the creation of a State composed of Mormons."[27]

Notwithstanding Dutton's vigorous opposition to Utah statehood, his essay is clearly the work of a perceptive social observer. Indeed, it may be the best nineteenth-century account of the sociology of the Mormon village. Because the agricultural resources of the region are limited not by land but by water, and because of the expense of building and maintaining irrigation works, Dutton writes,

> The conditions practically enforce a social organization having much in common with the ancient village communities of Europe, or the existing village communities of southern Russia or of India. A village is necessary in order to use the water effectively and economically. The ownership and location of lands must be subordinated to the general welfare, and cannot have that exclusively personal and absolute character which attaches to the ownership of land in more favored regions. Individual rights must be subordinated in an exceptional degree, and the whole community must be under an unusual amount of control. The social unit is no longer the individual, nor even the family, but the village community.[28]

And the dominant figure in the Mormon village is the bishop, who, though "appointed by the central authority of the church, without the knowledge or consent of the people whose affairs he is to administer," must be

> a man of force, and able to command the respect and obedience of his people. Nominally he is only the pastor of his flock and the agent of the church in matters purely ecclesiastical. He pretends before Gentiles to be nothing more than a counselor in secular matters, or, at most, a mere moderator of a small community, with no power of enforcing any measure. In reality his powers are very great, for while they are advisory in form and name, they are dictatorial in fact. He controls the occupancy of the land of the village, assigning to each man his field, and fixing his allowance of water. The lands being essentially communal, and worked to a large degree co-operatively; being, also, frequently changed, one field being abandoned and a new one opened, this arbitrary method not only works well, but is, on the whole, the best possible under the circumstances. The bishop also

initiates and supervises all public improvements, bridges, roads, saw-mills, dams, ditches, school-houses, etc., exacting contribution of labor, material, and money. He is the arbiter of all disputes. The Mormon never goes of his own accord into a court of law. If he quarrels with his neighbor, or seeks redress of grievances, his appeal is not to the courts but to the church. The bishop will surely listen to his case, and decide it as fairly as he can upon its merits. But if he goes into court he will find jury and witnesses against him, no matter what the merits of his case may be.[29]

Dutton's three years in Utah came during the period when settlements were being established in the harsh regions east of the High Plateaus and on the Little Colorado River in Arizona. He provides this account of the role of the Mormon hierarchy in the occupation of new lands:

[I]s a new village to be located and settled? Word is sent to the bishops of a dozen towns to name the men, who forthwith sell houses and gardens, abandon their fields, dispose of their standing crops, and converting the proceeds into wagons, provisions, tools, and clothing, bid adieu forever to their old homes, and marching hundreds of miles over mountains or across great cañons, begin life over again in the places selected for them. The church bids them go, and does nothing for them, unless, as frequently happens, they are in danger of starving before their first crop can be harvested.[30]

Mormon society obviously appeared more monolithic to an outsider like Dutton than it would have seemed to an insider aware of the tensions between the individual and the collective that exist in any community. The degree of control Dutton attributes to church leaders may approximate what they would have liked to possess but exaggerates the power that even so commanding a leader as Brigham Young was actually able to exert. Dutton also overstates the differences in motives between Mormons and the general American population. Despite the corporate emphasis in the Mormon settlement process, by the 1870s probably a majority of settlers in a new community were drawn by the hope of acquiring land and improving their economic situation—the same attractions that drew non-Mormon settlers to the West.

The eastern valleys of the High Plateau region were settled later and more sparsely than the central valleys, and only in recent years have they been connected by good highways. East of the middle range, a

Farm buildings, Widtsoe, 1936. Dorothea Lange photo, Library of Congress, USF34-1320-C.

long, narrow depression runs north and south between the Sevier and Paunsagunt plateaus to the west and the Fish Lake, Awapa, and Aquarius plateaus to the east. The northern portion of this depression is called Grass Valley, though the stream running through it bears the name of Otter Creek. Utah Highway 24 leaves Interstate 70 near Vermillion, midway between Richfield and Salina, passes through Sigurd and over a divide into Grass Valley, then climbs the wall of the Awapa Plateau—where the road to Fish Lake branches off—and continues on toward Rabbit Valley and Capitol Reef National Park.

Just past Koosharem Reservoir on this route, Highway 62 branches off to the right and runs down Grass Valley. Of the four settlements in this valley, Burrville, Koosharem, Greenwich, and Angle, only Koosharem is large enough to be considered a village. The valley, despite its near 7,000-foot elevation, lies in the rain shadow of the Sevier Plateau and is a region of little precipitation. However, its subirrigated bottomlands provide good livestock-grazing ground. The Sevier Plateau is almost as imposing on its eastern side as it is on the west. The Awapa Plateau appears from Grass Valley as a long, straight ridge rising at its south end to the section known as Parker Mountain.

Below Otter Creek Reservoir, Otter Creek joins the East Fork of the Sevier, which swings west into the gorge it has cut through the middle of the Sevier Plateau. South of the reservoir is the village of Antimony, situated in a meadow valley on the East Fork. This settlement was once known as Coyote but was renamed for a mineral deposit in the hills to the east. Despite the name, however, it is a Mormon farming-ranching village with nothing of the mining camp about it.

South of Antimony, the masses of the Sevier and Aquarius plateaus close in to form the narrow, volcanic-walled Black Canyon. Midway along this stretch of unpaved road lies the ghost town of Osiris, where the shell of a large gristmill stands on the banks of the East Fork. Beyond Black Canyon the terrain opens out again into a valley that rises gradually to the south toward Bryce Canyon National Park.

In the midst of this valley once stood the town of Widtsoe, named for agricultural scientist and Mormon Apostle John A. Widtsoe, who had proposed that agriculture was possible in some sections of Utah without irrigation. The East Fork Valley was one of those places, and the dry-farming colony, founded in 1910 and growing to a population of about a thousand by 1920, seemed to bear out Widtsoe's views for a time. However, with declining agricultural prices and uncertain harvests during the 1920s and a disastrous drought in the early 1930s, only a handful of hardy but impoverished residents remained by 1935. These last few were resettled in other locations with the assistance of a Depression-era federal program.

The well-known photographer Dorothea Lange was sent to Utah by the Farm Security Administration in 1936 to document various FSA programs. Widtsoe, then in the last stages of abandonment, was one of the sites Lange visited. Her photographs show unpainted frame buildings scattered across a brush-covered plain; an outhouse without a door beside a ramshackle barn; an aproned mother and child framed by rough boards in an open doorway; an elderly Danish immigrant woman, wrapped up against the cold April winds of the high valley, clutching in her hand her first old age assistance check.[31] Today the only visible remnants of Widtsoe are half a dozen frame structures, some fences, and the weed-grown former croplands where the native bunchgrasses have not been reestablished.

South of Widtsoe the valley rises to a ridge that connects the Paunsagunt to the Aquarius. This ridge forms the dividing line between the Sevier drainage and the valley of the Paria River, which continues south toward its confluence with the Colorado, running in places through almost inaccessible canyons between the descending terraces of the Paunsagunt on the west and the broken country rising to the Kaiparowits Plateau on the east. The Paria Valley is gradually being eroded into the ridge and will eventually "capture" the East Fork of the Sevier. Even now, some of its waters are diverted by means of a canal that runs through Bryce Canyon National Park and cascades down the eastern slopes of the Paunsagunt to water the fields around Tropic—the only place where water is transferred from the Great Basin to the Colorado drainage.

The Paunsagunt Plateau has a platform more than a thousand feet lower than its neighbors the Markagunt and the Aquarius, and much smaller in surface area, about twenty-five miles long and fifteen wide. But it sustains one of the finest forests in the Plateau Region and offers, as millions of tourists have discovered, some of the most breathtaking views. The scenic wonders of the Paunsagunt's Pink Cliffs were surprisingly late in coming to public attention. The first recorded Anglos to view the area were the members of a militia force from St. George, who, under the direction of James Andrus, pursued a raiding party of Indians across the Paria country in 1866. But the Andrus party were looking for Indians, not scenery, and were apparently not strongly impressed by the remarkable formations of the Paunsagunt.

John Wesley Powell, less sensitive to landscape aesthetics than his associate Dutton, mentioned briefly that the south rim of the Paunsagunt Plateau "is bounded by a line of beautiful pink cliffs" but says little more, though he does record an experience with the abruptness of the plateau rim. Having sought shelter under the pines during a violent rainstorm, the party then had to search in the mist for their horses:

> I go out to follow their tracks, and come near to the brink of a ledge of rocks, which, in the fog and mist, I suppose to be a little ridge, and I look for a way by which I can go down. Standing just here, there is a rift made in the fog below, by some current or blast of wind, which reveals an almost bottomless abyss. I look from the brink of a great precipice of more than two thousand feet; but, through the mist, the forms below are half obscured, and all reckoning of distance is lost, and it seems ten thousand feet, ten miles—any distance the imagination desires to make it.[32]

A government surveyor named T. C. Bailey wrote a description of the Paunsagunt rim in 1876, first noting the remarkable resemblance of the formations to architectural types.[33] But the first published appreciation, was, not surprisingly, Dutton's account of what he called "the great amphitheater of the Paria." Dutton, too, drew upon the language of art and architecture, depicting a landscape unpeopled yet filled with anthropomor-

phic elements, as he attempted to render a scene that represents both a natural sculpture without parallel and a geologist's object lesson in erosion:

> This process has left the strata in terraced cliffs facing the center of the amphitheater, and as we look across from the southern cape of the Paunsagunt to Table Cliff and Kaiparowits Peak, more than 30 miles distant, we behold the edges of the strata, sculptured and carved in a fashion that kindles enthusiasm in the dullest mind. At the base of the series the vermilion sandstones of the Upper Trias are seen in massive palisades and gorgeous friezes, stretching away to the southward till lost in the distance. Above them is the still more massive Jurassic sandstone, pale gray and nearly white, without sculptured details, but imposing from the magnitude and solidity of its fronts. Next rises in a succession of terraces the whole Cretaceous system more than 4,000 feet in thickness. It consists of broad alternating bands of bright yellow sandstone and dark iron-gray argillaceous shales, the several homogeneous members ranging in thickness from 600 to 1,000 feet. But the glory of all this rock-work is seen in the Pink Cliffs, the exposed edges of the Lower Eocene strata. The resemblances to strict architectural forms are often startling. The upper tier of the vast amphitheater is one mighty ruined colonnade. Standing obelisks, prostrate columns, shattered capitals, panels, niches, buttresses, repetitions of symmetrical forms, all bring vividly before the mind suggestions of the work of giant hands, a race of genii once rearing temples of rock, but now chained up in a spell of enchantment, while their structures are falling in ruins through centuries of decay. Along the southern and southeastern flank of the Paunsagunt these ruins stretch mile after mile. But the crowning work is Table Cliff in the background. Standing 11,000 feet above sea-level and projected against the deep blue of the western sky, it presents the aspect of a vast Acropolis crowned with a Parthenon. It is hard to dispel the fancy that this is a work of some intelligence and design akin to that of humanity, but far grander.[34]

The easternmost interior valley of the High Plateaus is Rabbit Valley, a circular oasis surrounded by the Thousand Lake, Fish Lake, Awapa, and Aquarius plateaus. Its deep alluvial soil is well watered by the Fremont River, though the 7,000-foot elevation limits the crops that can be grown to hay and short-season grains. The village of Loa—named after Hawaii's Mauna Loa volcano by a former Mormon missionary to Hawaii—still preserves some of the traditional Utah farm-village character with houses on the corners of the block, and the sensitively preserved Wayne Stake Tabernacle is worth a visit. At the east end of the valley, the village of Bicknell is situated above the Fremont bottoms. The settlement was originally known as Thurber but acquired the present name when an easterner offered a library to any Utah town that would adopt his name. Thurber and Grayson, in San Juan County, both took him up on the offer, so he directed one to take his name and the other his wife's, and Bicknell and Blanding each ended up with a new identity and what residents recall as a very small collection of books. East of Bicknell, the Red Gate marks the passage of the Fremont River through the uplift of Thousand Lake Fault. Just past the gate, a pioneer gristmill stands picturesquely amid Lombardy poplars, and farther east are the red-rock villages of Teasdale and Torrey.

The Fish Lake Plateau that forms the northern horizon of Rabbit Valley is a broad table about twenty-five miles square with an elevation of about nine thousand feet. Four major eminences rise above the platform to elevations in excess of 11,500 feet: the Fish Lake High Top at the western edge of the plateau, a lava-capped tabular mass two miles wide and twelve miles long; Mounts Terrel and Marvine, two peaks connected by a ridge and separated from the High Top by Sevenmile Valley; and Mount Hilgard some six miles farther east, past U.M. Valley (named for the brand of the Moroni United Order livestock herd that once grazed there). On the west side of the High Top, one of the most imposing mountain gorges in the plateau region supplies the headwaters of Otter Creek, draining into Grass Valley. Elsewhere on the Fish Lake Plateau, the higher peaks and ridges are surrounded by broad, gently sloping valleys filled with abundant grass and lined with forests of aspen and fir. More than a century later, these valleys are still as delightful as Dutton found them in 1875, when he described Sevenmile (which he called Summit Valley) as "a most eligible summer camping-place":

> In the daytime, throughout July, August, and most of September, it is mild and genial, while the nights are frosty and conducive to rest. The grass is long, luxuriant, and aglow with flowers. Clumps of spruce and aspen furnish shade from the keen rays of the sun, and fuel is in abundance for camp-fires. Thus the great requisites for Western camp-life, fuel, water, and grass, are richly supplied, while neither is in such excess as to be an obstacle to progress and examination.[35]

Fish Lake itself occupies a narrow valley east of the High Top. Here, too, Dutton's description remains apt:

No resort more beautiful than this lake can be found in Southern Utah. Its grassy banks clad with groves of spruce and aspen; the splendid vista down between its mountain walls, with the massive fronts of Mounts Marvine and Hilgard in the distance; the crystal-clear expanse of the lake itself, combine to form a scene of beauty rarely equalled in the West.[36]

Dutton describes Thousand Lake Mountain as a gigantic butte cut off from the Aquarius by the canyon of the Fremont River. From the north and west, however, it appears to be an extension of the Fish Lake Plateau. A ridge whose northern anchor is Mount Hilgard runs southeast across the Fish Lake table, dips to the saddle where Highway 72 crosses Hogan Summit, then rises again and widens to form Thousand Lake. This is the smallest of the High Plateaus, a table about six by ten miles from which rises a higher platform some two miles long, a mile wide, and 11,300 feet high. Because of its peninsular situation, its loftiness, and its relatively small area, Thousand Lake Mountain stands in especially striking contrast to its surroundings. From Rabbit Valley to the west, the Fremont River Gorge to the south, and the eroded desert to the east, the mountain rises abruptly from a treeless base to subalpine forest with scarcely a transition. The forest of mixed spruce-fir and aspen is almost continuous over the table, with few of the open meadows that characterize the other High Plateaus.

Thousand Lake Mountain does not have a thousand lakes. The few small bodies of water are scarcely more than ponds feeding thin streams that flow into the Fremont River or sink in the desert soil of Cathedral Valley to the east. Indeed, there is some conjecture that the name was applied by mistake, having been intended for the larger Aquarius Plateau to the south. The main access road leaves Highway 72 near Forsyth Reservoir and circles east around the roadless high top. At breaks in the forest, there are startling views across the desert to the Henry Mountains, forty miles east. A steep, rocky road drops down the east side of the mountain, passing in five miles from lush forest to the barren sand and gothic stone of Cathedral Valley. From Cathedral Valley the adventurous traveler can choose between two dirt roads, one following the Waterpocket Fold for twenty-five miles to Highway 24, the other running north for about the same distance to Interstate 70, following the inaccessible eastern escarpment of the Fish Lake Plateau and passing the lonely oases of Baker and Last Chance ranches along the way. Here, beyond the inner valleys of the plateaus, is the dramatic boundary that separates the High Plateaus from the eastern Utah Canyonlands.

5

STOP AND TELL ME,
RED MAN

W hen people of European stock entered the region of the high plateaus, they found it occupied by Utes and Southern Paiutes, peoples linguistically related but in most cases culturally distinct. Small Paiute bands lived in units ranging from extended families to small village communities within fairly well defined domains normally including both highlands and lower valleys: Shivwits, Uinkarets, and Kaibabits on the Arizona Strip; Paguits around Panguitch Lake; Paroosits in the Virgin River Valley; the Tonoquints band on the Santa Clara River; Moapas along the lower Virgin and the Muddy River in southern Nevada; Kumoits in Cedar Valley; and Kwiumpats on the Beaver River.[1] Most of the Utes were based north and east of the plateau region and were more mobile than the Paiutes, having acquired the horse from their association with the Plains tribes. However, the Pahvant and Sanpitch bands had developed a borderline Ute-Paiute culture in the valleys of the high plateaus, and the more powerful Tumpanawach made frequent forays south from their base on the shores of Utah Lake.

In addition to the living tribes, there were extensive material remains from the Fremont and Anasazi cultures that had occupied the region until the fourteenth century: pit houses and aboveground dwellings of stone, some still stocked with basketware, pottery, and figurines; remarkable rock art painted or incised on the natural canvases of thick-bedded southern Utah sandstone; and storage granaries high on the cliff walls—often called "Moqui houses" on the erroneous assumption that some presumably very small and agile people had actually lived in them.[2] Though these remains were centuries old, the dry atmosphere had kept them in such a state of preservation that it was easy to think the occupants had only recently departed.

Though their material culture was much less imposing than that of the vanished peoples who preceded them, the Paiutes had made a highly creative adaptation to their semidesert environment. They used the waters of small springs and intermittent streams to irrigate gardens of squash, maize, and beans. They propagated wild food plants such as mesquite and amaranth by transporting seeds to suitable sites, and systematically burned brush and grasslands to stimulate new growth and seed production. They developed cooperative arrangements among bands to allow access to the pine-nut harvest on other domains in years when the local crop failed (pinyon pines typically produce good crops only about two years out of six).[3] They used long nets woven from oose fibers to catch hares, and collected grasshoppers that were roasted and ground to a high-protein meal. They were skilled basketmakers, using willow strips to fashion harvesting and storage containers, winnowing and roasting trays, infant carriers, and even water jugs sealed with pitch.[4] Their shelters, covered with brush and bark, provided both shade and air circulation during the summer, and their blankets and robes made from narrow strips of rabbit fur gave protection against the winter chill. Nevertheless, theirs was a marginal subsistence economy at best, subject to the hazards of a harsh environment, both natural and social. Living in small groups, the Paiutes were vulnerable to raids by their more powerful neighbors. Their children were frequently stolen for the New Mexico slave trade—and sometimes sold by their families in exchange for badly needed supplies.

Most early travelers' accounts fail to appreciate the ingenuity of the Paiutes' strategies for survival, while emphasizing their poverty and misery. For example, the Yount-Clark narrative relates the discovery by the 1830–31 Wolfskill party of a lone rabbit hunter amid the snows of the Sevier Valley, "whose dwarfish stature & lean, half starved, nakid person, a heap of bones & skin, well corresponded with the region where he dwelt." He was persuaded to take the travelers to his people, "a groupe of the lowest & most degraded of all the savage hords of the west":

These people are an anomaly—apparently the lowest species of humanity, approaching the monky—Nothing but their upright form entitles them to the name of man—They had not a hatchet, nor any instrument to cut or perforate the softest wood—One discovery they had made, or had learned it from some more intelligent savage—They would get fire by rubbing together pieces of hard wood—But it was a long & tedious process—When they would fell a tree for fuel, or for any purpose they built a fire about its roots—& they cut it up with fire—To erect a dwellinghouse for their own abode & to shield them from the severe cold, they were accustomed to break off boughs & stick them in the snow & sloping the tops inward they would pile bushes on the top—Thus they were little else than animals in human shape—The name of their tribe is Piuch, a corruption of the word in the Eutau tongue which means Rootdiggers—They have but few words, & communicate chiefly by signs—They live in little clans scattered over a great extent of country. . . . Their food consists of occasionally a Rabbit, with roots & mice, grasshoppers & insects, such as flies, spiders & worms of every kind—Where nuts exist they gather them for food—They also luxuriate & grow fat when they find a patch of clover—On many kinds of grass they feed like cattle—They love to be covered with lice because they appropriate these for food.[5]

Culturally biased judgments of this kind were common, yet the very accounts in which they appear sometimes provide information that makes us call them into question. The Wolfskill party crossed the High Plateaus region during the winter, when despite their supposed superior culture they experienced their own struggle for survival. If they had not had their horses to eat, they might well have been driven to share the Paiutes' rather unappetizing diet.

Furthermore, some of the unsavory habits that travelers' accounts ascribe to the Indians may in fact have been a product of white incursions into their territory. Escalante portrays the Indians of Utah as being invariably peaceful and hospitable. Indeed, one reason the padres decided to return to New Mexico instead of pushing on to California was that they were anxious to organize a mission to the Tumpanawach of Utah Valley and the "Yutas Barbones"—bearded Utes, most likely Pahvants—whom they had met on the Sevier.

By the time of Jedediah S. Smith's 1826 visit to their territory, the formerly sedentary Tumpanawach had acquired the horse and a fair number of guns and were frequently at war with the Northern Shoshoni. Smith complained of "that savage disposition too prevalent among Indians" as manifest in their treatment of young Shoshoni women they had captured. Nevertheless, his impressions were for the most part positive. He found the Utes to be "more honest than any I had ever been with in the country," and described them as "cleanly quiet and active," making "a nearer approach to civilized life than any Indians I have seen in the Interior. Their leggings and shirts which are made of the skins of the Deer Mt Sheep or Antelope are kept quite clean."[6]

Smith formed a less favorable impression of the Sanpitch Utes, describing them as "rather above the middling size but in the mental state lower than any I have yet seen. . . . In appearance and action they are strongly contrasted with the cleanliness of the Uta's." Still, though shy they were not unfriendly. Smith tells of presenting a badger to an old Sanpitch woman on the assumption that she would take it home to her village. "But the moment it was presented she caught it in her hands and exclaimed we are all friends . . . and immediately tore it in pieces and laid it on the coals. When it was about half cooked she commenced eating making no nice distinction between hair pelts entrails and meet."[7]

Smith found Paiutes growing maize and squash on the Santa Clara River, and these same crops plus "some small green Water Melons" on the Muddy in southern Nevada. On the east bank of the Colorado River, opposite the mouth of the Virgin, Smith encountered the same "old Pautch farmer" both in 1826 and on his return trip in 1827, cultivating pumpkins, squash, beans, and wheat.[8] A California-bound party traveling some distance north of the usual trail in 1849 reported finding farms in Beaver Dam Wash with crops including maize, beans, wheat, pumpkins, squash, and sunflowers.[9]

So when Mormon missionaries were sent to the Santa Clara in 1854 to teach the Paiutes how to farm, they were actually coming into a long-established agrarian tradition. It appears likely, however, that agriculture, along with other traditional arts, had declined in the period between 1830 and 1850, largely as the result of traffic over the Old Spanish Trail. The New Mexico traders seized both Paiute crops and Paiute children at will. In response, the Paiutes grew more aggressive and began attacking isolated travelers and following the big caravans on the lookout for an opportunity to wound horses that would then be left behind for them to butcher.

A large force of Paiutes shadowed John C. Frémont's 1844 party from the Muddy River to the Santa Clara "like a band of wolves," killing one of Frémont's men at Beaver Dam Wash. Frémont's description reveals his own hostile reaction to their aggressiveness:

> In these Indians I was forcibly struck by an expression of countenance resembling that in a beast of prey, and all their actions are those of wild animals. Joined to the restless motion of the eye there is a want of mind—an absence of thought—and an action wholly by impulse, strongly expressed, and which constantly recalls the similarity.[10]

While the Tumpanawach Utes also must have suffered a cultural crisis as a result of the incursion of trappers and traders into their territory, some of them profited from the trade in horses and slaves. Wakara, "Chief Walker," in particular dominated traffic on the Spanish Trail much as the medieval "robber barons" dominated the Rhine.

Frémont met Wakara and his band of warriors in the course of his 1844 journey along the western base of the High Plateaus. The Utes impressed the explorer much more favorably than their Paiute cousins had done:

> They were all mounted, armed with rifles, and use their rifles well. The chief [Wakara] had a fusee, which he had carried slung, in addition to his rifle. They were journeying slowly toward the Spanish Trail, to levy their usual tribute upon the great Californian caravan. They were robbers of a higher order than those of the desert. They conducted their depredations with form, and under the color of trade, and toll for passing through their country. Instead of attacking and killing, they affect to purchase—taking the horses they like and giving something nominal in return.[11]

Wakara's version of the good life ended with the cessation of caravan traffic on the Spanish Trail and the coming of Mormon settlers into central Utah with attendant disruption of the slave trade. Wakara himself was baptized into the LDS Church and reportedly invited the Mormons to settle Sanpete Valley. Tensions nonetheless mounted until they erupted in the "Walker War" of 1853–54, when Utes raided the livestock herds of Sanpete and Utah valleys, burned Allred's Settlement (later resettled and known as Spring City), and killed two men at the Manti flour mill and four teamsters hauling wheat to Salt Lake City. Though there is no comprehensive record of Indian casualties, it is likely that in this as in most other conflicts many more Indians died than whites. At least six Utes were killed in a battle with the militia near Mount Pleasant on July 23, 1853, and eight were executed in retaliation for the murder of the teamsters.[12]

The hostilities tapered off in early 1854, and Brigham Young held a peace conference with Wakara and other Ute leaders at Chicken Creek in May in an attempt to resolve their differences. An interesting report of this conference is found in Solomon Nunes Carvalho's *Incidents of Travel and Adventure in the Far West*.

Carvalho, who came west with Frémont's 1853–54 expedition, was so exhausted by the winter journey across the High Plateaus that he chose to remain behind in Parowan when Frémont pushed on to California. After a two-week period of recuperation, he caught a ride to Salt Lake City with Bishop Henry Lunt of Cedar City, who was going to April LDS conference.

Carvalho left the city on May 6, in company with Brigham Young and a large party going to visit the southern settlements. Governor Young's first order of business was the peace conference with Ute leaders at Chicken Creek, near present-day Levan. Carvalho claims to have attended the conference and reports interestingly on the personalities and views of the Indians present. He describes Wakara as "a man of imposing appearance . . . attired with only a deer-skin hunting shirt, although it was very cold." Carvalho sketched portraits of several Utes on this occasion; that of Wakara has survived and shows a handsome, powerful head with penetrating eyes and a hawklike nose. The Ute chief appears to be in the full vigor of life, and there is nothing to suggest that he would be dead in less than a year.

While Carvalho presents a sympathetic report of the Indians' grievances, he also notes a vivid instance of their cruelty:

> When I returned to our camp, I saw a crowd around the Governor's wagon. I approached, and found that his excellency had just concluded a purchase from the Utahs of two children, about two to three years of age. They were prisoners, and infants of the Snake Indians, with whom the Utahs were at war. When the Governor first saw these deplorable objects, they were on the open snow, digging with their little fingers for grassnuts, or any roots to afford sustenance. They were almost living skeletons. They are usually treated in this way—that is, literally starved to death by their captors.[13]

As Brigham Young's caravan continued southward along the Mormon Corridor, they called upon Kanosh of the Pahvant band at Corn Creek. Kanosh permitted Carvalho to draw his likeness and also explained the circumstances of the Gunnison massacre the previous year. Carvalho describes the Pahvant chief as "well armed with a rifle and pistols, and mounted on a noble horse. He has a Roman nose, with a fine intelligent cast of countenance, and his thick black hair is brushed off his forehead, contrary to the usual custom of his tribe."[14] However, he does not present a very attractive picture of the Pahvants in general, calling them "a dirty degraded set of beings, scarcely deserving the name of human." Wakara's Tumpanawach companions, on the other hand, strike him as picturesque:

> The Utahs have a large number of horses, and when mounted for a journey they are caparisoned with bells and gaudy trappings. The men paint their faces with vermilion, except when they go to war—they then paint them black. They are curiously attired in buckskin shirts, leggings, and moccasins, beautifully marked with beads and porcupine quills. They generally travel bare-headed, with sometimes a single feather in their hair. They are very fond of red and blue blankets, and use them in the manner of a Roman Toga.[15]

John Wesley Powell brought a new and more scientific approach to the study of the Indians of the plateau region when he arrived in 1870. Indeed, he must be considered as one of the first true ethnologists. His report on the Uinkaret and Shivwits bands of Paiutes describes them as being "more nearly in their primitive condition than any others on the continent with whom I am acquainted."[16] And indeed, in their remote location near the Grand Canyon they must have been almost as isolated in 1870 as the Paiutes of central Utah had been when the Wolfskill party met them forty years earlier. The Shivwits had killed three members of Powell's 1869 Colorado River expedition, but Powell's report is free from bitterness, and perhaps more significantly free from the degrading animal comparisons employed by so many other travelers. Always he presents the Paiutes as sharing his own humanity, though with a profoundly different—and therefore interesting—culture. For example, he recognizes that his guides' reading of the landscape differs from his own both in degree and in kind:

> It is curious now to observe the knowledge of our Indians. There is not a trail but what they know; every gulch and every rock seems familiar. I have prided myself on being able to grasp and retain in my mind the topography of a country; but these Indians put me to shame. My knowledge is only general, embracing the more important features of a region that remains as a map engraved on my mind; but theirs is particular. They know every rock and every ledge, every gulch and cañon, and just where to wind among these to find a pass; and their knowledge is unerring. They cannot describe a country to you, but they can tell you all the particulars of a route.[17]

When the party comes upon a naked Uinkaret woman gathering seeds, Powell refers to her with Victorian delicacy as "one of the ladies resident in these mountain glades; she is evidently paying taxes, Godiva like."[18] He collects Paiute legends, admires their skills (he is especially impressed by the way the women can roast seeds in willow trays without burning the tray), and respects their adaptation to their conditions of existence. He cannot, however, entirely bridge the cultural gap that separates them from him. When the Shivwits who had killed Powell's companions come to parley, he fills his pipe with tobacco and passes it around the circle:

> When it has passed the chief, he takes out his own pipe, fills, and lights it, and passes it around after mine. I can smoke my own pipe in turn, but,

when the Indian pipe comes around, I am nonplussed. It has a large stem, which has, at some time, been broken, and now there is a buckskin rag wound around it, and tied with sinew, so that the end of the stem is a huge mouthful, and looks like the burying ground of old dead spittle, venerable for a century. To gain time, I refill it, then engage in very earnest conversation, and, all unawares, I pass it to my neighbor unlighted.[19]

Powell does not sentimentalize the Indians, and he recognizes a fundamental incompatibility between their traditional life-style and the opening of the West to agricultural and commercial development. In his economic geography of the arid region, he notes the Indians' practice of setting forest fires in order to drive the game, and proposes that they be prevented from hunting in forested areas.[20] Nor is he entirely immune to patronizing generalizations. Writing of the pueblo cultures whose ruins lay scattered over the land, he observes that "they had almost accomplished the ascent from savagery to barbarism when first discovered by the invading European."[21]

More subtly than other writers' crude comparisons of the Indians with animals, this remark of Powell's reflects the nineteenth-century tendency to interpret human society in evolutionary terms. From this point of view, Native American cultures belonged to a lower stage on the evolutionary scale than European civilization. When the Mormons entered the region of the High Plateaus, they brought with them an alternative model to account for the Indians' condition, viewing them as descendants of Book of Mormon peoples and therefore a chosen race but degraded through sin and ignorance. Until well into the twentieth century, Mormon hymnals contained a song text by W. W. Phelps that begins with the query,

O stop and tell me, Red Man,
Who are you, why you roam . . . ?

The Indian spokesman in the song—evidently enlightened beyond the general run of his people—replies by recounting a story of ancestral rebellion against the Truth and consequent decline to the present benighted and impoverished condition:

And long they've lived by hunting
Instead of works and arts,
And so our race has dwindled
To idle Indian hearts.[22]

Obviously neither the evolutionary nor the devolutionary model does much to encourage a sympathetic understanding of Native American cultures—nor, for that matter, does the Romantic concept of the Noble Savage that inconsistently tinges both models. However, there is a long-standing and currently much-debated tradition that the Mormons, because they viewed them as wayward Israelite brethren, treated the Indians more humanely than did other nineteenth-century Americans.[23] Brigham Young's famous dictum, "It is cheaper to feed the Indians than to fight them," is frequently cited as an enlightened policy, despite its implicit contempt for Indian character and culture.

And it was an enlightened policy compared to "The only good Indian is a dead Indian." Leonard J. Arrington maintains that while "Brigham's Indian policy did not encompass respect or recognition of the values and outlook of their culture," it was largely free from the "ruthless exploitation and genocide . . . all too common" in the nineteenth century.[24] Elizabeth Wood Kane testifies to the Mormons' general attitude of tolerance toward the Indians. She describes the arrival of a party of Pahvants just as the Kanes were preparing to dine with their hosts in Fillmore:

> When Mrs. Q. called us to supper, these gentry rose to accompany us. I looked helplessly at her. She said a few words in their dialect, which made them at once squat down again, huddling their blankets round them, with a pleasanter look on their dark faces than they had yet worn.
>
> "What did your mother say to those men, Mr. Q.?" I asked, curiously.
>
> "She said, 'These strangers came first, and I have only cooked enough for them; but your meal is on the fire cooking now, and I will call you as soon as it is ready.'"
>
> "Will she really do that, or just give them scraps at the kitchen-door?" I pursued, thinking of "cold-victual" beggars at home.
>
> "*Our* Pah-vants know how to behave," he answered. ". . . Mother will serve them just as she does you, and give them a place at her table."
>
> And so she did. I saw her placing clean plates, knives, and forks for them, and waiting behind their chairs, while they ate with perfect propriety.[25]

Indeed, Mrs. Kane suggests that the Mormons may be too indulgent:

> We have heard our English friends with country places, complain of the gypsies strolling through the country, camping here and there, and pilfering from friend or foe. But their grievance is a bagatelle compared to that the Mormons endure, under the infliction of a visit from a party of Indians.

They have the appetites of poor relations, and the touchiness of rich ones with money to leave. They come in a swarm; their ponies eat down the golden grain-stacks to their very centres; the Mormon women are tired out baking for the masters, while the squaws hang about the kitchens watching for scraps like unpenned chickens.

She adds, "I found the Mormons disposed to justify and excuse the Indians more than I thought the hideous creatures deserved."[26]

In a sermon delivered in Springville at the height of the Black Hawk War, Brigham Young criticized those Mormons who "felt like wiping out the Lamanites in these regions, root and branch," and preached a policy of reconciliation: "Do we wish to do right? . . . Then let the Lamanites come back to their homes, where they were born and brought up. This is the land that they and their fathers have walked over and called their own; and they have just as good a right to call it theirs to-day as any people have to call any land their own."[27] Fred A. Conetah, writing from a Ute point of view, grants that the Mormons "had a particular interest in Indians" and "a policy of converting the Indians and encouraging them to become farmers," but he maintains that fundamentally, "they wanted what all other intruders wanted—land and resources. If the Indians were in the way, they were pushed aside."[28] William R. Palmer, Mormon stake president and community leader in Cedar City, declared long before it was fashionable to do so that although Brigham Young's Indian policy "was intended to be humane," its real basis was

> Safety First for the Mormons. . . . As a policy it was good, but as a declaration of rights it had serious shortcomings. There was in it no recognition of Indian rights. The great pioneer sent colonies out to possess the lands peacefully if they could, or by force if they must.[29]

Estimates of the number of Indians living within the present borders of Utah in 1850 range from twelve thousand to thirty thousand.[30] That total would include not only the Utes and Paiutes but also the Shoshoni in northern Utah, the Gosiutes in the West Desert, and perhaps a few Navajos. (Navajos had not yet taken up residence in southeastern Utah in significant numbers; the region was then held by Weeminuche Utes and San Juan Paiutes.) While it is likely that diseases introduced by mountain men and Spanish traders had already reduced the native population from what it had been a century earlier, it seems clear that thirty thousand represents something close to the maximum population supportable with a hunting-gathering way of life.

The Mormons came to Utah fresh from a series of conflicts with their Gentile neighbors in Ohio, Missouri, and Illinois, conflicts that had in each case resulted in their forced expulsion, and Brigham Young was clearly anxious to stake out a territory where his people could develop in relative isolation. For this reason, even though the well-watered Wasatch Front valleys where they originally settled were probably the best sites for development between Iowa and California, Brigham early began to send out exploring parties to locate colonies throughout a large region. He looked first to the south, perhaps because of a mistaken notion that the area north of Salt Lake Valley was too cold to sustain agriculture, perhaps because the Shoshoni presented a more formidable barrier to expansion than did the Utes and Paiutes. (The image of the Shoshoni as more warlike than the Utes was not universal, however. George Brewerton wrote in 1853 that "The Eutaws are perhaps the most powerful and warlike tribe now remaining upon this continent."[31])

The traditional story of the first Mormon settlement in the high plateau region, at Manti, maintains that Chief Wakara invited the Mormons to come and teach his people how to farm.[32] It is difficult on the basis of the available evidence to determine the exact nature of this invitation or Wakara's authority to issue it. The Ute people were composed of autonomous bands with nothing resembling a central government. Even within individual bands, power seems generally to have been shared among a group of influential men rather than concentrated in a single individual.[33] The concept of an Indian "chief" may be largely an Anglo fiction, perhaps arising from a difficulty in understanding the Indians' social organization, perhaps, less excusably, merely a pretext for exploitation. If you could label a single individual as the chief and negotiate a concession with him, then you had a quasi-legal basis for arrangements that were in fact simply imposed on the majority of Indians without their consent.

Wakara most likely belonged to the Tumpanawach, but had an influence beyond his own band as evidenced in the fact that he died and was buried with high honors among the Pahvant. Early accounts identify Wakara as one of several brothers, including Tabby, Sowiette, Sanpitch, and Kanosh, among others, each of whom ruled one of the Ute bands as chief.[34] This, however, looks suspiciously like an imposition of a European dynastic model on a culture to which it was entirely alien. It seems more likely that if Wakara and other prominent Utes regarded one another as "brothers" it was only in the sense of belonging to the Ute People.

The Sanpitch, with few horses, were a low-status band among the Utes. In inviting the Mormons to settle among them, Wakara may have

Shivwits baptism, 1875. C. R. Savage photo, courtesy LDS Church Archives.

been motivated by a genuine desire to improve his impoverished brethren's condition—or by a more self-serving wish to have access to the settlers' livestock as a replacement for the buffalo that had been hunted to extinction in Utah.[35] Early accounts from Manti settlers indicate that the Indians welcomed their presence at first—especially during the exceptionally harsh first winter, when the settlers' frozen cattle provided a steady supply of meat.[36]

The view of the little band of 224 Mormon pioneers who dug shelters in the south slope of Temple Hill in November 1849 was that they were entitled—both by the general doctrine of appropriation and improvement and by specific license of Chief Walker—to possess the land they improved as their own. In return, they were willing to set aside some land for the Sanpitches and teach them how to farm, or, as one Mormon preacher put it in 1856, "wash up and learn to work."[37] And a few Indians did take up farming while others were employed as herders. Most of the Sanpitches, however, refused to make so radical a change in their life-style, an unwillingness the settlers could not comprehend since they understood labor in this sense to be the basis of life.

The Mormons' title to Sanpete Valley became more firmly grounded when, after Wakara's death, a Ute variously called Seignerouch or Arropine agreed to the following document:

Be it known by these presents that I, Seignerouch (Arropine) of Manti City, in the County of Sanpete and Territory of Utah, for and in consideration of the good will which I have to the Church of Jesus Christ of Latter Day Saints, give and convey unto Brigham Young, trustee in trust for said church, his successors in office, all my claims to and ownership of the following described property, to-wit: The portion of land and countries known as Sanpete County, together with all material and timber on the same, valued at $155,000; ten horses valued, $500; four cows, $120; one bull, $40; farming tools valued $10; in all $155,765, together with all the rights, privileges and appurtenances thereunto belonging or appertaining. I also covenant and agree that I am the lawful claimant and owner of said property, and will warrant and forever defend the same unto the said trustee in trust, his successors in office and assigns, etc.[38]

It would be interesting to know exactly what Arropine thought he was agreeing to when he scratched his mark at the end of this document, and what the Sanpitches thought—if they were aware at all—of his claim to represent them in thus disposing of their ancestral lands. In any event, the legal document does not seem to have made much difference in the actual state of affairs in Sanpete Valley. Settlers continued to move into the region, and despite attempts to settle the Sanpitches on Indian farms at Twelve Mile Creek and in Thistle Valley they apparently continued a nomadic life but tended to cluster near the towns, where they regularly begged for food and clothing and sometimes frightened the residents by hostile gestures.

Conventional wisdom held that Anglo settlement was not necessarily injurious to the Indians. Especially in the West, where settlements were confined to relatively small tracts of irrigable land, there seemed to be plenty of room for the Indians to continue their traditional way of life if they preferred to do so instead of acquiring the "superior" culture of the whites. What was not taken into account was the fact that, though the Indian population was small in relation to the vastness of the land, it was generally in equilibrium with the resources available to a hunting and gathering economy. The valley lands that were suitable for agriculture were also among the most productive sources of seeds, berries, and game, and the streams diverted for irrigation were the best fisheries. When the settlers preempted this land and water, compelling the Indians in some instances to winter in colder regions, the Indians' traditional resources were significantly reduced. In addition, the settlers, in a subsistence economy themselves, turned to the lakes and streams for fish and to the foothills and mountains for deer and small game to supplement their own diets, thus further depleting the Indians' food supply. When domestic livestock were introduced to the range in large numbers, no portion of the Indians' traditional resources was left sacrosanct, and they were reduced to increasingly desperate measures to eke out an existence.

This partly unconscious attack on the Indians' economic base was further aggravated by a profound difference in worldview. Like the broader Anglo-American culture, the Mormons took it for granted that property and agriculture were the foundations of society. From their point of view, the Indians were incorrigibly lazy, since they expected to live on what the land yielded naturally rather than cultivating the earth to increase yields, and incorrigibly dishonest, since they had no respect for the whites' property rights. From the Indians' point of view, however, the world looked very different. Far from being lazy, they were destined to an unremitting struggle for the necessities of life, and their traditions took for granted the sharing of scarce resources. John Wesley Powell quotes as a widely repeated proverb among the Utes and Paiutes, "What matters it who kills the game, when we can all eat of it?"[39] Since they were accustomed to gathering whatever edibles the earth offered, it is hardly surprising that they found the produce of the settlers' gardens a tempting resource. And cattle must have seemed wonderfully appealing game—slower than deer and carrying much more meat.

Furthermore, while the Indians had a concept of territorial rights, they had no concept of individual property rights in the Anglo-European sense. For Anglo-Europeans, to own property means exclusive possession. For the Indians, agreeing to allow others to settle among them represented a willingness to share their territory, not to surrender use of it. While the Mormons had experimented, and would continue to do so into the 1870s, with schemes of communal ownership, the ethic of private property proved too deeply implanted to be removed. And despite Brigham Young's repeated counsel to feed the Indians, it must have grated upon many a settler to see Indians helping themselves to the products of the settlers' toil.

And so both parties felt themselves ill used. The Sanpitches viewed with growing apprehension the continuing influx of Mormon settlers into the valley and the establishment of settlements on one after another of the perennial streams. The festering resentments erupted into open hostilities on April 9, 1865, in Manti, when John Lowry pulled Jake Arropine off his horse. While almost all accounts agree in identifying this event as triggering the ensuing conflict, there is wide disagreement on the details. Some accounts have it that Lowry was drunk and looking for a fight. Others maintain that Jake Arropine was inciting other Utes to violence, boasting that he would kill Mormons and eat Mormon beef, and that when Lowry told him to be quiet Arropine moved to put an arrow to his bow. Lowry himself, in a statement written several years later, maintained that the Utes were seeking a pretext for hostilities that would have broken out in any event.[40]

After the scuffle, Jake Arropine reportedly rode to the home of James Tooth, where a Sanpitch leader, called Autenquer by the Utes but better known in Utah history as Black Hawk was having Sunday dinner.[41] Black Hawk, had evidently been troubled for some time by the displacement of the Utes and had made efforts as early as 1863 to unite the Ute bands in resistance to the white advances. A smallpox epidemic among the Sanpitches during the winter of 1864–65 had intensified the unrest, as the Indians blamed the devastating disease on the whites. The tinder was ready for the spark, and Black Hawk seized the opportunity to establish himself as a war chief.

In retrospect, the Black Hawk War can be seen as the last desperate struggle of the Utes to preserve their ancestral lands and life-style. The little band of rebellious Indians (estimated at no more than forty men at the beginning, swelling to perhaps as many as two hundred as early successes brought recruits not only from other Ute bands but from the Paiutes and Navajos) were fighting the tide of history and had no chance for ultimate victory. But for several years the uprising constituted a serious threat to Mormon settlements in central and southern Utah.

The "war," such as it was, was fought throughout the region of the High Plateaus. Only a handful of episodes could be considered pitched battles, and those few usually turned out badly for the Utes. Their chief successes came in surprise raids aimed at livestock herds or vulnerable individuals or families outside the "forted up" towns. The Utes' deep knowledge of the plateau terrain enabled them to enter the valleys without warning, complete a raid, and disappear into the mountains before organized pursuit could be assembled. Of the estimated four thousand head of cattle and horses captured by the Indians, no more than a few dozen were recovered, even though large militia parties often went in pursuit. The livestock was taken for the most part to the wide dry valleys east of the Wasatch Plateau, where the horses were traded to other bands or kept as mounts for Black Hawk's men, who enjoyed a beef-rich diet during the three years the conflict continued at its height.

Between sixty and seventy whites were killed in the Black Hawk War, depending on where one draws the spatial and temporal boundaries. Indian casualties were probably substantially higher. The first blood was spilled the day after the quarrel between John Lowry and Jake Arropine, when Peter Ludvigsen was killed while rounding up cattle at Twelve Mile Creek. As the Indians were driving the captured cattle eastward through Salina Canyon, they came upon Barney Ward and James P. Andersen, who were later found scalped and stripped. The pursuing militia was ambushed in the Salina Canyon narrows, where William Kearns and Jens Sorenson were killed.[42]

Other raids followed in swift succession, causing widespread alarm among the settlers and inducing many of them to withdraw from isolated ranches into the towns. The Wilson and Given families had recently settled in Thistle Valley, a favorite camping and hunting ground for the Utes situated between the northern portion of the Wasatch Plateau and the foothills of Mount Nebo. At the outbreak of hostilities, A. G. Wilson moved his family to the safety of a larger community, but John Given was determined to remain on his land. On the evening of May 25, 1865, a war party traveling north killed a sheepherder named Jens Larsen near Fairview. At daybreak the next morning, they surrounded the Givens' willow hut and shot through the walls, killing Given, his wife, and their nineteen-year-old son. Their three little girls, ages three, five, and nine, were killed by tomahawk blows to the head. Two young men who had been working for Given escaped to sound the alarm. When the militia arrived from Fairview and Mount Pleasant, they found not only the six stripped and mutilated bodies, but also several crippled calves in a nearby corral. Evidently thinking them too young for a forced drive, the Utes had broken their backs before making off with the older animals.

This event and the October attack at Ephraim epitomized the Indians' brutality in the minds of the settlers. On October 17, a raiding party led by Black Hawk himself rode down Ephraim Canyon, killing William T. Hite and Soren Jesperson and chasing several other men to the safety of the town. Then the Indians circled west into the fields, where Soren Sorenson, Martin and Hansine Kuhre and their two-year-old son, and Hansine's sister, Elizabeth Petersen, were harvesting potatos. Sorenson had been acquainted with Black Hawk during more peaceful times, and the chief rode up to him and began to talk, explaining that what the Indians mainly sought was the Ephraim cow herd. While this conversation was going on, other Indians killed the Kuhres and the Petersen girl before Sorensen's shocked eyes. Sorensen was permitted to escape, and when a party came from Ephraim to recover the bodies they found the Kuhre baby, unharmed, beside the corpses of his parents.

Brutality was not confined to one side in the conflict. Several Ute women and children were killed during what became known as the "squaw fight" in Grass Valley in July 1865.[43] But the most grisly episode of the war was the massacre of virtually an entire village of Paiutes at Circleville in April 1866. Four Circleville residents, two of them thirteen-year-old boys, had been killed and the community cattle taken by Indians on November 26, 1865. Circleville was remote from other settlements, and its defenders were few and poorly equipped. Situated near the junction of the two main forks of the Sevier River, it was also on major Indian trails. War anxiety was intense in the community.

On April 21, 1866, there was a skirmish between a group of Paiutes and the militia at Fort Sanford, seventeen miles farther up the Sevier. When news of this encounter reached Circleville, suspicions immediately focused on a neighboring Paiute village, even though the settlers' relations with this group had previously been peaceful. The community militia surrounded the Indians, disarmed them (one Paiute was killed when he resisted arrest), and took them to the town, where the men were kept under guard in the log meetinghouse and the women and children in a cellar. Under interrogation, some of the Paiutes reportedly told of a massing of Indian forces for an attack on Circleville, which could only have intensified the residents' apprehensions. Then the Paiute men made an attempt at escape, during which most or all of them were fatally wounded by the guards. According to an account written later by Oluf Christian Larsen, "The next consideration was how to dispose of the squaws and papooses. Considering the exposed position we occupied and what had already been done it was considered necessary to dispatch everyone that could tell the tale. Three small children were saved and adopted by good families."[44] Evidently, the women and other children were "dispatched" by bringing them up from the cellar one at a time and cutting their throats. So much, then, for white "civilization" as opposed to Indian "savagery." It is symptomatic that there are no reliable records of the number of Paiutes who died in this slaughter. Bishop William J. Allred reported that sixteen were killed and four children permitted to live, but Albert Winkler suggests that this "may be considered the minimum possible figure."[45]

The battle at Gravelly Ford on the Sevier River above Salina in June 1866 probably represents the turning point of the Black Hawk War. On June 10, Indians raided the cattle herd at Scipio, killing two herdsmen. They then drove some five hundred head of stock eastward toward their refuge beyond the Wasatch Plateau. They were intercepted at the Sevier by a party of militia under the command of William B. Pace, but managed, as usual, to get the livestock through the river and safely into the mountains. Indeed, the Utes more than held their own, as Pace's troops were surrounded and running low on ammunition when some seventy cavalry arrived from Fillmore to relieve them.

The Utes' cattle raid was a costly success, however, as Black Hawk received a wound that disabled him for some time, and from which he never entirely recovered.[46] Deprived of vigorous leadership, Black Hawk's band began to dwindle in numbers. Other circumstances were also combining to undermine his cause. After more than a year of raids, the settlers had largely gathered into the larger, fortified towns, and the local militias in central Utah were increasingly supplemented by better-equipped forces from the more populous communities on the Wasatch Front. Under Brigham Young's direction, the residents of Utah and Heber valleys undertook a concentrated campaign to send large quantities of beef and flour to the hungry Utes on the Uintah Reservation, who had been victimized by a series of corrupt or incompetent Indian agents and by the failure of the federal government to deliver promised supplies. This campaign evidently achieved its intended aim. By relieving the destitution of the main body of Utes, it slowed the stream of recruits Black Hawk had depended upon to maintain his fighting force.

While sporadic raids continued through 1866 and 1867, some of them carried out by Navajos and Paiutes in southern Utah who were not actually part of Black Hawk's band, the Utes' power of sustained warfare was clearly on the decline. In August 1867, Black Hawk appeared on the Uintah Reservation and announced to Col. F. H. Head, the Indian superintendent, that he desired peace. Apparently as a gesture of submission, he asked Head to give him a haircut.[47]

What was perhaps the most dramatic and surely the strangest episode of the Black Hawk War occurred after the cessation of hostilities. Still suffering from the effects of his 1866 wound and perhaps sensing that he did not have long to live, Black Hawk announced in 1869 that he wanted to visit all of the communities that had been injured by the war and personally ask the residents' forgiveness. William Probert, who served as an escort for one leg of this penitential tour, wrote that

> accompanied by a few (seven or eight) warriors, Black Hawk visited every town and village from Cedar City on the South to Payson on the north and made peace with the people. On this mission of peace he was provided with an escort, usually from two to six citizens, from town to town.[48]

101

Pahvants at Kanosh, 1901. G. E. Anderson photo, courtesy Brigham Young University photo archives.

At Parowan, where some of his followers had conducted a raid in the fall of 1868, after Black Hawk himself had sued for peace, he was met by the martial band, whose music, according Maria Taylor, "seemed to please him very much. Black Hawk explained that he had been very ill and his young men had acted without his knowledge or authority in their efforts to raid the cattle."[49] At Holden he spoke for an hour on the causes of the war. Then, with a larger escort than usual, he traveled over the pass to Scipio, where feelings were still high because of the killing of the herdsmen in 1866. By the time he reached the towns of Fountain Green and Fairview, at the north end of Sanpete Valley, the strain of his journey was clearly telling upon him, and those who saw him there left descriptions indicating that he had "a very sallow complexion" and was "a wreck physically."[50] Black Hawk made his final journey in 1870, traveling from the Uintah Reservation to Spring Lake, in Utah Valley, where he had reportedly been born. Here, by most accounts, he died and was secretly buried on the mountainside by his followers.[51]

The costs of the Black Hawk War were substantial in relation to the means of the hard-pressed settlers, and the human suffering was heavy on both sides. The campaigns were fought entirely by volunteer militia under the general leadership of the Nauvoo Legion, a Mormon paramilitary organization formed in Illinois and continued in Utah. The U.S.

military authorities in Utah Territory refused to recognize the Nauvoo Legion, and the Indian campaigns were carried out with negligible government assistance. However, in 1917 Utah Senator Reed Smoot succeeded in amending a pension act for Indian war veterans in order to make Black Hawk War veterans eligible for pensions. These small payments were welcome sources of income for many elderly men and women during the 1920s and '30s.

In addition to hastening the removal of the Utes to the Uintah Reservation, the ultimate product of the Black Hawk War was a body of heroic legend. Almost every village in central Utah has in its local lore accounts of miraculous interventions, daring rides, or clever stratagems that averted what would otherwise have been a massacre. Boys as young as ten or twelve had been called upon to stand guard duty or carry messages. For many of them, this adventurous period constituted the most memorable time of their lives. Black Hawk veterans continued to hold an annual encampment until well into the twentieth century, a three- or four-day gathering in late summer that rotated among several towns. These festivities normally included a parade, a rodeo, and campfire evenings where old men stayed late, talking about the war in particular and pioneer times in general.

The reservation Utes have largely lost the identity of their ancestral bands and now regard themselves as members of the Uintah Band as distinguished from the White River and Uncompahgre bands from western Colorado who share the reservation. The Uinta Basin was designated as an Indian reservation on the basis of a perception that the region was too cold and barren to have any value as farmland—in the words of an 1861 exploring party, a "vast contiguity of waste . . . valueless except for nomadic purposes, hunting grounds for Indians and to hold the world together."[52] Then, in a predictable pattern, valuable minerals were discovered, beginning with gilsonite in 1885, and areas were withdrawn from the reservation to allow developers free rein. During the same period, ranchers moved their herds onto the reservation grazing lands, sometimes in return for nominal lease payments, sometimes without any payment at all. Shortly after the turn of the century, large portions of the best land were thrown open to white settlement, on the theory that the fewer than two thousand Utes who remained by then did not need all of that land, and that if they would turn farmers they could do very well on individual allotments of eighty acres. This opening of the Uinta Basin soon made the Utes a minority population on their own reservation. When the populous Wasatch Front began to exhaust its natural water supply, covetous eyes were turned toward the Strawberry River and other tributaries of the Duchesne, and a still-continuing series of transbasin diversion projects began.

The Utes have not been without their victories. In 1911 and again in 1933, they were awarded compensation for various land claims, and in 1950, after years of litigation, they won the largest award for Indian claims made to that time, almost $32 million. In recent years, court decisions affirming Ute rights in the entire territory of the original reservation boundaries, combined with a growing activism among the Utes, have made the white residents of the Uinta Basin increasingly nervous.

The history of the Paiutes, always more scattered and impoverished than the Utes, has in some respects been even sadder. While the Utes were given a large reservation with hunting and fishing lands that enabled them to preserve in some degree their traditional way of life, the Paiute bands, when they were allocated any land at all, were typically given small plots of desert terrain insufficient even for their subsistence economy. In the 1950s, the Paiutes were "terminated" as a tribe and for thirty years had no existence as a distinct people in the eyes of the federal government. But persistence in a hostile environment has always been a prime Paiute quality. Not only did the bands preserve their identity throughout this period, in significant measure they even maintained their ties to traditional territories—ties the Utes have largely lost.

An interesting measure of the strength and persistence of Paiute culture has been the drift of the Koosharem and Kanosh Indian communities from a Ute to a Paiute identity. Many of the Pahvants and Sanpitches, however reluctantly, joined the move to the Uintah Reservation in the 1860s and 1870s, where their descendants were assimilated into the Uintah Band. But some Pahvants, including Chief Kanosh, remained at the Indian farm on Corn Creek. Others, together with some Sanpitches, maintained residence near the villages of Koosharem and Greenwich in Grass Valley.[53] In the nineteenth century, the Pahvants and Sanpitches were clearly numbered among the Utes, even though they employed some desert survival practices characteristic of the Paiutes. Carvalho lists both Kanosh of the Pahvants and "a San Pete chief" as participating with other Ute leaders in the 1854 Chicken Creek peace conference.[54] Peter Gottfredson evidently thought of the Corn Creek and Grass Valley communities as being composed of Utes in 1914, when he observed a Bear Dance held jointly by the two communities. But the descendants of these Pahvants and Sanpitches have now come to think of themselves as Paiutes and have closer associations with the other Paiute bands in central and southern Utah than they do with the Utes of the Uinta Basin.

6

STREAMS EVER COPIOUS

Aperennial Utah legend holds that irrigated agriculture by Anglo-Americans had its beginning in July 1847, when the Mormon pioneers diverted the water of City Creek onto their fields in the Salt Lake Valley. The claim is somewhat dubious. By the 1840s, a good many American adventurers had settled down as *rancheros* in the Southwest and California, where the hispanic population had been growing irrigated crops for several generations, and the Indians for centuries. It seems likely, too, that some early Oregon settlers must have supplemented the natural rainfall with irrigation, particularly in the drier interior valleys. Moreover, the Mormon pioneers may not have realized the full implications of their water diversion at the time it occurred. They flooded the earth in order to soften it for plowing. It is not clear exactly when they realized that irrigation would be an ongoing necessity.

But whether or not the Mormons were the first irrigators, they unquestionably developed a distinctive though somewhat inefficient irrigation technology that gave the Utah landscape a different look from other regions of the West. Villages were established on the alluvial fans at the mouths of canyons, sometimes even straddling the creek (a location the residents learned to regret later when the floods came). Small creeks were preferred settlement sites because their waters were easier to divert and control than larger streams such as the Bear and Weber and Provo rivers.

The first diversions were usually relatively low on the stream, allowing irrigation of bottomland only, and were typically the work of what might be termed folk engineering. Diversion dams might be simply a row of large rocks placed across the creek bed to direct some of the water into the irrigation ditch. Since many settlements lacked trained surveyors and instruments, canal routes were surveyed by such rough and ready methods as a carpenter's level attached to a long, straight plank, or a tube filled with water. The canals were the product of pick and shovel work supplemented by horsedrawn plows and scrapers.

In order to bring water to the benchlands, later diversions were made at higher points on the creek. These needed larger and better-engineered dams, and the canals often traversed rugged country that required tunnelling through hills, building flumes across gullies, and in some cases even hanging a stretch of canal on the face of a cliff. Many of these irrigation works were constructed almost entirely without money (except for the purchase of such essentials as blasting powder) by cooperative labor, with settlers working for "shares" of the water. Some early canals in central and southern Utah represent nothing short of heroic achievements. For example, the settlers of Cleveland spent more than four years building a twenty-six-mile canal to their dry townsite. During the construction period, all water for household use and domestic livestock had to be hauled six miles in barrels. The settling of Emery required bringing the waters of Muddy Creek through a tunnel that took more than three years to dig. With no trained engineering assistance, the builders made their calculations, started from opposite sides of the hill, dodged numerous cave-ins of the treacherous Mancos shale, maintained the correct level inside the tunnel by sighting over lighted candles, and joined the two segments almost perfectly.

The most remarkable achievement among these low-capital, labor-intensive reclamation projects, however, was the Hurricane Canal. From the earliest times in "Utah's Dixie," the Hurricane Bench had been recognized as desirable agricultural land in a region where most level ground was either saturated with alkali or subject to periodic flooding. But it was situated high and dry above the Virgin River gorge where it emerges from the Hurricane Cliffs. In 1893, "using nothing more complicated than a wheelbarrow,"[1] the Dixieites set to work. For eleven years, they chiseled their way through solid rock or hung flumes on the canyon wall. It took nine tunnels and several trestles before the eight-mile-long canal was completed in 1904.

In some instances, the later, larger canals replaced the earlier diversions, but not always. After a decade or so, there might be a dozen or more diversions on a single creek, each of them built and managed by a different company, and with cumulative claims far in excess of the dependable streamflow. For example, the first settlers on Cottonwood Creek, in Emery County, dug the Blue Cut Canal in 1877 to irrigate the bottomland between the present towns of Orangeville and Castle Dale. Several miles upstream and a year later, Erastus Curtis and his family began what was later called the Starr Ditch. Downstream from the Blue Cut, the West Town Ditch, Seely, Olsen, Wilcox, Jeffs, Wilsonville, Higby, Wilberg, and Biddlecome ditches were all constructed between 1878 and 1885. These were low diversions designed to irrigate relatively

106

small plots of land near the creek. The first high-line diversion was the Clipper Canal, begun in 1878 to bring water to the Orangeville townsite. The Mammoth Canal and the Great Western, both constructed in the mid-1880s, made possible the cultivation of the benchlands north and south of the creek.

With the completion of these canals, the irrigable land exceeded the water supply. The users of the small riverbottom ditches had a prior claim to irrigation water, but the high-line canals were in a position to divert the entire stream during seasons of low runoff. As local historian Montell Seely puts it,

> The upstream users, even though they came later, had first access to the creek so naturally they took what water they wanted and this often left the downstream users short changed. The waste water and seep water from the farms upstream ran back into the creek, and in the fall the only water the downstream users had was this adulterated seep water.[2]

In a process repeated with variations on numerous Utah streams, Cottonwood Creek farmers invoked the authority of both church and state to resolve the conflict. Mormon Apostles John Henry Smith and Anthon H. Lund and Emery Stake President Ruben G. Miller prepared a referees' report which they submitted to non-Mormon Judge Jacob Johnson of Spring City. In 1902, Johnson issued a decree awarding a "first class" water right to those who had homesteaded before 1884 and a "second class" right to those who had come later. In addition, a "third class" right was given to the water users on the Great Western in consideration of the great expense in constructing that canal. First-class rights were allocated among the various canals on the basis of one cubic foot of water per second for each sixty acres of land. Second- and third-class users were entitled to the available surplus water, which in effect meant that they could irrigate only during the high water season in the spring and early summer. By 1909, all of the major canal companies except the Blue Cut had merged into the Cottonwood Creek Consolidated Irrigation Company. In 1937, the Blue Cut Canal stockholders joined the consolidated company, and the three classes of water were reduced to a single class based on stock held in the company.[3]

Some consolidation of canals accompanied the consolidation of irrigation companies, but many of the older diversions remain in use. One of the distinguishing marks of the Utah landscape has been the presence of multiple canals, one above another, each with its own streamside thicket of trees, shrubs, and willows, and its own riparian wildlife. Even the main canals are seldom very large, but there is a progressive division into smaller and smaller distribution ditches, down to the individual farm's headgate.

In order to insure that all users get the portion of the streamflow they are entitled to, the irrigation companies employ watermasters to make regular rounds of all the headgates. A traditional measuring device was a small weir made of boards, rather like a box open at both ends, installed on a fairly level stretch of ditch not far below the headgate. Inside the weir, the water would pass over a level board through an opening whose width was determined by the number of water shares held. The watermaster's goal was to keep the flow through this opening at the same level for all the users on the system. During high water, the flow might be several inches deep, and no one worried much about precise adjustments. Late in the season, however, it might shrink to an inch or even less, a stream too small to do much good but nonetheless jealously guarded. This was the time when half an inch's difference could provoke violence.

Some irrigation companies, rather than attempt to provide a continuous flow to all users, employed a system of "water turns" by which the entire flow of a ditch would be given to a farmer for a certain period of time in each cycle depending on stock held in the company. Cycles typically revolved once each week, though some systems had longer cycles.

For the town lots, irrigation by turn was the norm even where the surrounding fields enjoyed a continuous flow. Early each spring, the watermaster would distribute a list of water turns to every user. Normally these would be rotated from week to week so that they came at different hours of the day and night. If a water turn began at three o'clock in the morning, the householder would be at the ditch on the minute, gum boots on his feet, a shovel in one hand and a lantern in the other, ready to break the upstream neighbor's dam. Then for the two or four or ten hours of the turn, the irrigator would work feverishly in an effort to give the entire lot "a good soak." When water turns came during daylight hours, they often involved the entire family, with one member nursing equal streams along each furrow in the vegetable garden while others filled the depressions around the fruit trees and currant bushes and rose bushes and peonies, and flooded the lawn and the cow pasture. All the while the younger children splashed barefoot in the grass.

The technology of irrigation brought with it a whole set of social institutions and folk traditions. One tradition that has attained the status of foundational myth is that the Mormon pioneers transformed a barren desert into a lush garden. But Richard H. Jackson has persuasively demonstrated that the myth of the desert transformed was largely a creation of the period between 1855 and 1880, when church leaders were trying to recruit settlers for the harsher regions of southern Utah. Contemporary reports by the 1847 pioneers do not suggest that they perceived the Salt Lake Valley as a desert. Wilford Woodruff, for example, wrote, "We gazed with wonder and admiration on the most fertile valley."[4] Thomas Bullock reported that the company had to wade "thro' thick grass for some distance" before finding "a place bare enough for a camping ground, the grass being only knee deep but very thick."[5] William Clayton commented on the abundant water and soil of a "most excellent quality."[6]

The members of the 1849 exploring expedition led by Parley P. Pratt were also favorably impressed with the agricultural prospects of the southern valleys, as we have seen. They liked the broad alluvial plains at the base of the high plateaus and the mountain streams flowing from the canyons. They had had no experience with the irrigation requirements of southern Utah, with its low rainfall and high evaporation rate, and they obviously greatly overestimated the water supply. Or perhaps they were carried along by a faith that God would "modify and mollify" the climate to accommodate their needs—the Mormon version of the widespread nineteenth-century American belief that "rain follows the plow."[7]

When John Wesley Powell made his influential study of the arid region in the 1870s, he noted that "the belt of country lying between Great Salt Lake and the Wasatch Mountains" enjoyed "a rainfall much greater than the general rainfall of the region," though still requiring supplemental irrigation for productive agriculture.[8] The remainder of Utah, however, Powell characterized as classically representative of the arid region, where "the extent of irrigable land is dependent upon the volume of water carried by the streams." He estimated the potential agricultural lands of Utah at less than three percent of the total area.[9] At the same time, however, Powell saw some distinct advantages to irrigated agriculture:

> Crops thus cultivated are not subject to the vicissitudes of rainfall; the farmer fears no droughts; his labors are seldom interrupted and his crops rarely injured by storms. This immunity from drought and storm renders agricultural operations much more certain than in regions of greater humidity. Again, the water comes down from the mountains and plateaus freighted with fertilizing materials derived from the decaying vegetation

and soils of the upper regions, which are spread by the flowing water over the cultivated lands.[10]

Powell also predicted the construction of upstream storage reservoirs to increase the water supply during the later part of the irrigating season. Such reservoirs in the high mountain valleys were to be preferred over lower-elevation storage, which "is somewhat wasteful of water, as the evaporation is greater than above." In a remark that takes on considerable irony in light of the huge, low-elevation, high-evaporation storage reservoir that now bears Powell's name, he cautioned, "This wastage is apparent when it is remembered that the evaporation in an arid climate may be from 60 to 80 inches annually, or even greater."[11]

The notion that the climate and water supply would improve as the land was cultivated went hand in hand with the Mormon settlement of the West. Utah folklore is rich with legends that seem to bear out this process, and it is probably true that streamflow increased, for reasons to be examined below. But some stories greatly exaggerate these changes. A Sanpete Valley tradition has it that when settlers first arrived at the site of Ephraim, there was scarcely enough water in Pine Creek to support a single family, but the streamflow grew along with the settlement. In contradiction to this legend, however, a nineteenth-century history quotes Ephraim's original settler, Isaac Behunin, as saying, "Pine creek had more water and the location was better for a town than anywhere in the valley."[12] The Daughters of Utah Pioneers history of Beaver County declares, "When the first pioneers came to this valley, it is said that one could step across the Beaver River in almost any locality. But through years of effort and planning, the water resources have developed to an astonishing degree."[13] James S. Brown, recalling in 1900 a journey he had taken along the Mormon Corridor in 1849, writes of camping on the future site of Springville:

> I remember that we thought the place would be capable of sustaining eight or ten families, or a dairy, believing there was not enough water for more.
>
> From Hobble Creek we passed on from one small stream to another, expressing our opinion as to the capacity of the water supply; and in no instance did we suppose that there was water sufficient for more than fifteen families, judging from what we could see then. Again, the barrenness of the country was such that it did not seem that more than seventy-five or a hundred head of cattle could find feed within reach of water. Now thousands of head of horned stock and horses are sustained at the same places.[14]

However, other travelers in the same 1849 party wrote in their journals of finding several sites with sufficient streamflow to support towns.

The climate of the western United States is subject to wet and dry cycles of several years' duration. If a settlement was established at the beginning of a wet cycle, the expectation that God would "temper the elements" might seem to be borne out for a period of time. But when a dry cycle returned, the community would face a crisis.

The Powell study of the arid region was influential in dispelling the notion that rain follows the plow. Powell's fundamental assumption was that aridity was the permanent condition of the Rocky Mountain region, and that institutions and technology must be developed to accommodate that reality if the region was to be developed. At the same time, Powell had to deal with the widely observed phenomenon that streamflow did indeed tend to increase during the early years of settlement. This aspect of the study fell to Powell's associate G. K. Gilbert, who began his report by declaring, "The residents of Utah who practice irrigation have observed that many of the streams have increased in volume since the settlement of the country. Of the actuality of this increase there can be no question."[15] He noted that records had been kept of some streams over a period of more than twenty years, and that "in many places the service of a stream was doubled, and in a few it was increased tenfold, or even fiftyfold." Gilbert also charted what he took to be a permanent rise in the level of the Great Salt Lake.

In seeking to account for these phenomena, Gilbert granted as "tenable" the notion that the climate of the Great Salt Lake basin might give grown moister during the period between 1847 and 1877. However, he hastened to add that

> so far as I entertain the idea of a change of climate, I do so without referring the change to any local cause. It is frequently asserted that the cultivated lands of Utah "draw the rain"; or that the prayers of the religious community inhabiting the territory have brought water to their growing crops; or that the telegraph wires and iron rails which gird the country have in some way caused electricity to induce precipitation; but none of these agencies seem to be competent. The weather of the globe is a complex whole, each part of which reacts on every other, and each part of which depends on every other.[16]

Gilbert preferred to think that "human agencies" were primarily responsible for the increased streamflow and attempted to trace the observed changes to particular causes. He proposed that the cutting of timber and

the introduction of grazing stock on the watersheds had the effect of re-
ducing both evaporation and absorption, thereby increasing runoff. Further, irrigators had removed beaver dams and other obstructions from
the streams and "opened up" springs formerly lost in bogs, and these
measures had also contributed to increased streamflow. Gilbert painted
an optimistic picture of the continuing benefits of these practices:

> Not alone are the agricultural facilities of this district improving, but the
> facilities in the whole Rocky Mountain Region are improving and will im-
> prove. Not only does the settler incidentally and unconsciously enhance
> his natural privilege, but it is possible, by the aid of a careful study of the
> subject, to devise such systematic methods as shall render his work still
> more effectual.[17]

With a longer historical perspective than Gilbert had at his disposal, we
now recognize some of the shortcomings of his analysis. The rise in volume of the Great Salt Lake that he viewed as permanent was merely the
product of a wet cycle. Since 1877, the lake has during several dry cycles
fallen lower than it was when the Mormon pioneers arrived in 1847,
and during the wet cycle of the mid-1980s it rose even higher than the
level Gilbert had termed "exceptional."

Gilbert's analysis of ways in which settlement may increase streamflow is plausible, but once again a longer experience of irrigated agriculture in the arid region suggests some additional factors he failed to take
into account. Nearly all of the usable streamflow in Utah descends from
the high-elevation watersheds of the mountains and high plateaus, the
only areas in the region where annual precipitation exceeds evaporation. Some of this water comes directly from snowmelt and the runoff
from rainstorms, which tend to be concentrated in the spring and early
summer or to come in floods of short duration. The more steady portion
of the streamflow derives from perennial springs, whose natural reservoirs are charged by water percolating into the soil. The denuding and
compacting of the soil that Gilbert identified as causes of increased
runoff will in the long run reduce the amount of water that reaches the
underground reservoirs, eventually leading to a reduction in the flow of
springs.

With this model in mind, we are in a better position to understand
both the increase in streamflow that Gilbert observed in the first years
of settlement and the reductions that followed toward the end of the
nineteenth century and into the twentieth. In a pristine environment,
water absorption is maximized and runoff is minimized. Therefore,

streamflow will be relatively low during periods of runoff but relatively high during those parts of the year when streams depend on springs. As the watershed is altered by grazing, logging, and other human activities, runoff is increased. But because the water-bearing underground strata have been charged over a long period of high absorption, springs will continue to flow abundantly. The result of these combined circumstances will of course be a noticeable increase in streamflow. Eventually, however, the underground reservoirs will become depleted and the flow from springs will decrease. This not only reduces the total amount of streamflow but also changes its character, resulting in a wider variation between high flows during seasons of runoff and low water at other times of the year.

This is exactly what happened in many Utah watersheds. Increased streamflow during the early years of settlement led to overdevelopment of irrigated land. Then the combination of damaged watersheds and natural dry cycles produced devastating droughts in the 1890s, again in the period around 1915, in the early 1930s, and in the 1950s. Where suitable reservoir sites are available, efforts have been made to mitigate the fluctuations in streamflow by constructing reservoirs to hold spring runoff for use later in the growing season. But to a significant extent, these are only expensive (and where built at low elevations wasteful) attempts to compensate for the loss of the natural storage system that once helped to equalize streamflows throughout the year.

Despite the vital importance of water both to the Utah economy and to the Utah imagination, many residents still do not understand the relationship between a healthy watershed and useful streamflow. During drought periods in central and southern Utah, one can still occasionally hear seriously intended proposals to strip all vegetation from the watersheds in order to maximize streamflows—this despite the terrible lessons of the Sanpete Valley floods in the early years of the twentieth century and the Davis County floods of the 1920s, directly caused by the denuding of mountain watersheds.

Whoever would seek to grasp the essence of rural Utah must understand the water: its scarcity, its fragility, its power to transform barren land to garden, meadowland to gully, highland to lowland. From its mysterious source in the alpine snowbanks, still frigid in midsummer, it flows both through surface rills and underground to mirror tarns, to saturated hollows and boggy ponds where salamanders slither in the mud. From weeping ledges and sweetly gushing limestone springs, it gathers in willow-fringed brooks and follows an intricate network of draws, ravines, canyons, with streams merging and growing as they flow to lower elevations while alpine fir changes to blue spruce and riverside birch along the banks. In the lower reaches of the mountain canyons, narrow-leaf cottonwood and box elder appear, and in the valleys big Fremont cottonwoods mark the meandering course until the creek cuts through a reef and disappears into the deep gorges of the Colorado drainage or suns itself lazily to extinction in the valleys of the Great Basin.

This is the natural pilgrimage, but hardly less deeply embedded in the landscape now are the earthworks erected at glacial moraines or canyon narrows to form reservoirs that have their own kind of beauty, rising in the spring to reflect greening aspen groves then shrinking through the summer to reveal a jigsaw puzzle of crazily cracked clay. Where the canyons approach the valleys, a thin silver sheet of water flows over a mossy diversion dam, while from the deep, still pool behind the dam a canal begins its slow winding journey, gurgling its peaceful song. A hymn still frequently sung by Mormon congregations declares,

> Lo! in the desert the flowers are springing;
> Streams, ever copious, are gliding along.
> Loud from the mountaintops echoes are ringing;
> Wastes rise in verdure and mingle in song.[18]

There is something awe-inspiring about the transforming power of irrigation water, whether in the red fields of Sevier County, or an isolated ranch at the edge of the San Rafael Swell, or only a couple of chokecherry bushes, kept wet by the overflow of a mossy stock trough at a trickling desert spring. Foliage seems more lush and abundant in a place like Fruita, where the orchards run up against the walls of Capitol Reef, than it does in regions where green is the common color. And even though they are in a sense artificial, irrigation works tend to become naturalized over time. Probably not one in a hundred of those who splash in the waterfalls that tumble down the east side of the Paunsagunt Plateau just inside the boundaries of Bryce Canyon National Park realizes that this is a manmade diversion rather than a natural stream, so completely have the works of man found a home among the works of nature.

When Wallace Stegner gave the title The Sound of Mountain Water to his book on what it means to be a westerner and a western writer, he was thinking primarily of water running free in mountain streams, a fine symbol for the freedom and openness of the West. He writes, "I discovered mountain rivers late, for I was a prairie child, and knew only flatland and dryland until we toured the Yellowstone country in 1920." There, on the banks of Henry's Fork of the Snake, he "stood beside this river with its spray in my face and watched it thunder into foam, smooth to green glass over sunken rocks, shatter to foam again."[19] A love for free-flowing water in the mountain creeks has formed part of Stegner's wilderness ethic ever since.

But Stegner also came to appreciate the quieter music of the water that sustains the Mormon landscape. He has written appreciatively of the deep peacefulness of a central Utah village, with "only the rattle of the cottonwood leaves and the grassy gurgle of water in the irrigation ditch."[20] And he captures memorably the rich visual effects of a Plateau Country family gathering in a desert transformed by irrigation:

> Inside the gate is deep shade. We are looking into a half acre of big Fremont poplars that lean over a log ranch house and all but obscure the cliff behind. Through the grove, quicksilver bright, the ditch flows through grass that must be periodically flooded to keep it so green. Scattered and clustered through the grove are fifty or sixty people. They make a picture like a Renoir picnic or a Seurat promenade *sur l'herbe*, but different, special, simpler and homelier, quintessentially red-ledge Mormon.[21]

Water is a central symbol in Maurine Whipple's powerful novel *The Giant Joshua* through its account of the St. George pioneers' long struggle to control the erratic flow of the Virgin River.[22] The river, now sinking to a stagnant trickle, now roaring with flood-fury that crushes the puny diversion dams and tears away the fields, epitomizes the hostile natural environment, while the unpalatable spring water that seeps from the red ledges and waters the gardens but corrupts the innards of the settlers symbolizes the internal tensions within the community.

While Whipple grew up on the iron-laden water of the Virgin River Valley, Virginia Sorensen as a child drank from the sweet limestone springs of Sanpete Valley. In Sorensen's finest novel, *The Evening and the Morning*, an expatriate Utahn named Kate Alexander awakens on the twenty-fourth of July, 1922, to the ringing bells of the Manti Pioneer Day celebration and utters the wish, "If only a great poet could be born here and make the kind of poetry the story of the water deserves!"[23] By "the story of the water" she means the essential story of rural Utah, the oasis villages with tree-lined streets, "barns . . . clustered at the hearts of the blocks," the aroma of ripe raspberries in the air, and the ever-present murmur of the roadside irrigation ditches.

115

Sorensen's three Manti books are charged with memories of water. For example, midsummer plunges in Main Ditch:

> She and Esther had always known, on any hot summer day, where a dam would be raising the water. In black bloomers and undershirts, they splashed and dived, and the water from the mountain was icy from great heights and swift motion. They came out shuddering, their lips plum blue, and lay on the grass in the hot dry sun, smelling crushed mint and listening to the tumble of the water. Over them moved western clouds, clouds that never interfered with each other but were complete individuals like the people who came to live under them.[24]

In a community dependent on irrigation, the watermaster, as Sorensen has said, was "an official of great importance."[25] By the same token, the water thief—the individual who put his own needs above those of his neighbors—was a threat to the entire social fabric. The title story of *Where Nothing Is Long Ago* tells of the killing of a water thief and the killer's vindication by the community. The victim is doubly marginal—not only a water thief but one who has "fallen away from the faith." His killer, Brother Tolsen, is, like the bishop and other respected members of the community, of Danish extraction and a churchgoing Mormon. The story is told in retrospect by a narrator who as a young child was playing in Bishop Petersen's garden when Brother Tolsen arrived to report his deed to the bishop before turning himself in to the sheriff (which was, the narrator says, "entirely proper in all eyes"). Later that day, she listens intently as her parents discuss the killing:

> "But why did he hit him like that?" Mother asked my father. "It's not like Brother Tolsen to strike anybody. Such a gentle man!"
> "Twice he had turned Brother Tolsen's water off his fields in the night. *Twice!*" My father spoke with the patience of a man obliged to explain violence to a woman. "Brother Tolsen says he had no notion of hitting so hard, but he hit him with a shovel, after all."[26]

Forbidden to attend the funeral or the trial, the narrator—in the tradition of the artist as curious and observant child—tries to piece together an understanding of events from fragmentary impressions. Some things she misunderstands:

> I was absolutely certain for years afterward that two piles of bloody rabbits' ears I saw on the courthouse lawn at the time of Brother Tolsen's trial had

something to do with the killing he was being tried for. They hadn't. They were merely tokens of the fact that the annual county rabbit hunt had gone off according to schedule.[27]

But of course the bloody ears *do* have something to do with the killing. Sorensen is using a naive narrator to make key thematic points obliquely. The annual, competitive rabbit drives, like the killing of the water thief, reflect the ineradicable violence at the root of society.

The narrator as child does not comprehend all of this, but the narrator as adult, looking back, is able to place the events in a larger context. At the beginning of the story, she refers to a newspaper clipping her mother has sent to her describing another water-thief killing. In this instance, the aggrieved farmer had shot the thief and then turned the gun on himself, and her mother had commented, "Dad and I don't see why he had to shoot himself, too. Do you?" The narrator then reflects:

> That's a very Western query. A poem written by Thomas Hornsby Ferril begins: "Here in America nothing is long ago . . ." and that's very Western, too. People out West remember when important things were settled violently, and they remember the wide, dry wastes before the mountain water was captured and put to use. Even now, the dry spaces . . . are always there, waiting to take over; dryness hugs the green fields, pushing in, only the irrigation ditches keeping it at bay.[28]

But even as a child, the narrator had held herself somewhat apart from the community's way of looking at things. This had gained her, in her family, a reputation of being "morbid." And it enables her to pose the question that brings the story to its conclusion:

> One other memory remains. I recall an evening, months after the trial was over, when my parents and I were driving along the road where his fields lay and saw Brother Tolsen working with the little streams that were running among his young corn. Dad and Mother waved and called to him. He lifted an arm to answer, and I saw that he held a shovel in the other hand. "I wonder if he bought a new shovel," I said suddenly.
>
> For a minute, the air seemed to have gone dead about us, in the peculiar way it sometimes can, which is so puzzling to a child. Then Mother turned to me angrily. "Don't you ever let me hear you say a thing like that again!" she said. "Brother Tolsen is a good, kind man!"[29]

"Where Nothing Is Long Ago" stands on its own as a work of fiction. But it also draws meaning from history. There is scarcely a town in Utah that has not had, somewhere in its past, a violent dispute over water rights. Most cases have been resolved as quietly as possible and consigned to the dark unspoken underside of the community's memory. But occasionally one survives in a literary record—for example, the anonymous folk ballad titled "The Recent Kanab Tragedy," memorializing an event that occurred on July 23, 1899:

In Kanab they will always remember
This Twenty-Fourth of July
For this year there's no celebration,
No band plays and no pennants fly.

The speeches they give in the Church house,
Do not boast of our brave Pioneers;
There's no shouting, no dancing, no picnic,
But there's sorrow and mourning and tears.

For two of the town's best men are lying
In their coffins awaiting the earth;
[*Line illegible where paper was folded*]
There's no room in our hearts now for mirth.

It happened because of hot anger—
A quarrel about their water right,
William Roundy accused Dan Seegmiller
Of stealing his turn in the night.

So Roundy jumped up on his pony,
Rode right down to Seegmiller's door;
He shouted, "Come out and I'll show you,
You'll not steal my turn any more!"

And Dan, little thinking of trouble,
Came out with his babe in his arm;
His wife Emma stood there beside him,
Neither yet felt the faintest alarm.

Then Roundy quick lifted his shotgun—

Aimed it straight at Dan Seegmiller's heart;
Emma screamed and ran forward to stop him,
[*Another illegible line*]

Dan fell to the ground with his boy,
Weeping, poor Emma knelt down,
Not knowing if both husband and baby
Were dead beside her on the ground.

Roundy turned then and rode to his own house,
Where he kissed his wife fondly goodbye,
Then out into the yard he staggered,
By his own cruel hand there to die.

So today there is no celebration,
Kanab has no thought for Pioneers;
Two fine men now lie in their coffins—
No wonder the town's bathed in tears![30]

Other reports of this murder-suicide indicate that the ballad-writer has taken some poetic license. Roundy apparently shot Seegmiller in his farmyard after an exchange of angry words, rather than at his doorstep without warning, as the ballad suggests, and there is no indication that Seegmiller was holding a child when he was shot. On the other hand, the killing was in some respects more vicious than portrayed here. Roundy severely wounded Seegmiller with the first shot, then pumped two additional shots into him as he attempted to escape.[31]

It is interesting that the Kanab murder took place on July 23, the day before Pioneer Day, while what Sorensen calls "the Tolsen trouble"[32] occurs on July 25. Late July is often a critical time for Utah farmers, when the hottest average temperatures of the summer coincide with rapidly diminishing streamflows. But the conjunction of these water crimes with the major Utah commemoration of the coming of the Mormon pioneers has thematic implications exploited by both Sorensen and the anonymous ballad-writer. In "The Recent Kanab Tragedy" the shock of the crime disrupts the normal Pioneer Day celebration, making the day painfully memorable. In Sorensen's story, Brother Tolsen comes running into Bishop Petersen's garden during the bishop's water turn, while he is explaining to the narrator the centrality of the water to his Mormon convictions:

Bishop Petersen said that to leave the lovely land of Denmark one had to be very certain it was to God's Kingdom he was coming. He himself had been sure of it when he heard about the mountain water, so pure, so shining, so cold, so free. Whenever his turn came to speak at Testimony Meeting . . . he spoke about the water. It was to him, next to the Gospel itself, the unmistakable sign of the Kingdom.[33]

Sorensen thus uses the carefully regulated water as a symbol of Mormon solidarity in order to emphasize the marginality of the lapsed-Mormon water thief, thereby making her story an examination of belonging and not belonging. But the main point of "The Recent Kanab Tragedy" is precisely that the killer and his victim were both community insiders, "two of the town's best men." The Seegmillers and Roundys were large and prominent families in southern Utah, and the feud over water rights therefore threatened to divide the community. The ballad, evidently composed shortly after the events it commemorates, can be viewed as an attempt at healing the community wounds.

Violent confrontations such as these are only the tip of the iceberg. More common is a general, often unspoken awareness of who can and who cannot be trusted to take his fair share of the water. My mother, speaking of a prominent rancher in the town where she grew up, once said, "He wasn't the kind of man you'd want to have upstream from you, if you know what I mean." The local lore of many communities includes stories about clever retaliation against a notorious water-hog, for example, the legend from Tooele Valley recreated by John Sterling Harris in "The Whittler." In Harris's poetic version, the trickster Josh runs a hardscrabble farm down the ditch from his pious and prominent neighbor Obediah Pratt:

Now Obie was a water hog
That took his share and a little more.
He always turned the water in early
And kept it a little late.
Of a night you'd lose your stream
And find it running in Obie's place.

At the end of Obie's water turn one Sunday morning, he purposely neglects to release the water down the ditch, expecting in that way to get some additional use before Josh comes up to break his dam. Serene in the confidence that he has his world well under control, Obie puts on

120

his Sunday clothes and goes off to conference in Tooele. But Josh decides upon a little revenge. Instead of taking the water,

> He went to the house and changed his clothes,
> Hitched up the rig and went to conference too,
> Though he hadn't been to church in years.
> He sat in the balcony grinning down
> On Obie, who was sitting on the stand.
> Obie saw him too, and was first surprised,
> Then fidgety, and frantic finally,
> But he couldn't leave the stand—
> Not while Brother Grant was talking,
> And Brother Grant talked a long, long time.[34]

When Obie finally gets home, he finds his garden washed out and his cellar flooded.

In recent years there have been some changes in the story of the water in central and southern Utah. Larger, government-sponsored and bureaucratically managed irrigation projects have appeared alongside and sometimes supplanted the traditional community-controlled systems. On some watersheds, large reservoirs capable of holding more than a single year's runoff have helped even out the wet-dry cycles. But there are still numerous watersheds without significant storage facilities, where the farmers anxiously watch the creeks shrink day by day in early July, wondering whether they will be able to water the hay one more time before the stream fails. "Streams ever copious" expresses a wish rather than a reality.

Technological developments such as concrete-lined canals and pressurized irrigation systems have greatly improved the efficiency of water use, but have exacted some penalties as well. Some hydrological systems—most notably that of the Sevier River Basin—were dependent on the inefficiencies of stream irrigation. Water wasted by upstream users returned to the system for reuse downstream. When upstream users adopt more efficient methods such as sprinkler irrigation, they can irrigate more land with the same amount of water, but there is no return flow to the river, and therefore the downstream users find themselves short-changed.

Other costs are perhaps more aesthetic than economic. Concrete-lined canals do not have ditchbank thickets, and as a result the picturesque hedgerow effect is gradually disappearing from the Utah landscape. With more and more towns installing pressurized systems, the pleasant music of the roadside irrigation ditches is heard less often, and the trees that depended on seepage from the ditches are dying. While Utah remains an oasis landscape where the human story will always be the story of the water, it is hard to compose a hymn of praise to a pipe.

7

A WIFE FROM
SANPETE COUNTY

Highway 89, the main street of Sanpete Valley, climbs a juniper-covered ridge north of Fairview, crosses the divide between the Sevier Basin and the Utah Lake drainage, and drops down into Thistle Valley, passing an old sheep barn and a bleak rural subdivision before entering the subirrigated meadows around Indianola. Driving this route a summer or two back, I came up behind a slowly moving self-propelled haywagon, one of those Rube Goldberg contraptions that pick up the bales, assemble them into a compact unit, and dump them at the stack entirely by mechanical means—a wonder to anyone who ever strained his back and wore his overalls ragged by hefting bales from the field to the wagon and from the wagon to the stack. Half irritated at being held up, half charmed as I always am by big machines, I followed awhile before attempting to pass. Then, just as I was looking to get around the haywagon, it slowed further and turned off the highway into a farm lane. As I went by, accelerating, I caught a momentary glimpse of the operator, a slim female figure in a plaid shirt and blue jeans with her hair tied back in a ponytail.

I don't know why I should have been surprised to see a young woman driving a piece of farm equipment. No doubt an unreflective masculine bias led me to assume a man would be at the controls, though it was certainly not the first time I had seen a woman engaged in farm work. I grew up among women who drove tractors, mended fences, milked cows, rode in cattle-roundups, and groomed calves for livestock shows. Still, this momentary encounter with the girl on the haywagon, coming at the end of a day spent exploring Sanpete backroads, led me to reflect upon my lifelong admiration for country women. I mistrust horses; I have never owned or desired a pair of cowboy boots, or for that matter other "western" apparel (except for an ambition in early childhood, never yet fulfilled, to possess a Pendleton shirt with pearl snaps), and a little country and western music goes a long way with me. Nevertheless, my heroines—to adapt a line from the Willie Nelson song—

Family harvest scene. Courtesy Utah State Historical Society.

have always been cowgirls. I like rodeo queens, though not rodeos, and I cannot resist a small-town parade, with banners strung across Main Street and girls in white Stetsons riding confidently on horseback, or in pastel dresses and nervous smiles clinging unsteadily to homemade floats, or in short skirts and tasseled boots twirling batons at the front of high school bands.

And it is not only the young girls. I admire bleached-blonde waitresses at crossroads cafes, sunburned housewives driving pickup trucks, old women working in their gardens or leaning over fences to talk. There is an energy in country women, a vitality that sustains the small-town social fabric. They are the managers of house and yard, caretakers of children and grandchildren and sometimes of aged parents, on-call extra hands for farm and livestock (when they are not in fact the primary farm workers), and often employed full-time outside the home as well. In addition, they usually take the lead in civic improvements, in neighborly charity, in artistic and cultural activities.

The tradition of these omnicompetent women runs all through rural Utah. It is embodied in the pioneer legends of the Virgin River settlements that provided the material for Maurine Whipple's 1942 novel *The Giant Joshua*—and in the remarkable career of that daughter of the Virgin River country, Juanita Brooks, who kept her manuscripts in the same basket with her ironing and frequently rode the bus all night from research trips to Salt Lake or Los Angeles in order to be home in St. George in time to cook breakfast for her family.[1]

Then there were the five women who constituted the entire town government of Kanab in 1912, before women were allowed to vote in much of the nation. Elected on a joke, they took their offices seriously and put into effect ordinances prohibiting animals from running loose in the streets, outlawing the liquor trade, and banning "the use of flippers and slings within town limits, thus protecting our feathered friends." Mary W. Howard, who served as mayor, declared that "nine-tenths of the people never knew before who the members of the Town Board were, or that there even was a Board, but you can ask any child on the street who the present Board is, and they can tell you every one of our names for we are discussed in every home for good or ill." Lest it be thought that they neglected their domestic responsibilities for their civic duties, Howard pointed out that three of the five women bore children during their two-year term of office. She added,

> We all do our own home work, make our own carpets, rugs, quilts, soap and all other things that pioneer women have to do. I clerk in the store part time, and do my own work, which at this season includes bottling fruit, preserving, pickling, drying corn, etc., etc., between times; and then there are my religious duties which I try not to neglect. I am local superintendent of Religion Class, teacher of the second intermediate department in Sunday school and treasurer of the Relief Society.
>
> I, and my two boys, which is all the family I have, each received a badge of honor for never being late nor absent from Sunday school last year, and have made the same record so far this year, so you will see that I haven't much leisure.[2]

Sanpete County, among the earliest settled of the Utah hinterlands, has a rich store of these legends of good women. For example, there was young Mary Lowry, the belle of Manti, who was alone with her paralyzed grandmother when Chief Walker burst into the house and demanded her hand in marriage. Hoping to gain time, she told him she was already married, and in response to his insistence on knowing who her husband was she named her brother-in-law, Judge Peacock. After this, she had no alternative but to actually marry Peacock in order to preserve the settlement from Walker's wrath.[3] Or there was Sarah Ann Peterson, wife of Ephraim leader Canute Peterson, who had the gargantuan task of preparing a feast for Black Hawk and his warriors when they arrived at her home unannounced. Well satisfied with the dinner, Black Hawk then repaired to a shady place by the creek to talk peace with the town's leading men. Grace Johnson writes, "History had been made. But

125

to Sarah Ann Peterson it was just another day. Wearily that night she washed her dishes, 'set' her bread, scrubbed her floor and dragged her tired feet to bed."[4]

With its severe winters, short growing season, Indian troubles, and a perennial shortage of irrigation water, Sanpete early became a society humorously attached to hard times. During the lean seasons, the diet staples were lumpy dick (made by stirring flour in boiling milk) and bread spread with lard instead of butter. Even in better times, meals usually consisted of "bread and"—bread and gravy, bread and radishes, bread and onions, bread and milk. Then there were carrots, which were called "Sanpete bananas": raw carrots, boiled carrots, stewed carrots, shredded carrot salad, and for dessert carrot cake with carrot icing. Parents throughout the territory were said to counsel their sons, "Every man ought to marry a wife from Sanpete County, because whatever happens she's seen worse."

The first Sanpete settlers were mostly from the eastern United States, but there followed an influx of Mormon converts from Scandinavia. In addition to the usual adjustments to a new language and culture, these immigrants had to deal with a plethora of patronymics-turned-surnames. The most often repeated story, with innumerable variations, of the confusion caused by these names has a Mormon apostle from Salt Lake City conducting a conference in Ephraim (or Spring City, or Moroni, or Mount Pleasant, or Gunnison) and announcing, "The benediction will be offered by Brother Petersen"—whereupon a hundred men rise to their feet. Somewhat taken aback, the visiting dignitary says, "I meant Brother *Peter* Petersen." And fifty of the men sit down.

In the Scandinavian tradition, the Sanpeters dealt with the problem by devising an extensive system of nicknames. There were occupational names: Pete Butcher, Charlie Well-driver, Pete Pigkiller, Joe Dobemaker, Painter Hansen, Creamery Rasmussen, Alice Sheeppelt, Salt Peter (who peddled rock salt, Dixie molasses, and Castle Valley honey). There were names derived from dwelling places or personal appearance: Chris Cellar (who lived in a dugout during his first years in Ephraim), Annie on the Hill, Scotty Water-eye, Big Mart, Dirty Mart, Big Mary Ann, Little Mary Ann, Long Soren, Fat Lars, Chris Tallerass. There were names that imply judgments of character: Soren Chickenheart, Chris Goldigger, Peephole Soren, Karen Scrook (in Danish a *scruk* is a brood hen known for her ill temper),[5] Bulldog Anderson. And there were names whose origins we can only guess at: Gopher Lars, Alphabet Hansen, Absolutely Anderson, Faithful Andrew, Chris Squirt, and Lead Pencil Peterson.[6]

Once established, a nickname could become a firmer identity tag than the official name. A wife would often be known by her own given name attached to her husband's nickname. And a nickname could persist through several generations. For example, Olaf Coffee Pot got his name from his fondness for a beverage much favored among the Danes but prohibited by the Mormon Word of Wisdom. His sons were known throughout their lives as Grant Coffee Pot and Angus Coffee Pot, even though they were not coffee drinkers.[7] A much-repeated story is meant as a commentary on the strength of the nickname as functional identity tag:

> A stranger, stopping at the Wise Bench on Ephraim's Main Street, inquired after a Jacob Jensen. No one could help him, but the stranger persisted. "I have his address. He lives in the South Ward, four blocks east of Main Street. Are you sure you don't know Jacob Jensen?" Jake-butcher, one of the old-timers idling on the Wise Bench suddenly straightened up, scratched his head and said, "Hell, that's me."[8]

The "Matter of Sanpete" is a rich body of dialect stories, many of them centering on "Brother Petersen," the generic Sanpete Dane, square-headed, pious, kindly, viewing the world with eternal wonder, and never quite at home with the English language. For example, Brother Petersen offers a prayer for moisture in a special fast meeting during a drought: "Now, Lord, you know ve are haffing a very dry season. If ve don't get some rains pretty soon, all de crops vill dry up and blow avay. But, Lord, ve vant a nice, yentle rain dat soaks down to de roots, not like dat tunder-bumper you sent last summer—de vun dat filled up de Gobblefield Ditch vit mud. And if you tink about it, Lord, you vill see dat it is a good ting for you as vell as us. If ve don't get no crops, you don't get no tithings."

Brother Petersen has various incarnations, depending upon the story-teller. One of Ephraim-bred Woodruff Thomson's staple characters is Bishop Anderson, who regularly gets to his feet in testimony meeting to offer thanks for his blessings:

> My bruders and sisters, I vant to bear you my testimony of de goodness of de Lord. He has blessed me abungelegan. When I first come to dis country I vas sooo poor. I didn't haf a ting. I vas yust as poor as a churchmouse. Und now I haf tree vives, tree cows, tree sows, and a barrel of molasses. Und de Lord's had his hand in it.[9]

In the tale cycles of the good Ephraim storytellers, certain characters reappear, representing attitudes toward life. For example, there is Peter

Sunby, the pessimist, whose hen laid thirteen eggs, "Und every one of dem eggs, except twelf, didn't hatch."[10] Or the happy trader Jim Daddy Niels, who invested an inheritance in a dairy herd then "traded the cows for goats, the goats for geese, the geese for rabbits, the rabbits for an old Ford truck which was rather cute until he wrecked it." When Prohibition came, Jim opened a speakeasy in the "Rez" section of Ephraim. "Once when the local marshal raided the place, Jim was just in the middle of brewing a big batch of beer with water and malt. 'Come in, Joe'—it was Joe Muns Nielson who was the marshal then—'Come in, Joe, come in, Joe,' said Jim, 'I was just going to give Papa a bath.'"[11]

A good share of the Sanpete stories revolve around the relations between men and women. They may deal with the women's domestic triumphs:

> One time after conference or meeting, Bishop Anderson was over at my grandfather's place for dinner . . . and my grandmother was famous for her mustard. . . . It was just the whole mustard seed ground up, and you mix it with some cream to make a nice cream sauce. And it was, it was really strong. You take a little touch of that and it was about as strong as horse-radish. Well, Bishop Anderson apparently didn't know the virtues of Grandma's mustard and so he had a piece of meat and he took a great big gob of mustard and put on the meat and . . . put it in his mouth and said, "Oh! O Das, O Das, O Lord! Lord, save my nose, my eyes are gone already!"[12]

Or with a husband's relief at being freed from a shrewish wife, as when Yappafoot Franson raised eyebrows in the town by remarrying only three months after Sister Franson's death. "One of his friends said, 'Vell, Yappa, how is it dot you marry so soon?' And he says, 'Vell, I am not one who holds a grudge.'"[13] Or with women's responses to male authority figures, as when Sister Hansen and Sister Petersen sit in the Petersen kitchen sipping coffee while they listen to LDS general conference on the radio. They become a bit uneasy during Church President Heber J. Grant's sermon on the Word of Wisdom, and Sister Petersen says, "Vell, Gretta, maybe ve should stop drinking de coffee."

"Vell, Helga, I don't know, I don't know."

"Maybe ve could try de kind dat has de caffeine taken out."

"I don't know, Helga. I tink President Grant vould still say dat vas a sin, and if I'm going to sin I'd rather sin vit de Hills Brothers."

Other stories treat the theme of women put upon by lazy husbands. For example, there is Sister Paulsen, who speaks appreciatively of her husband's kindness: "Many is de time dat Pol vould vaken me very yently and tell me, 'Dortea, it's time to milk de cows.' And ven I got de chores done he vould meet me at de door yust like a Patriarch and gif me his blessing before I made de breakfast."[14]

Woodruff Thomson reports,

> Grandpa Thomson was surely helpful. He was awfully good to Grandma all the time. He would always catch the sheep and hold them while she sheared them. . . . My father worked at the court house in Manti for a long time. . . . When Father couldn't get home Mother would have to milk the cows. One time Grandpa had come down . . . to the corral, and Mother had a bad back anyway and was carrying two big pails of milk. He said, "Dastine, das too bad you haf to carry all dat milk," as he walked along beside her.[15]

Though Thomson tells such stories with relish, he maintains that Sanpete men actually worked just as hard as the women. When similar stories are recounted by women, they have a slightly sharper edge—for example, Edith Christiansen on the helpfulness of Hans Rasmussen:

> He vould alvays sit right dere on de back porch smoking his pipe and vait for her to come from milking de cows. And right ven she vould get to the step he vould yump up and lift dose heavy buckets of milk right up to de separator so she could separate all dat milk vile he set dere in his lovely big rocking chair and vatch her and tell her she vas a good voman and so good a vorker.
>
> Den dere vas dat time dat she broke her own axe handle vile she vas chopping vood to keep her good husband varm and bake de kind of breat dat he like de best. She hurt her hand real bad too ven she broke de axe. And Bruder Rasmussen, de good man he vas, didn't get vun bit mad at her for breakin' de axe. He yust told her not to cry, dat she could haf a little of de milk money to buy a new axe handle, so she could go right on chopping vood. And he even vent out in de buggy shed and got some axle grease to put on her hand so it vould heal up quick.[16]

The experience of Sanpete women form the core of Virginia Sorensen's three Manti books. For example, there is the plural wife abandoned as a consequence of the "Manifesto" issued in 1890 by LDS Church President Wilford Woodruff, directing Mormons to conform to the anti-polygamy laws. The woman supports herself by running a corner grocery and lives in a single room behind the shop. The neighbor-

hood children call her "the Darling Lady" not out of affection but because she always addresses them as "darlings." The narrator remembers that as a child deeply involved in the network of family she had found the Darling Lady's isolation unsettling:

> When the bell tinkled, she came through a dark-green curtain hanging over a door behind the counter. She came like a small, soft mole appearing gently in the grass. She never appeared suddenly, and was always blinking, as if really emerging from the dark. In what deep strange recesses she led her life, behind that curtain, one could only imagine. But her mysterious existence there troubled us, sometimes, and we asked each other, "Where are her *folks?*"[17]

There is no lack of "folks" in the life of Christine Eriksen, powerful matriarch of a family of "big Eriksen boys and their pretty selected wives," who "all cook exactly alike"—like their mother-in-law.[18] Though her sons are prosperously established on their own farms, Christine maintains control of the clan from the big house where they all gather for Sunday dinners and other ritual occasions:

> She had butchered three pigs herself this autumn and did her own curing, for no "boughten" ham or bacon satisfied her. She kept three cows and sold the milk to Jens, making a strict tabulation of her earnings. She kept her bull, too, saying it was handier for the boys to bring their heifers here than to any other of the family establishments. And it seemed curiously fitting to her that the boys should still come to the source of their own lives for the seeding of their herds.[19]

Then there is Kate Alexander, the wife from Sanpete County as frankly sensuous woman and rebel. Kate learns to her sorrow the price of a woman's rebellion against community mores, reflecting that "if there is rebellion at all, it is better in a man":

> It is necessary that you be a man, she thought, without so many soft places on you. But if nature had got mixed up, somehow, and you were not a man and yet you had the rebellion in you and you lived in a place where women were women and they had a place to stay and must stay there—then something had to happen, and it happened, and when it happened it was all wrong. . . . If you were a woman and a rebel the only thing you could tear to pieces was your own life.[20]

Yet she also has the capacity, finally, to come to terms with her existence. Sitting at the novel's end beside the young granddaughter who

has inherited her lover's flaming red hair, Kate remembers the time in her own childhood when she had won a prize for memorizing the first chapter of Genesis:

> *And behold, it was very good,* she thought again. Perhaps our old allegories were not so bad, after all. Each one making what order he could from his own chaos. It could mean that, couldn't it? There had been a woman and she loved a man and through this love men and loves were multiplied. Perhaps one traveled in a great circle from love to love, first receiving and taking comfort only, as a child does, and finally coming to the love given to another child and no longer received. And behold, and behold, and behold, it was very good. And the evening and the morning were the sixth day, morning after evening so one could never make the mistake of thinking anything ended without being also a new beginning.[21]

Early settled, Sanpete Valley provided from its surplus population the seeds of many later settlements, spreading up the Sevier Valley during the 1860s and crossing the Wasatch Plateau to Castle Valley by the late 1870s. Like the ancient Greek colonies in the western Mediterranean, these new communities for a time retained close ties to the mother town, maintained and renewed by the annual reunions held each summer on top of the plateau. For example, what was originally intended to be a single settlement on Cottonwood Creek split into two when the predominantly Anglo-American settlers from Manti tended to locate on the south side of the creek and the predominantly Scandinavian settlers from Mount Pleasant, Spring City, and Ephraim on the north side. The resulting villages of Orangeville and Castle Dale reenacted the rivalry that has always existed between Manti and the other Sanpete towns.

The women who pioneered the new settlements brought with them the resilience and independence of their Sanpete heritage. Hanna Olsson Seely, the Swedish immigrant whose husband, Orange Seely, was the first Mormon bishop east of the Wasatch Plateau, left behind a new house and prominent social position in Mount Pleasant. For her, the first sight of the treeless plain strewn with prickly pears that was to be her home for the remainder of her life was a traumatic experience. Years later she confessed, "The first time I ever swore was when we came to Emery County and I said, 'Damn a man who would bring a woman to such a God-forsaken country.'"[22] She may have been angry, but she was not demoralized. Starting with a one-room log cabin, she eventually had a spacious central-hall adobe house, with red plush furniture and a store-bought carpet in the front room. Though rather frail in health, she bore and reared nine children, and at age ninety still looked elegant in a black dress with spotless white lace collar and cuffs.[23] When visitors called, she would never show herself until she had put on a clean apron over her dress.

Mary Ann Rowberry grew up in a comfortable upper-middle-class home in Gloucestershire, England, and immigrated with her parents to Fountain Green in 1869. There she married Charles Brown, who had also come from western England. Responding to a settlement call from Mormon church leaders, Charles crossed the Wasatch Plateau in 1879 and took up a homestead on Huntington Creek. Mary Ann's introduction to the new settlement is best given in her own words:

> In July of 1880 my husband came for me and what kind of a home do you suppose I came to? There were four dugouts situated along Huntington Creek and my husband had made arrangements with Noah T. Guymon for the use of one of these. Before we arrived some one had locked three pigs in the dugout that we were to occupy. It was night when we landed. I was weary and conditions which confronted me were too much. I broke down and wept. The ditch broke during that first night of mine in Castle Valley. This necessitated that my husband should take the shovel and go to work on the ditch early the next morning, leaving me alone to clean the dugout. During the day I scraped and scraped soil out of it with a hoe, but there was no way of eradicating the pig pen stench except to let nature take its course. So we were obliged to camp in wagons for several weeks.[24]

During the year that Charles was in Castle Valley alone, developing their homestead, Mary Ann labored as a household helper in Fountain Green, accumulating five dollars in cash, three hundred pounds of flour, and ten bushels of wheat. The cash was used to help Charles obtain his U.S. citizenship papers so he could get title to their homestead. They lived on the flour and planted the wheat as the first crop in their new land. Mary Ann recalled the harvest in these terms:

> The following autumn my husband returned to Fountain Green and cradled wheat to earn our bread stuff, and while he was gone I harvested our crop of grain grown from the ten bushels of wheat. This is how I did it. I turned the water down a row at a time on the patch to loosen the soil then pulled up the grain by the roots and stacked it by hand, for it was too short to cut. I placed my baby on a quilt in the field where I could watch her

while working. Uncle Samuel Jewkes thrashed with the first thrasher in the country. He said my grain stack looked like a mound of mud. When the grain was thrashed there were nine and a half bushels.

The homestead laws required that the family live on their land. Charles excavated a dugout in the side of a hill, and then, because they had lost their oxen, Mary Ann tied a rope around her waist and helped drag cottonwood logs into place to support the roof. They lived in this dugout for nine years, with rattlesnakes at the door and scorpions in the bedding, before moving into a one-room above-ground house. With characteristic understatement (for she was a wife from Sanpete County), Mary Ann described moving day as providing a "sense of exultation" that is "easier left to the imagination than to describe it."

My own grandmother was a wife from Sanpete County. Born in Spring City in 1869, Minnie Acord lost her mother to spotted fever when she was fifteen months old and was placed in the home of a family named Ashworth. Spring City in the 1870s and '80s was a prosperous and fashionable town, home of Orson Hyde, the resident Mormon apostle in Sanpete Valley, but young Minnie grew up in poverty. Her father, a cattleman of some means who had moved his base of operations to a ranch on the Sevier River near Glenwood, contributed virtually nothing to her maintenance, and the widowed Sister Ashworth, a warm but strict Cockney woman, was forced to take in sewing and washing to support the family.

At the age of eighteen, Minnie married Ole Louis Ungerman, a thirty-year-old childless widower, and in the early 1890s they moved across the plateau to Castle Dale, where Louis's father, Henning, had been called as bishop in 1882. Shortly after the turn of the century, Louis and Minnie purchased a few acres of ground and a small frame house on "the Bench" above Castle Dale, where she remained after Louis's death in 1922. She had borne eleven children, ten sons (three of whom died in infancy) and my mother, born when Minnie was forty-five and Louis fifty-seven. Through all the years of her marriage and beyond, there hung on one side of the front-room chimney a large framed photograph of Louis as a young man, and on the other side a matching photograph of his deceased first wife, whom the children knew as Aunt Mariah. My mother once had the temerity to ask if she resented the prospect of sharing her husband with another wife throughout eternity. "Not that lovely woman," Grandma stoutly declared.

It was during our Sunday afternoon visits to Grandma Ungerman's place when I was a young child that I first developed a conscious admi-

Sanpete County Fair, Manti, 1926. G. E. Anderson photo, courtesy Utah State Historical Society.

ration for country women. Not Grandma, whose strength I took for granted, but the handsome Johansen girls, who lived in a big brick house just beyond a fence lined with wild currant bushes. By Johansen was a cattleman with extensive rangeland on the mountain and in the desert. He had no doubt expected to produce a family of boys to assist him, but instead he had six daughters before getting, finally, a son. Long before the son arrived, however, By had discovered that farm-bred women can do anything men can do, and had made ranchers of his daughters.

Grandma Ungerman, who knew perfectly well that women were capable of doing men's work but who held the traditional view that they shouldn't *appear* as if they could, used to click her tongue at the idea of the Johansen girls wearing blue jeans and working in the hayfield or riding in the roundup. But they looked plenty feminine to me as they walked up the road from church in their pastel summer dresses. And when I peeked through the currant bushes and caught sight of them in their blue jeans later in the day, they still looked just fine. The tart, pulpy taste of wild currants still brings back the sensation of peering through the thick bushes, hoping for a glimpse of the Johansen girls.

Several years later when my friends and I used to sweep through the valley on Sunday afternoons in search of social conquests, the big Johansen house took on an even stronger appeal, since the two youngest girls were near our age. Though these and the other farm girls and coal miners' daughters we pursued were of Castle Valley stock, most of them had Sanpete ancestry, and the bloodlines were strong. So intense was their vitality that I occasionally find myself fantasizing that they still exist just as they were then, still riding horseback down farm lanes or making fudge on the coal range on winter evenings or strolling in their Sunday dresses along dusty summer roads lined with Lombardy poplars in some country of the young from which I alone have been exiled.

In another, only slightly less improbable fantasy, I sometimes imagine my sons coming to me for advice on the future direction of their lives. I see myself assuming a patriarchal manner, dignified and wise as I clear my throat and intone, "Every man should marry a wife from Sanpete County . . ."

8

VALLEY AT THE WORLD'S END

When I was a boy, we had a neighbor who had grown up in Boulder, so I absorbed early the stories of the place's extreme remoteness and isolation: the high passes and deep gorges and slickrock reefs that made it inaccessible to motor travel; the winters when its residents were entirely cut off from the outside world for weeks at a stretch; the mail that came by packhorse until the mid-1930s; the pickup truck carried in piece by piece, reassembled, and run on packed-in gasoline. The Boulder of my imagination was built up from overlays of hidden valleys in many of the books I read and the movies I saw, from Zane Grey's *Riders of the Purple Sage* to James Hilton's *Lost Horizon*, and took its place alongside such other romantic and unvisited refuges as Robbers' Roost and the Nine Mile of my grandfather's freight road stories. Someday, I knew, I would be a rancher and live an existence of perfect happiness in such a place, with rich green fields protected by impassable red rock walls.

The secret valley—or its counterpart, the undiscovered island—has had a perennial appeal for the western imagination. Its prototype is doubtless the Garden of Eden, but like all powerful archetypes it is capable of generating different meanings in different cultural settings, from Sherwood Forest in the Robin Hood legends to the ideal Christian humanist society of More's *Utopia*; from the Arcadian simplicity of Shakespeare's Forest of Arden to the luxurious but ultimately limiting and unsatisfying life of Samuel Johnson's Happy Valley or Voltaire's Eldorado. The Romantics seized upon the secret valley as an image of primitive innocence—Thoreau's Walden Pond or Yeats's Lake Isle of Innisfree—or of perfect fulfillment as in Coleridge's Xanadu or Alain-Fournier's Lost Domain. The popular Western novel, with its Romantic roots, is well stocked with secret valleys ranging from outlaw hideouts to rock-rimmed, spring-fed oases where some noble stallion rules his wild herd.

John Fowles calls this recurrent motif the "Sacred Combe," "a place

Rip-gut fence, Boulder Valley. Photo by the author.

outside the normal world, intensely private and enclosed, intensely green and fertile, numinous, haunted and haunting, dominated by a sense of magic that is also a sense of a mysterious yet profound parity in all existence."[1] With so many imaginative overlays, it is hardly surprising that these places at the world's end, if they exist at all, often prove somewhat disappointing when you actually arrive and must reconcile your expectations with the actuality. Perhaps for this reason, I was in no hurry to visit Boulder. I had poked into any number of out-of-the-way Utah valleys before I ventured over what was then the only paved road, Highway 12 from Escalante.

This, however, proved to be one of the rare expectations not disappointed in fulfillment. When I crested the last sandstone ridge and caught my first sight of the intensely green pastures and hayfields nestled among honey-colored slickrock hills, the primitive "rip-gut" fences running up and down the slopes, the copious streams flowing through the meadows, I was struck by an almost overpowering feeling that I would remain here forever. I would write to my wife and children, inviting them to join me if they chose, but I would never leave this valley at the world's end.

I did leave it, of course, after only a few hours' stay, but with a sensation of exile, and I can still frighten my wife by suggesting that we retire

Lower Calf Creek Falls, Escalante Canyon. Photo by the author.

there someday. I have since learned that others have been struck in a comparably dramatic way by one element or another in this landscape of extreme contrasts that nevertheless somehow achieve a perfect harmony. For some it may come at the end of a difficult hike to one of the arches carved from the Navajo sandstone in the Escalante Canyons, or perhaps in the intense sweetness of an *au naturel* plunge into the basin at the bottom of Calf Creek Falls, compelling a return to the site again and again. Others have found a way to take up residence in a place with practically no economic opportunities in the usual sense—painters who require the ambience of the Plateau Region's light and color, or others for whom the southern Utah essentials of orchard, pasture, and slickrock provide a sufficient compensation for most of what the outside world values. One artist I know divides his year between Salt Lake City and the ranching hamlet of Grover, under the eastern slopes of the Aquarius Plateau. Another actually commutes each week from a farm in Boulder—complete with hand-crafted timber barn and a pasture full of shaggy Highland cattle—to a professorship on the Wasatch Front.

Boulder Valley is situated in a cove of the Aquarius Plateau, which forms a lofty barrier to the north and west. To the east, the valley is walled in by the reefs and bluffs of the Circle Cliffs, while to the south are the deep gorges of the Escalante Canyons. The Aquarius is a massive table extending almost forty miles from east to west and about thirty miles from north to south in the central mass, with a narrow peninsula called Table Cliff reaching ten miles farther south to the saddle that separates the Aquarius from the Kaiparowits Plateau.

The Aquarius is deceptive. It is difficult to find a viewpoint that captures its full magnitude. From the crest of the Waterpocket Fold, virtually the entire eastern escarpment is visible, but it is a distant view. On the west side, the 7,000-foot valley of the East Fork of the Sevier is shut in by the plateau's shoulder. Only at the south end, near Bryce Canyon, does the valley open out to provide an impressive vista of Table Cliff, rightly characterized by Clarence Dutton as resembling "a vast Acropolis crowned with a Parthenon."[2] While the north front of the Aquarius appears massive enough from Rabbit Valley, its gradual rise is less dramatic than the mesalike abruptness of its neighbor, Thousand Lake. The Aquarius is connected to the Awapa Plateau, a broad, rather featureless table that curves around the western and southern sides of Rabbit Valley from Fish Lake Plateau to the Aquarius. Because the eye travels from the 7,000-foot valley floor to the 8,000-foot Awapa, the 11,000-foot elevation of the Aquarius is visually diminished.

The upper platform of the Aquarius, called Boulder Top, is accessible from Rabbit Valley by way of graveled roads that lead from Loa and Bicknell and join on the Awapa. The fifteen-mile route winds up the gradual western slopes, passing from the sagebrush flats and pinyon-juniper woodlands of the Awapa through the ponderosa-pine belt (narrower here than it is on the Aquarius's eastern and southern slopes) and into the quaking aspens and spruce-fir forests and the characteristic mountain meadows of the High Plateaus. Only the last portion of the climb, where the road is cut into a 500-foot lava cliff, gives a sense of the Aquarius's true loftiness as you realize that you are looking *across* the summit of the Sevier Plateau to the peaks of the Tushar beyond.

Boulder Top is an area of some fifty square miles with an average elevation of 11,000 feet, the largest continuous high-elevation platform in the High Plateaus region. Yet the dominant sensation on its rolling expanse is not of great altitude but of being on a far northern plain. During the most recent ice age, Boulder Top was covered by a massive ice cap, and dozens of small lakes occupy the remaining depressions among clumps of stunted alpine fir on a boulder-strewn tundra-like landscape. There are no peaks. The highest point, 11,322-foot Bluebell Knoll, is merely a low hill beside the road.

The earliest description of the Aquarius Plateau to enter the literary record occurs in a report prepared by Franklin B. Woolley, a member of the St. George militia assigned to explore the region east of the High Plateaus in 1866. The expedition's route led from Kanab through Johnson Canyon and across Skutumpah Valley to the upper Paria Basin, then over the saddle between Table Cliff and the Kaiparowits Plateau to the Escalante River drainage. The party did not reach Boulder Valley but traveled up Pine Creek and ascended Boulder Top from the west side.[3]

Five years later, Jacob Hamblin, the Mormon scout, traveled much the same route into the Escalante Basin on a contract to deliver supplies to John Wesley Powell's second Colorado River expedition at the mouth of the Dirty Devil. Hamblin mistook the Escalante for the Dirty Devil and tried to follow it to its confluence with the Colorado, but found the canyon impassable.

The next summer, Powell sent his brother-in-law and cartographer, Almon H. Thompson, to recover the boat they had stashed at the Dirty Devil in 1871. Thompson climbed the slopes of the Aquarius Plateau and discovered that the Escalante and Dirty Devil were separate rivers, with the Henry Mountains and forty miles of desert between them. Strangely, both of Powell's river expeditions had failed to discover the mouth of the Escalante. Thompson continued north across the Aquarius, then followed the Fremont/Dirty Devil east and south to its confluence with the Colorado. Because of its numerous lakes, he named the Aquarius for the "waterbearer" of the Zodiac. He recorded his impressions of the region in his diary entry for June 10: "The landscape from the divide we came over is beautiful. The mountain slopes a little west of south . . . up to the sand rock, a distance of 20 miles, and is 20 miles wide. Slope quite easy. Creeks every mile or two. Often groves of aspen and pine and clear meadows. Is a perfect paradise for the ranchers."[4]

For Clarence Dutton, coming to the region five or six years later, the Aquarius represented the culminating experience of the High Plateaus, and his remains the classic description:

> The Aquarius should be described in blank verse and illustrated upon canvas. The explorer who sits upon the brink of its parapet looking off into the southern and eastern haze, who skirts its lava-cap or clambers up and down its vast ravines, who builds his camp-fire by the borders of its snow-fed lakes or stretches himself beneath its giant pines and spruces, forgets that he is a geologist and feels himself a poet.

Dutton would have caught his first view of the Aquarius from the peaks of the Fish Lake Plateau, where he began his explorations in the summer of 1875. It is likely that he also visited the Sevier, Paunsagunt, and Tushar plateaus before making his way to the Aquarius. Perhaps this had created a sense of anticipation:

> From numberless lofty standpoints we have seen it afar off, its long, straight crest-line stretched across the sky like the threshold of another world. We have drawn nearer and nearer to it, and seen its mellow blue change day by day to dark somber gray, and its dull, expressionless ramparts grow upwards into walls of majestic proportions and sublime import. The formless undulations of its slopes have changed to gigantic spurs sweeping slowly down into the painted desert and parted by impenetrable ravines. The mottling of light and shadow upon its middle zones is resolved into groves of *Pinus ponderosa*, and the dark hues at the summit into myriads of spikes, which we know are the storm-loving spruces.

When he at last crossed this "threshold of another world," Dutton found his expectations fully satisfied, with "forests of rare beauty and luxuriance" and flowers strewn across the meadows "like the hues of a Persian carpet."[5]

This "perfect paradise" for ranchers was not long in being discovered. Settlers came to Rabbit Valley and Escalante in the mid-1870s, and by the end of the decade several stockmen had moved their herds

Orchard, pasture, slickrock, Boulder Valley. Photo by the author.

east from the Sanpete and Sevier valleys and established bases near the Aquarius. They knew nothing of the exotic name A. H. Thompson had given the plateau. They called it Boulder Mountain because of the lava boulders strewn across its slopes, and Boulder Mountain it remains in popular usage.

It still took some time to reach the secret valley nestled in the southeastern cove of the plateau. Ranchers no doubt recognized the value of the natural grazing drift between the Aquarius's high meadows and the winter range in the Circle Cliffs area, but the difficulty of access must have given them second thoughts. Richfield cattlemen Nick Johnson and August Anderson brought five hundred head of stock into the upper reaches of Boulder Creek Canyon in 1879. Within a year or two, according to a local history, "herds of cattle, sheep and horses began trailing in by the thousands, as it was wonderful grazing land all over the country. Stock was turned loose to fatten and increase, calves were left for their mothers to wean, no losses except for an occasional thievery."[6]

Still, there were no permanent habitations. In 1887, Nick Johnson "squatted on 160 acres on the west side of the Boulder Valley"—squatted because there would be no survey permitting official homestead entry for several years. The next year, Johnson traded his claim to John King for a harness. "Two months later, John King sold the place to

Henry Haws for ten yearling steers valued at $6.00 each."[7] George and Henry Baker, Willard Brinkerhoff, and Amasa M. Lyman also took up land in the valley in 1888, followed by other hardy souls over the next few years. A school was established in 1896 and a sawmill in 1900. Regular mail service did not begin until 1906, with a twice-weekly pack-horse from Escalante that continued until 1933.[8]

Good soil is a somewhat scarce resource in the slickrock region east of the High Plateaus. And where there is soil, there is seldom water. Though Boulder Valley is interrupted at many points by knobs and domes and cross-hatched ridges of thick-bedded sandstone, there are several thousand acres of irrigable land in the valley that slopes from the base of the Aquarius Plateau to the Escalante Canyons. While the elevation at the townsite is more than 6,600 feet, a southern exposure and the protection against north winds provided by the plateau give the valley a milder climate than would otherwise be expected.

Boulder Creek is the finest stream generated on the Aquarius, draining a sizeable basin south of Boulder Top. It gathers waters from numerous lakes in the spruce-fir forest and flows through a wide, meadow-bottomed canyon amid groves of ponderosa pine to emerge near Boulder village. The village comprises a dozen or so houses dispersed across a two-by-four-block grid that also contains an old schoolhouse that is now a community center, an LDS chapel, a couple of stores, a drive-in restaurant, and two motels. On a hillside at the north edge of the village are the remains of an Anasazi settlement, now incorporated into a state park.

Boulder was never a typical compact Mormon farm village with homes clustered on the townsite and residents commuting to their fields. Rather it was a ranching community, "one mile wide and ten miles long" in the irrigated valley,[9] and claimed as its range "about 600 square miles of the roughest country in the State. The standard terms for measurement seem inappropriate in this case as most of the landscape seems to stand on end and defy surveyors instruments."[10]

Four roads now connect the once roadless valley with the outside world—four amazing roads. The Civilian Conservation Corps first eased Boulder's isolation by building the "Upper Road" to Escalante. This circuitous route goes west and north from Boulder Valley, winding up through the forested canyons of the Aquarius to the notorious Hell's Backbone, a narrow ridge dividing the chasms of Sand Creek and Death Hollow. Across a deep crevasse in this ridge, the CCC built a timber bridge that seems to hang in space. From Hell's Backbone, the road winds around the side of 10,115-foot Roger Peak, skirts Wide Hollow, and then turns south to follow Pine Creek Canyon down to Escalante.

143

Hell's Back Bone bridge, Aquarius Plateau. Photo by the author.

The route requires forty-five miles to cover an airline distance of less than fifteen.

After completing the Upper Road, the CCC, in response to demands for an all-season route, began construction of "Lower Road," a more formidable engineering project that formed the basis of the present Utah Highway 12 from Escalante to Boulder. This route swings southeast from Escalante to skirt a massive monoclinal fold of white sandstone, then turns north, crests a ridge, and drops by a looping dugway down the slickrock slope into the Escalante River Canyon. The single-lane concrete bridge over the Escalante was built low to permit flood waters to run over its top, a clever design for flash-flood-prone desert country that has endured now for more than fifty years. A short distance from the river crossing, an improved campground lines the banks of sparkling Calf Creek. From the campground it is a three-mile hike to Lower Calf Creek Falls, a 126-foot waterfall with a wide pool at its base, icy cold on even the hottest summer days.

The road leaves Calf Creek Canyon by way of a two-mile dugway blasted into the solid rock of the eastern wall. The route then runs along the top of the Hogback, a ridge dividing Calf Creek Canyon from Dry Hollow. In places this ridge is barely wider than the road, affording simultaneous views, for those who have the nerve to enjoy them, into the precipitous thousand-foot-deep gorges on both sides. The Hogback gradually widens into Home Bench, from which the road crosses yet another sandstone ridge and offers a sudden vista of Boulder Valley, its green floor strikingly vivid against rock walls that look like huge twists of honey candy.

This is the most dramatic approach to Boulder and served as the main link to the outside world from its opening in 1940, though it was not fully paved until 1971. It reduced the distance to Escalante to only thirty miles and was passable—though sometimes barely so—throughout the year, while the Hell's Backbone route was closed by winter snows.

The Civilian Conservation Corps also built a road across the eastern shoulder of the Aquarius to the ranching hamlet of Grover in the Fremont River Valley. Now incorporated into Highway 12 and paved in the late 1980s, this route intersects Highway 24 near Torrey and provides a direct link between Bryce Canyon and Capitol Reef national parks. More important, however, Highway12 is arguably the most scenic road in America. Leaving U.S. 89 south of Panguitch, it climbs through Red Canyon to the wide mountain-meadow valley between the Sevier and Paunsagunt plateaus, where the access road to Bryce Canyon National Park branches off to the south. The highway actually traverses a corner of the park and the characteristic Pink Cliffs formation as it drops down Tropic Canyon and into the Paria Basin. After passing through the farm villages of Tropic, Cannonville, and Henrieville, the highway ascends "The Blues" to the saddle between Table Cliff and Kaiparowits Peak and enters Upper Valley in the Escalante drainage.

The early explorers of the region, including the St. George militia in 1866, Jacob Hamblin in 1871, and A. H. Thompson in 1872, all crossed this pass. The modern traveler will be struck, as Franklin B. Woolley was in 1866, by the contrast between the "sharp, steep" clay ridges of The Blues and the secluded charm of the Upper Valley. Woolley wrote,

> Arrived at the Summit of the divide the Scenery at once changes as if by magic, to a beautiful park green grassy meadows, groves of timber on Sloping hill sides, streams of clear cold mountain water shedding into a Small open Valley forming the Centre of the picture, very refreshing after the barrenness of the Pah Rear side.[11]

From the Upper Valley, the highway descends through an overgrazed and badly eroded landscape to Wide Hollow and the town of Escalante. Then comes the remarkable thirty-mile stretch from Escalante to Boulder. From Boulder the road ascends Boulder Creek Canyon for about five miles, then swings east, passing through groves of aspen and fir and crossing Deer Creek and Steep Creek canyons to a 9,500-foot summit, with several spectacular viewpoints along the way. The highway then descends gradually through a ponderosa pine forest and pinyon-juniper woodlands to the ranches of Grover, less secluded than Boulder but similar in the pleasing contrast between the irrigated crop and pastureland and the sandstone knobs, domes, and reefs. Several small creeks run down the eastern slopes of the Aquarius and through canyons carved in the Waterpocket Fold to water desert ranches to the east.

At Point Lookout, near the summit of Highway 12, the modern traveler is almost directly below the point on Boulder Top from which Franklin B. Woolley surveyed the landscape to the east and south:

> At noon on Sunday . . . we came suddenly out on to a high bold promontory of the S. Eastern face of the mountain overlooking the country to N.E., E. and S.E. and South, In some directions probably for a distance between one hundred and two hundred miles. Immediately under us and down the black volcanic precipice forming the South Eastern face of the

Mountain, and more than a thousand feet below are three Small lakes surrounded by groves of timber beautifully Situated on A Small plateau of 1 or 2 miles extent on the mountain side that seems to have sunk down from the upper level of the mountain.

The highway in fact crosses this depressed plateau. Even from this lower viewpoint, it is still possible to appreciate the immense scope of the panorama Woolley described:

> Below these lakes again, down another precipice to the S.E. is the Colorado Plateau Stretching as far as the Eye can see a naked barren plain of red and white Sandstone crossed in all directions by innumerable gorges similar to those mentioned before. Occasional high buttes rising above the ground level, the country gradually rising up to the ridges marking the "breakers" or rocky bluffs of the larger streams. The Sun shining down on this vast red plain almost dazzled our eyes by the reflection as it was thrown back from the firey surface.[12]

Clarence Dutton experienced similar sensations as he viewed the Circle Cliffs and Escalante Canyons from a similar, or perhaps the same point on "the southeastern salient" of Boulder Top:

> It is a sublime panorama. The heart of the inner Plateau Country is spread out before us in a bird's-eye view. It is a maze of cliffs and terraces lined off with stratification, of crumbling buttes, red and white domes, rock platforms gashed with profound canyons, burning plains barren even of sage— all glowing with bright color and flooded with blazing sunlight. Everything visible tells of ruin and decay. It is the extreme of desolation, the blankest solitude, a superlative desert.[13]

This sense of awe mingled with a shudder of revulsion is characteristic of Dutton's descriptions of the desert regions east of the High Plateaus. He obviously relished his experiences among the well-watered meadows and lush groves of the plateau highlands, but while he could admire the sweeping desert panoramas he evidently had little desire to venture into this forbidding landscape. In his introductory overview, he contrasts the "moist climate with an exuberant vegetation and many sparkling streams" of the High Plateaus with the "grotesque forms," the "endless repetitions of meaningless shapes," the "belts of fierce staring red, yellow, and toned white" of the desert, where "a few miserable streams meander in profound abysses" and "the surface springs will not average one

147

in a thousand square miles."[14] In the view of the San Rafael Swell from the eastern rim of the Wasatch Plateau he found "a peculiar kind of impressiveness and even of sublimity" but in the final analysis perceived it as "a picture of desolation and decay; of a land dead and rotten, with dissolution apparent all over its face."[15]

From the Aquarius, Dutton writes, "the radius of vision reaches out perhaps a hundred miles, where everything gradually fades into dreamland, where the air boils like a pot, and objects are just what our fancy chooses to make them." With a geologist's eye, he traces the "colossal crags and domes," the "row of cusps like a battery of shark's teeth on a large scale" of the Waterpocket Fold for ninety miles, from its emergence from the eastern slopes of Thousand Lake Plateau to where it "is lost to view beyond the Colorado."

> Directly east of us, beyond the domes of the flexure, rise the Henry Mountains. They are barely 35 miles distant, and they seem to be near neighbors. Under a clear sky every detail is distinct and no finer view of them is possible. It seems as if a few hours of lively traveling would bring us there, but it is a two days' journey with the best of animals. They are by far the most striking features of the panorama, on account of the strong contrast they present to the scenery around them. Among innumerable flat crest-lines, terminating in walls, they rise up grandly into peaks of Alpine form and grace like a modern cathedral among catacombs—the gothic order of architecture contrasting with the elephantine.

The view of the Escalante Canyons to the south Dutton describes as "dismal and suggestive of the terrible. . . . The rocks are swept bare of soil and show the naked edges of the strata. Nature has here made a geological map of the country and colored it so that we may read and copy it miles away."[16]

Evidently Dutton was content to read this great geological map from a distance and felt no desire to make a closer examination. The traveler who wishes to venture into this "superlative desert" can now easily do so by way of the fourth road from Boulder, the Burr Trail. This route, the center of much controversy in recent years between Garfield County officials who wish to pave it and wilderness advocates who want to discourage motorized travel in the region, runs for sixty-six miles from Boulder to Bullfrog Marina on Lake Powell. It goes down a valley trending southeast from Boulder, crosses a low divide to Deer Creek, then climbs a bench and descends into The Gulch. It follows narrow, red-walled Long Canyon for five miles through the Circle Cliffs and emerges into what Dutton, viewing it from the Aquarius, called "a spot which is about as desolate as any to be found on earth."[17]

This is the elliptical plain about ten miles wide and twenty miles long enclosed by the Circle Cliffs. On the site it is less forbidding than Dutton thought. The deep, sandy soil supports a fair growth of bunch-grass, and there are pinyons and junipers on the higher benches. The plain's eastern boundary is the massive reef of the Waterpocket Fold, which the Burr Trail crosses by way of a series of switchbacks that drop seven hundred feet down a narrow crevice. Near the summit of the reef, a foot trail leads from the road into Muley Twist Canyon, once the chief pack-train route between Escalante and the Colorado crossing at Hall's Creek.

At the eastern base of the Waterpocket Fold, the road divides, with one branch running southeast to a junction with State Highway 276 near Bullfrog. The other, less-traveled branch follows the Waterpocket Fold north to an eventual junction with State Highway 24 just east of Capitol Reef. There is access from this road to the southern and western slopes of Mount Pennel and Mount Ellen, the dominant peaks of the Henry Mountains. The road also provides access to remote ranches on Oak Creek and Pleasant Creek. These, too, are secret valleys, with green fields nestled against the steep slopes of the Waterpocket Fold and points that afford a view beyond the reef to the blue heights of the Aquarius. If Boulder, with its four roads, should ever become too crowded, the isolation-seeking imagination can always fall back upon these magic places even farther towards the world's end.

9

THE BACKHOUSES
OF ESCALANTE

"A little farm well cultivated near homes, I know,
is your doctrine, and it is mine and ever was."
—Pioneer Bishop Henry Lunt of
Cedar City to Mormon Apostle George A. Smith[1]

I n early November 1934, a young man of twenty rode into the town
of Escalante on a Navajo burro. His legs reached almost to the
ground on either side of his unlikely mount, and he led a second
burro laden with camping gear and artist's supplies. Strangers were not a
common sight in the town, which at that period still lay at the end of a
long and difficult road, but Everett Ruess attracted more attention than
most because of his novel mode of transportation, his immediately en-
gaging personality, and his distinctive trade. Peddlers found their way
over Table Cliff from time to time, but probably no one had ever come
to Escalante before with a stock of watercolors and block prints.

Ruess would have experienced the characteristic sights and sounds
and smells of late autumn in a Mormon farm village of substantial brick
houses on the corners of the blocks and roadside irrigation ditches
choked with fallen leaves. The unsurfaced streets, a quagmire in wet
weather, would have been deep in dust in the drought season of 1934.
The weathered gray barns in the interior of the blocks were crammed
with hay hauled in from the fields that spread across the river valley
north of town and extended south along the base of Fifty Mile Mountain. Horses leaned across pasture fences and snorted and whinnied at
the odd little procession, while from somewhere came the cackling of
chickens, the squeal of a hog on butchering day. The musky perfume of
burning leaves hung heavy in the dusty air, mingled with the scent of
ripe apples and the acrid odor of branding season.

Riding down from Upper Valley, Ruess would have entered the town
from the west and come past the Star Amusement Hall and the little
cluster of business houses at the intersection of Main and Center streets.
He would have seen the white sandstone LDS meetinghouse down the

street to his right, and the red brick school in the middle of a block to his left. He made his camp under the riverbank cottonwoods north of town and remained for a week or so, poking tentatively into the slickrock canyons and climbing the Straight Cliffs. On Sunday morning, November 11, after writing letters to his family announcing vague intentions of crossing the Colorado to Navajo country or possibly circling back to the north through Boulder, he broke camp and rode down the plain at the base of Fifty Mile Mountain. A week later, he spent a couple of nights with two sheepherders near the head of Soda Gulch then went on in the direction of Hole-in-the-Rock. He was never seen again.

Everett Ruess grew up in a middle-class Los Angeles family. His father was a philosophically minded public servant, and his mother had artistic interests. Everett's elder brother Waldo had what might be thought of as a typical upbringing for his time and place and went on to a successful career in the diplomatic service and in international business, but Everett from an early age strained against conventional expectations. A kind of latter-day Thoreau, but not content to "travel much in Concord," Ruess was driven throughout his short life by wanderlust and cycles of emotional highs and lows. In the summer of 1930, at the age of sixteen, he hitchhiked to Carmel, where he explored the Big Sur country and cultivated the acquaintance of local artists. Then he crossed over to the Sierras and camped for several weeks around Yosemite. He spent the next winter and spring in Monument Valley, then drifted south and west to the San Francisco Mountains near Flagstaff, north across the Grand Canyon and the Kaibab Plateau, west to Zion Canyon, back to the Grand Canyon, then south to the Tonto region. After a few months at home, he returned to Arizona in March 1932 and worked his way north to the Navajo Reservation, then to Mesa Verde in Colorado, then west to the Grand Canyon. He hitchhiked to Los Angeles in September and enrolled at UCLA but dropped out after a semester. He spent the summer of 1933 in the Sierras and the fall and winter in San Francisco, making several acquaintances in the artist community there, including Maynard Dixon, Dixon's wife Dorothea Lange, and Ansel Adams. In the spring of 1934, Ruess returned to Monument Valley, purchased two burros, and made his way slowly west, visiting Navajo Mountain and Rainbow Bridge, joining an archaeological expedition for a time on a dig in Tsegi Canyon, going to the Hopi villages for the August rain dances, then catching a ride with a Hopi silversmith to the intertribal ceremonies at Gallup, New Mexico. Returning to the Hopi country, he drifted to Flagstaff and Oak Creek Canyon then crossed the Grand Canyon again and reached Bryce Canyon in mid-October.[2]

151

Farm village street scene, Escalante. Photo by the author.

Ruess's letters indicate that he stayed for several days in the village of Tropic, under the Pink Cliffs of Bryce, with the family of park ranger Maurice Cope. Though he spent much of his time wandering alone in the wilderness, Ruess was by no means antisocial. He cultivated acquaintances wherever he went and did not hesitate to accept hospitality when it was offered—and sometimes even when it was not. He described his time with the Copes as "great fun" as he rode out with one of the boys looking for lost cows, feasted on apples and engaged in apple fights in the Tropic orchards, went to the Saturday night dance, and attended church services at the local Mormon ward, where the national economic crisis formed the chief topic of discussion.[3] In a letter sent to his brother from Escalante, he hints at a romantic interest in Tropic, writing, "If I had stayed any longer I would have fallen in love with a Mormon girl."[4]

He enjoyed similarly pleasant experiences in Escalante. To his parents he wrote, "I have had plenty of fun with the boys of this town, riding horses, hunting for arrowheads, and the like." He attended a showing of *Death Takes a Holiday* at the Star and sat up late with newfound friends around a campfire feasting on roasted venison and potatoes and munching pine nuts, which were abundant that year.[5] It was as if, on the verge of an absolute isolation, Ruess were taking one last, deep draught of human society.

Ruess's family, accustomed to his wanderings, did not become alarmed for some time, but on February 7 they wrote to the Escalante postmistress, Mildred Allen, to inquire whether there had been any news of their son. A search party organized by Mrs. Allen's husband, Garfield County Commissioner H. Jennings Allen, found Ruess's burros grazing in Davis Gulch, one of the lower tributaries of the Escalante River, together with signs that Ruess had camped there for some time. However, there was no other evidence of either Ruess himself or of his heavy pack outfit except for prints of his size nine boots and the letters NEMO and the date 1934 carved on a pictograph panel, and again near the doorway of an Anasazi ruin. In the months that followed, searchers combed the plateaus and canyons on both sides of the Colorado without success. Despite the discovery over the years of various scattered items that might or might not have been part of Ruess's camp gear, and sporadic unconfirmed rumors of a young white man living with a Navajo bride in some remote corner of the reservation, no definite trace of Everett Ruess has ever been found.

The mystery of his disappearance added to the romantic appeal of his youth, and his passion for natural beauty soon turned Ruess into a legendary figure. A collection of his letters and poems titled *On Desert Trails with Everett Ruess* was published by *Desert Magazine* in 1940. In his 1942 book *Mormon Country*, Wallace Stegner, while noting that Ruess was "not a good writer" and "only a mediocre painter," found "something almost magnificent in his single-minded dedication" to beauty. Stegner declared, "Everett Ruess is immortal, as all romantic and adventurous dreams are immortal. He is, and will be for a long time, Artist in Residence in the San Juan country."[6] The legend was renewed for a later generation by W. L. Rusho's *Everett Ruess: A Vagabond for Beauty* (1983), published with the cooperation of Waldo Ruess and with the impeccable conservationist credentials of Gibbs Smith as publisher, an introduction by John Nichols, and as afterword "A Sonnet for Everett Ruess" by Edward Abbey. (Ruess himself, incidentally, despite his love for the wilderness, was not so impeccable, leaving tin cans scattered around his campsites, scratching his own messages on pictograph panels, and sometimes appropriating artifacts from Anasazi ruins.)

The California Ruess family had links to New England transcendentalism. Mrs. Ruess's brother was Emerson Knight, a well-known San Francisco landscape architect, and it seems likely that Waldo's name was also a tribute to Emerson. Mr. Ruess was a graduate of Harvard Divinity School and had served for a time, like Emerson, as a Unitarian minister. Everett Ruess combined an Emersonian idealism with

Thoreau's passion for direct experience in nature, and his poems show a strong influence of Whitman. When his Mormon friends in Tropic and Escalante inquired into his religious views, he described himself as "a pantheistic hedonist,"[7] which seems to come pretty close to the mark. Certainly he was a thoroughgoing romantic.

Aldous Huxley argues in his essay "Wordsworth in the Tropics" that romanticism could not have developed in a genuine wilderness, where the power of nature is so overwhelming that humans must of necessity erect defenses against it. Only in a thoroughly humanized, "safe" landscape like Western Europe or nineteenth-century New England could nature be understood as beneficent teacher and source of inspiration. Once established, however, romantic attitudes can be transplanted to the wilderness, which is exactly what happens in much American nature writing.

Such transplantation entails risks, both artistic and personal. Indeed, from one point of view the life and probable death of Everett Ruess should serve as a warning to romantics. To attempt an existence in harmony with nature at Walden Pond is one thing, with Concord only a couple of miles away and concerned neighbors who leave bags of groceries at your door to supplement the uncertain produce of the bean patch. But Thoreau in the desert is another matter. Of course, Everett Ruess may have disappeared intentionally in order to cut all ties with his past life and assume a new identity. But all the probabilities suggest that he died in the Escalante canyons. Perhaps he was murdered for his gear or out of suspicion by cattle rustlers or renegade Navajos. Perhaps he fell to his death from one of the innumerable and unsearchable cliffs, or died of exposure or thirst on some rimrock he had clambered up but could not descend. His bleached bones may yet be found by a cattleman or hiker in some trackless spot.

Added to the characteristic romantic underestimation of the real dangers in nature, there is also the death wish that forms the dark underside of romanticism. Ruess alarmed the archaeologists at the Tsegi Canyon dig by his carelessness in clambering up and down cliffs or perching himself on a precarious rim to make a sketch.[8] In a letter to a friend written a month or so before his disappearance, Ruess declared, "In my wanderings this year I have taken more chances and had more wild adventures than ever before."[9] His last letter to his brother contains several passages that take on an ominous tone in retrospect:

As to when I shall visit civilization, it will not be soon, I think. I have not tired of the wilderness; rather I enjoy its beauty and the vagrant life I lead,

154

more keenly all the time. . . . Do you blame me then for staying here, where I feel that I belong and am one with the world around me?

"Often, as I wander," he writes, "there are dream-like tinges when life seems impossibly strange and unreal." And he declares, in explaining why he will not return to "the routine and humdrum" of conventional urban life, "I would prefer anything to an anticlimax."[10] No wonder, then, that John Nichols writes of Ruess, "Eventually, it is probable he lost all understanding of natural scale or human endurance. And along the way that ordinary awareness of danger we human beings carry must also have dissolved from his consciousness."[11]

There are many things to wonder at in the strange career of Everett Ruess, but I keep coming back in my own mind to his last days and nights in Escalante and his associations with the local young people. I wonder what were the topics of conversation around the campfires on the banks of the river, and how Ruess's feelings for the southern Utah landscape compared with those of people who had known the place all their lives. Everett Ruess was born on March 28, 1914. My mother was born exactly one month later, on April 28, and my father on May 30 of the same year, both of them in Mormon villages less remote and isolated than Escalante but otherwise similar, with a horizon defined by the plateau highlands on the west and wide expanses of desert reefs and canyons to the east. The girls Ruess danced with and went to church with in Tropic could have been like my mother. The boys he hunted arrowheads with at Escalante could have been like my father, who spent much of his boyhood exploring the dry hills and hollows.

By the age of twenty, however, my father's dreams were reaching out toward the world beyond the High Plateaus. He wanted to experience firsthand the excitement and tireless energy of great cities, attend the New York theater, see the movie studios of Hollywood. The urban life Everett Ruess had rejected was the life my father at the same age longed to possess, but without rejecting the life he had known amid plateaus and canyons, long views, and unpeopled spaces. What would they have talked about, Everett Ruess and my father, if they had met around a southern Utah campfire on an autumn night?

The main road into Escalante now is Utah Highway 12, which climbs The Blues from the Paria Valley and crosses the wide saddle between Table Cliff and Aquarius Peak into Upper Valley, the approximate route

Aquarius Plateau near Hell's Back Bone. Photo by the author.

followed by the earliest explorers and by Everett Ruess. For most of the community's history, however, the link to the outside world was by way of a steep, unpaved road over the 9,200-foot ridge that joins Table Cliff to the Aquarius Plateau. This route, hacked out by the original settlers in 1875, retained its importance until 1958, when the state highway department, tired of trying to keep the high pass open through the winter, completed the more roundabout but lower-elevation present highway.

Each landmark along the twenty-eight miles of the old mountain road has a place in local lore. From Johns Valley on the East Fork of the Sevier, site of the abandoned dry-farming settlement of Widtsoe, the route leads up Sweetwater Canyon through Lime Kiln Flat, the Pines, and Ford Stuck to the summit, where the Forest Service installed a telephone box in 1912 to enable travelers to call home and report they had made it this far, or to request help if they were in trouble.[12]

From the summit ridge, the earth falls abruptly away to the east, opening up one of the great panoramas in this panoramic region. The long sweep of mountainside is timber-clad except where eroded headlands break through in crenelated pink and white cliffs. At lower elevations, the ponderosa pines give way to pinyon/juniper woodlands, then to the maze of slickrock canyons draining into Lake Powell, where, sixty or seventy miles away, the tour boats from Wahweap plow their heavy wakes up and down as they haul tourists to gawk at Rainbow Bridge. In the middle distance to the left, you can see the Waterpocket Fold running diagonally across the desert like a great barrier reef, and beyond it the five blue humps of the Henry Mountains. To the right, the dome of Navajo Mountain looms on the distant horizon.

The eastern descent is longer than the climb up Sweetwater, since Escalante is almost two thousand feet lower than Widtsoe. From the summit, the road drops down past Heaps Slide and Conference Flat, where a large party was snowed in on their way to Salt Lake City for LDS General Conference in 1893, then on through Horseshoe Bend, the Bench, the Greens, and the campground at Twin Trees, halfway down Main Canyon.

When you reach the town of Escalante, you find the vista sharply reduced. Mormon pioneers did not select settlement locations primarily for the view, and Escalante sits in a trough that trends, like most other landforms in the region, from northwest to southeast. Only toward the southeast, where the gaze is drawn by the pronounced horizontal strata of the Straight Cliffs, do you get the sense of a long view.

Anyone who knows the Mormon farm village will find much that is familiar in Escalante: the geometrical grid of large blocks and wide

House with backhouse, Escalante. Photo by the author.

streets (laid out by the North Star, in the absence of regular surveyors' points); the substantial brick houses set well back from the road on the corners of the blocks, with barns and pastures on the town lots; the Mormon meetinghouse near the village center. One element you will not find, not anymore, is open irrigation ditches running along the roadsides. Like many other Utah towns, Escalante recently installed a pressurized irrigation system, and as a result the road margins that used to be grassy are now bare, and the trees that depended on seepage are dying or dead.

Still, there is considerable arboreal variety, with Carolina poplars, weeping willows, and ash trees shading the dooryards, and apples, pears, apricots in the backyard orchards. However, you do not see what is sometimes thought to be the hallmark of the Mormon village: straight, tall rows of Lombardy poplars. In place of these shallow-rooted and water-loving trees, the dominant species in Escalante is the black locust. These trees, with their ragged outline, deeply sculptured bark, and dark foliage, are everywhere, and you soon discover that the older residents hold them in special esteem. One old cowman I talked with several years ago said, "Maybe they're not the nicest tree, but they can stand the drought. They can stand the wind."

On an unpaved side street in Escalante, you can still hear the sounds Everett Ruess might have heard almost sixty years ago: a young rooster trying to learn how to crow, the bleating of lambs somewhere on the next block, the stamp of hoof and swish of tail as a horse in a nearby corral attempts to shake off the flies. For this is a functioning farm village. Along with a diminishing few other Utah settlements—Scipio, Levan, Paragonah—Escalante still has livestock on the town lots, hay in the barns, wheat and oats and barley in the inside-out granaries. There are even a few complete blocks. A complete block, in a Utah farm village, is one that still has four barns, one on each of the four original lots. Some outbuildings are in a rundown condition, and several of the old brick and adobe houses are empty and boarded up, but as southern Utah towns go Escalante is relatively well kept, with clean and flower-filled dooryards, abundant gardens, and only moderately cluttered barnyards.

If you spend some time in Escalante, admiring the fine old houses, sensing the scale of the community, feeling the rhythms of its life, you will sooner or later be struck by the unusual number of backhouses. I do not mean the kind of outhouse that serves as a substitute for indoor plumbing. A few old "crannies" do in fact survive, but most of them have disappeared—and few will regret their passing. Nor do I mean woodsheds, toolsheds, pigpens, or chicken coops, though these too are present in Escalante. But these outbuildings belong to the barnyard and are usually built of rough lumber. The backhouses I refer to belong to the dooryard and are typically constructed of the same materials as the house. Under the names of wash house or summer kitchen, such structures were common in nineteenth-century towns. They had various uses: as laundry room or canning kitchen; as storage pantry; as guest room, or mud room, or dairy; occasionally as a studio for crafts such as rug weaving; in short, for any activity that needed to be close to but not necessarily in the house.

The backhouses of Escalante are not unique, but I know of no other Utah town where so many of them remain, or where even houses constructed in relatively recent times often have them. Even public buildings have backhouses. The surviving tithing house, now a pioneer museum, was built next to the old LDS meetinghouse (1885-1953), of the same white sandstone in the same vernacular adaptation of classical architectural forms, the one structure essentially a miniature version of the other. And when an LDS seminary building was erected behind the North Ward meetinghouse in 1940, it was constructed of the same red brick in a style to harmonize with the larger building.

Escalanteans tend to take the backhouses for granted, as if it were perfectly natural for a big house to have its accompanying little house. And indeed these structures represent a link to the very roots of the community. Older Utah towns often had their origins in a fort, but in Escalante, settled after the Indian troubles were over, the first dwellings were built on the town lots. These original homes were dugouts, made by excavating a hole perhaps twelve feet square in the desert clay, then building up a roof of poles and brush covered with dirt. A dugout was a dark and airless place, subject to muddy drizzles from the roof during heavy rains, but it provided a refuge from summer heat and winter cold. When a permanent house was completed, the dugout was often converted to a root cellar and an upper room built above it of sawed logs, or native rock, or, later, adobe-lined brick. Thus the backhouses of Escalante reflect the continuity of community life from the founders to the present day.

The 1866 St. George militia party who were the first recorded Anglo-European visitors to the site of Escalante named the region Potato Valley because of an abundant growth of the sweet-rooted plants known as Indian potatoes. Almon H. Thompson named the Escalante River on his 1872 expedition to the mouth of the Dirty Devil. Thompson returned to the region in 1875 with a mapping party and found a group of men digging a canal to bring water to the land north of the creek. He noted in his diary, "met four Mormons from Panguitch who are thinking of establishing a settlement in the valley. Advised them to call the place Escalante."[13]

Although some preliminary work was done in 1875, the actual settlement of Escalante occurred in 1876, the centennial of the Dominguez-Escalante expedition. Therefore it is perhaps fitting that the town should have been named for the explorer who first reported on the terrain of the plateau and canyon country. It seems rather odd, however, that an Anglo-Saxon Mormon village should bear the name of a Spanish Franciscan padre, especially in view of the fact that Escalante never saw the river and basin that bear his name, never came within fifty miles of Potato Valley. Moreover, there is another Escalante Valley in southern Utah, west of Cedar City on the route actually traveled by the Dominguez-Escalante party, and it has been a longstanding source of confusion to have the same name applied to two distinct regions.

When Lowry Nelson first visited Escalante in 1923 during his study of the sociology of the Mormon village, he found that few residents knew the origin of the town's name. Some assumed it was an Indian name.[14] Today almost everyone knows where the name came from, but many townspeople still anglicize the pronunciation by omitting the final vowel, calling their town Escalant. Other residents are embarrassed by this pronunciation, regarding it as a sign of ignorance. But why should the Spanish pronunciation be preferred? Nobody expects the residents of Paris or Montpelier, Idaho, or Provo, Utah, to use the French pronunciation of their towns' names. And, indeed, even those who think they are pronouncing Escalante "correctly" do not say the word as hispanics would. Escalante got its name by an accident of history. The settlement could just as easily have kept the name Potato Valley. Or it might have been named for one of the early settlers—Schowtown or Liston or Shirtsville—or for a Mormon church leader, like neighboring Cannonville, or for an outsider who offered a library, like Bicknell and Blanding. Or it could have been called Moqui, the nickname of the Escalante High School athletic teams, and the term commonly applied throughout southern Utah to Anasazi relics. Escalante, as a name, is not intrinsically better or worse than these others, though after a generation or two any place name comes to seem inevitable. Still, why not prefer the local form, Escalant, which is unique to this place?

The entire question of naming is interesting. Who has the right to name a place? The first discoverers? (But what does "discovery" mean in a land that has been inhabited for centuries by a succession of peoples?) Officials of the state? The permanent inhabitants? In the Escalante region, as elsewhere in southern Utah, many places have two names, the "official" name found on maps and the name used by the local people. So, as we have noted, the Aquarius Plateau is called Boulder Mountain. The Kaiparowits Plateau is better known locally as Fifty Mile Mountain. Table Cliff Plateau is commonly known as Escalante Mountain, and its summit, which C. E. Dutton described as resembling "a stairway for the Titans, leading up to a mighty temple,"[15] is Barney Top.

It might seem that the local names are less "poetic" than those bestowed by John Wesley Powell's well-educated explorers, but in fact they reflect a different kind of poetry, an imagination no less vivid but more down-to-earth, and a capacity for wry understatement that outsiders sometimes fail to appreciate. The author of a 1949 *National Geographic* article on the Paria Valley remarked rather patronizingly that when local ranchers ventured into the wilderness they were "too busy hunting stray cattle to note its beauty."[16] He therefore bestowed the name "Kodachrome Flat" on a colorful area south of Cannonville known to local people as "Thorny Pasture." Through the prestige of the *National Geographic*, Kodachrome Flat has become the official designation and now appears on all the maps. Nevertheless, far from reflecting a genuine sensitivity to the landscape, it is merely a vulgar appropriation of a commercial trademark. Thorny Pasture—a humorous reference to the sharp-angled rock formations—is a far more imaginative name.

161

The original settlers of Escalante were for the most part second-generation Utahns with a good deal of pioneering experience. In her community history, Nethella Griffin Woolsey writes,

> They had battled flood and drouth in the hot, arid lands of the St. George country and in the basin of the Muddy River in Nevada and in the deserts of Arizona. They had been literally starved out of these parts and had moved to Panguitch in hopes of gaining a foothold there. When their crops froze, they decided on the move to Potato Valley, hazardous but promising.[17]

Their first plan was to establish the town on a level site north of the creek, but they decided to build instead on rising ground south of the creek in order to save the better land for farms. The skimpy streamflow of the Escalante River meant that farmland would be sharply limited at best, perhaps three thousand acres, but this deficiency was compensated for by the vast expanse of grazing land. The terrain decreed that Escalante should be a stockraising community, with only enough feed produced on the irrigated land to supply domestic needs.

As was typical of Mormon settlements, the population of Escalante grew rapidly during the first few years, and the townsite was expanded to accommodate approximately two hundred families with the standard arrangement of four houses to a block. Homestead laws required settlers to live on their land for several months each year until they secured legal title. But the preferred model in Escalante, as in other nineteenth-century Mormon communities, was to have a home in the village, and by the time of Lowry Nelson's 1923 study he found no families residing on farms. The general preference for village life, however, did not mean the people lacked experience in the outer country. Herders spent weeks at a stretch in the mountains or the desert, and whole families might pack up and move to "the ranch" for the summer.

While Escalante's remote situation in an undeveloped territory formed part of its appeal to the first settlers, there was evidence from the very beginning of a desire for connections with the outside world and a place on the road to somewhere. A group of Escalante men discovered the notch in the wall of Glen Canyon that came to be known as Hole-in-the-Rock. Escalanteans persuaded leaders of the 1879 San Juan colonizing expedition that it was possible to take teams and wagons directly across the canyon country instead of following the longer route of the Old Spanish Trail. As a result of this advice, Escalante gained its first influx of travelers—and the San Juan pioneers were sub-

jected to their winter-long ordeal, surely one of the longest short-cuts in the history of travel.

The first few years of pioneering in a new land make extraordinary demands on human strength and endurance because so many tasks must be accomplished before the community can become self-sufficient. There are surveys to complete, roads to build, diversion dams and irrigation canals to construct, ground to break, crops to plant, shelters to erect. During the first summer, the Escalante settlers lived in their wagon boxes or in hastily built willow shelters. When cold weather came, they moved into the dugouts, much as the Anasazi who inhabited the region centuries before had done. The second season brought the establishment of sawmills in the mountains, and the Escalanteans moved out of the earth and into one- and two-room cabins made of sawed logs. Many of these structures were still inhabited fifty years later, and a few remain today, though now usually as outbuildings.

Indeed, though characteristically small in dimensions and sparsely appointed, a well-built log cabin is a highly durable and adaptable structure. Woolsey describes "the typical log cabin of the eighteen-seventies and eighties" as being "almost as movable as the modern trailer house":

> If a house was vacated for any reason, and a man needed a home, he traded for the house, got his neighbors to help him put some log skids under it, hitched a four-horse team to the skids and dragged the house to his lot. Or if it was a large log house, he might put lengthy logs between the front and back running-gears of his wagon, jack up the house and slide it onto the log platform and let it ride on wheels. Characteristically, a log house would have a history of two or three moves. For instance a sawed-log house on the Job Hall farm was rebuilt into a barn. Years later someone wanted the barn moved away. So he gave it to Mike Schow for moving the barn and clearing up the mess. The barn became the "big room" of Mike's house until he decided to build a brick house. He traded the house to Johnny Davis for a horse. Johnny moved the house to his homestead in Proctor. After he was through homesteading, Johnny traded the logs to Clark Veater to build a two-room house at his cow-camp at the Soda, now owned by Gail Bailey. The house is still in constant use.[18]

In keeping with the typical development pattern of the Mormon village, the next step beyond the log cabin was the central-hall house built of

163

rock or adobe. By the 1890s, kiln-fired bricks were being manufactured in Escalante—at first in a pale salmon color but later in deep red tones that harmonize beautifully with the surrounding landscape. (The Edward Wilcock house, built in 1893 at the corner of First South and First East streets, has a lower story of the earlier brick and an upper story of the later.) Most of the imposing two-story houses that stand at the corners of the blocks were built between 1890 and 1910. In Escalante, as in many other central and southern Utah communities, these years were a "golden age" of growth and prosperity. During this period, sheep and cattle populations were at their peak on the largely unregulated range, and after the nationwide depression of the early 1890s beef and wool prices were generally good. These were the years when the fall cattle drives stretched for miles down the desert, and when wagon trains laden with wool labored over the mountain each summer on their way to the Marysvale railhead.

It was doubtless during this period also that much of the damage was done to the range. There was an almost universal tendency to overestimate the carrying power of western ranges. Partly this was because the native bunchgrasses appeared to be so tough and durable, and partly because, in the dry climate, past years' growth, instead of decaying, remained available as a kind of naturally cured hay. Therefore, a new range was like an immense and seemingly inexhaustible haystack. But once the old growth was consumed, close grazing of new growth gradually weakened the extensive root systems required for survival in a land with less than ten inches of precipitation per year. Over a period of several years, the bunchgrasses gave way to "cheatgrass" and other less nutritious plants. It is difficult for any people to accept the idea that they have injured the land they love, and many in Escalante still blame the deterioration of the range on a decline in rainfall—even though local precipitation records kept since 1902 do not substantiate such a trend.

The livestock economy of Escalante suffered a double blow in 1918–19 with a severe winter and the collapse of high wartime prices. Woolsey quotes cattleman Alfred Sherman:

"In 1918 the men started on the fall ride to drive the cattle from the summer range on the Fifty-mile Mountain to the winter pasture in the desert. A man came down with the flu so they could not make the drive." (The deadly epidemic of Spanish influenza of that year was raging.) "Then came the hard winter (heavy snow). Next spring when we went to gather the cattle on the mountain, we found nearly all of them dead in piles. Then the bottom

Farm village scene, Escalante, 1936. Dorothea Lange photo, Library of Congress USF34-1351-C.

dropped out of the market and the ones we could deliver we got no pay for."[19]

There was a partial recovery in the 1920s, which was wiped out by the Great Depression and drought of the '30s, then another upturn in the 1940s and '50s. But each recovery crested at a lower level than the preceding one and found the diminished numbers of livestock concentrated in the hands of fewer owners. The sheep industry has virtually disappeared as an economic factor in Escalante, though some sheep are still maintained on the town lots to keep the weeds down. There are still cattle on the range but in much reduced numbers.

Escalante's very remoteness has been an attraction over the years, not only for geologists and wilderness lovers, but also for those interested in the social structure of isolated communities. Dorothea Lange found her way to Escalante in 1936 in the course of her landmark work for the Resettlement Administration—perhaps drawn also by curiosity about Everett Ruess, whom she had known. She photographed business buildings on the unpaved main street, the hydroelectric plant that oper-

165

ated only during the evenings and on washday, farm buildings against a backdrop of slickrock ridges, pioneer residents posed beside the homes they had established in the wilderness, and young children in their Sunday best emerging from the old rock meetinghouse.[20]

Rural sociologist Lowry Nelson chose Escalante for his study of the Mormon village "because it was assumed that by virtue of its extreme geographic isolation and the comparative recency of settlement it would more nearly approximate frontier conditions than any other community in Utah." In 1923, when Nelson began his investigations, Escalante "was the end of the road."[21]

Nelson's thesis is that the Mormon village was "a social invention" compounded "from the ideologies of millennialism, communism, and nationalism which they derived from the social environment of the early nineteenth century, and the Old and New Testaments."[22] The values and social organization defined by this model seemed to be amply demonstrated in the original settlement of Escalante. Although the first settlers staked out land claims of 160 acres each—the standard acreage permitted by the homestead laws—they did this not merely for their own benefit but in the interests of the community. Nelson writes, "According to the testimony of James Schow, they all agreed that they would subdivide these holdings into farms of 22 1/2 acres each in order that other settlers might come in and get land. They were primarily interested in establishing a community rather than large individual tracts."[23]

Nelson found that by 1923, Escalante, though less than fifty years old, had already passed its prime and entered a stage of social and economic stagnation. However, some signs still remained of the founders' egalitarian ideals. Despite some consolidation of land holdings, there were still 124 farms, most of them containing less than fifty acres. Eighty-seven families were running beef cattle on the range, and fifty-four had sheep, while 140 maintained at least one milk cow and some chickens on the town lot. But some significant differences in living standards had developed. While the more prosperous had well-built and spacious brick homes, Nelson found more than a third of the families inadequately housed, including one family of eight children in a two-room cabin. He concluded, "The low standard of housing in the village in 1923 suggests that the second and third generations had not contributed to the building of the community in the same proportion as did the 'founding fathers.'"[24] Nelson further observed a predictable association of certain family names with certain economic and social levels:

Those with the largest families lived in the smallest houses, possessed the fewest books, and so on. With their high birthrate they are the people whose progeny will inherit Escalante a few generations hence. It is not likely that their young people will go beyond the high school education provided in the town. They may migrate elsewhere in larger numbers than the children of the other families but in terms of numbers, should they remain in the village, they will surely come to possess it finally.[25]

The general picture that emerges from Nelson's 1923 study is of a town gone to seed. He quotes one resident as saying, "It is easy to make a living in this community."[26] Nelson attributes this to the livestock economy, which did not make heavy time demands except at certain seasons of the year. As a result, "there was what may be termed a great amount of 'under-employment' in the village; or in other words, a large accumulation of leisure time."[27] The fact that this available time-resource was not being employed to improve living conditions was seen by Nelson as further evidence of social decline.

That there were Escalanteans who relished their leisure is borne out in community lore. Local historian Nethella Griffin Woolsey recounts the anecdote of a visitor to the town who, in view of "the broken fences and general rundown look of many houses," was perplexed to find a large group of men squatting against a wall and whittling. "Is this all you fellows have to do?" the stranger demanded; whereupon Hyme Bailey, the town wag, drawled, "We don't even *have* to do this, mister, if we don't want to."[28] Indeed, there is a kind of taste for the ramshackle in many Utah villages, and the village "characters" tend to be those who embody this quality. In Escalante, in the early years, such a figure was Napoleon Bonaparte Roundy, a sheepman with extensive holdings, two wives, and the biggest house in town, but who went about dressed in worn and ragged clothing and boots held together with baling wire. An entire cycle of Escalante stories celebrates the colorful disarray and sharp wit of "Pole" Roundy.

The 1930s marked a crucial transition time for Escalante. The Great Depression and drought devastated the economy, ruined the local bank, and cost many stockmen their land and herds. More than two-thirds of the residents were receiving some form of government relief in 1935.[29] At the same time, however, Depression-era programs brought some significant civic improvements. Two Civilian Conservation Corps camps were established in the area, bringing the first substantial influx of outsiders into the community, some of whom married local girls. Among other projects, they built roads from Escalante to Boulder and into the plateau highlands. Another program financed a culinary water system to replace the individual wells, cisterns, or simple "ditch-dipping" that had prevailed until that time.

When Lowry Nelson returned to Escalante for a follow-up study in 1950, he found that the almost self-sufficient economy of a quarter century earlier had given way to the money economy of the larger society:

> In 1950 Escalante no longer grew, ground, processed, or made many of the things it needed in daily life. The flour mill was no more. Home baking was by no means universal. Dairy cows were fewer in number. Even fresh vegetables from California were now brought in during the winter. Trucks bearing oil and gasoline, bakery and dairy products, radios and ranges, furniture and hardware, and a thousand other items, daily began to pound the new highway which connects Escalante with the Great Society.[30]

Livestock numbers had fallen from ten thousand cattle and thirty thousand sheep in 1923 to only four thousand cattle and fewer than seven thousand sheep in 1950, with ownership of land and livestock concentrated in fewer than one-fourth of the families. Where the economy in 1923 had depended almost entirely on farming and stockraising, the largest factors in 1950 were government employment and welfare payments. Eighteen percent of the population depended on public welfare—and this, as Nelson noted, in "the most prosperous period ever known" in the nation as a whole. While the total population had declined by only a hundred people between 1923 and 1950, the town had exported virtually all of its natural increase. And as Nelson had predicted, the out-migration rate was highest among the best-educated portion of the population: "Of 387 graduates of the local high school since 1937, only 41 still resided in the village in 1950."[31]

Nelson did find housing standards substantially improved by the building of new homes and the installation of electricity and piped-in water. Two-thirds of the homes had indoor bathrooms; almost every household had a radio, and most received a daily newspaper from Salt Lake City. At the same time, however, Nelson reported a decline in the sense of community. In place of "the 'we feeling' which was so manifest in conversation and behavior" during his first visit to Escalante, he was now "equally impressed with the lack of such a sense of identification." He attributed this change to "the increased occupational stratification" and "the increased concentration of the available resources in few hands."[32]

In recent decades, some of the trends identified by Nelson have continued and intensified. Escalante's isolation has been further reduced by improved highways, increased ownership of cars and trucks, and the coming of television. After 1950, Escalante, like many other rural communities, entered what might be termed a "second-stage" depopulation. The first stage of depopulation occurs when a community must export its natural increase, making for an aging populace even though the total numbers may remain fairly stable. In the second stage, there is an actual decline in population. By the time Escalante reached its centennial in 1975, its population had fallen to little more than half of what it had been at the peak. A section of Nethella Griffin Woolsey's community history is titled, "Chief Export—People." She sums up the trend in these terms: "Young people have gone to find employment, educational opportunity, and a fuller life. Middle-aged people have gone for employment and interest. Older people went to live near their sons and daughters. To name them all would fill a book."[33]

Escalante moved into its second century amid mixed economic signs. A lumber mill, built at the edge of town to process the ponderosa-pine timber of the Aquarius Plateau, became the major employer. However, because of a combination of market conditions and uncertain timber supplies the mill has suspended operations at this writing. Still, there are more young families in the community today than there were twenty years ago, and there are even modest signs of prosperity in the form of a new high school, new homes, modern farm equipment, and a remarkable number of fine horses.

Escalanteans have always taken a special pride in their horses. The 1942 WPA-sponsored *Utah: A Guide to the State* characterized Escalante as a "horse town" where "people ride on horseback from one part of town to another, and newsboys deliver papers on horseback."[34] At that time, however, the horses still served a primarily utilitarian purpose as draft animals or cow ponies, and their numbers fell sharply with the coming of trucks and tractors. Lowry Nelson's 1923 survey counted 717 horses with 135 owners. By 1950, the number of horses was down to 176 and the number of owners to only 37. A cursory survey of local pastures suggests that the horse population has risen substantially since 1950 and that the favored breed is now the quarter horse. There are extensive public stables near the community racetrack and rodeo grounds, and horse trailers—some of them very large and luxurious—are parked beside many homes.

Nelson counted ninety new houses constructed in Escalante between 1923 and 1950, all of them within the town limits. He noted,

"Escalante remained a compact village in its original form. There was no tendency toward establishing homes on the farms."[35] As recently as 1964, only one family lived year-round on a farm.[36] Since then, however, probably most of the new houses have been located outside the original town limits. It is difficult to estimate how much of this change is to be attributed to a decline in community life and how much simply to improved transportation, which makes the village facilities more easily accessible to those living out of town. It would seem, however, that the ideal of the ranch—of living on one's own spread, at a distance from neighbors—has taken precedence over the earlier ideal of the close-knit village. In the town, many of the original quarter-block lots have been subdivided, so that the life-style of the community is at once more expansive and more congested than it used to be. (The households are more numerous and smaller, a common pattern throughout the country.) Despite the fact that the chief local industry is a lumber mill, there is a preponderance of mobile homes and factory-built houses. It is a commentary on the way we live now that so many people choose to haul a prefabricated house from a factory hundreds of miles away rather than using local materials and local craftspeople to build something more harmonious with the landscape.

The greater part of Escalante's natural increase is still compelled to leave the town to obtain employment. Escalante experiences the same anguish as other small towns at this continuous exporting of its youth, but in addition there is bitterness growing out of a sense that the potential for economic development has been stifled by outside interests. There were high hopes several years ago for development of the vast coal reserves of the Kaiparowits Plateau to fuel a large electrical generating plant. When these plans were canceled because of environmental concerns, several prominent environmentalists were hanged in effigy in Escalante—and some of the local people would have been happy to hang them in person if it had been possible. More recently, battle lines have been drawn over the efforts of wilderness advocates to prevent drilling and mining activities in the Box Death Hollow area and to restrict logging on the Aquarius, and over plans by Garfield County officials to improve the Burr Trail that crosses the desert from Boulder to Lake Powell.

Escalante's location is both its chief resource and the major limiting factor in its development. No town in North America is situated in the midst of a more dramatic landscape, yet Escalante remains off the main tourist track. The wilderness enthusiasts who have discovered the grandeur of its canyons and plateaus do not bring much money into the

local economy—and often prefer, moreover, to keep the beauty of the region a secret among themselves. For them, the difficulty of access is part of the Escalante country's charm. The reefs and canyons that have been a road-builder's nightmare are irresistibly appealing to those who seek the preservation of what little remains of more or less pristine wilderness. At the same time, the environmental lobby generates massive resistance to the development of extractive industries. The most emphatic voice for wilderness interests has been a coalition known as the Southern Utah Wilderness Alliance. The feelings of some local people can be gauged from the number of bumper stickers one sees in Escalante bearing the motto "S.U.W.A. SUCKS."

Thomas Hardy, who made a literary career out of interpreting the decline of rural England for the rapidly urbanizing Victorian age, characterized the fundamentally different responses of rural natives and outsiders in these terms:

> The town-bred boy will often appreciate nature more than the country boy. But he does not know it in the same sense. He will rush to pick a flower which the country boy does not seem to notice. But it is part of the country boy's life. It grows in his soul—he does not want it in his button-hole.[37]

Hardy's images require some modification to fit the late-twentieth-century situation. Today's "town-bred" nature lovers prefer to enjoy the flower in its living, natural condition instead of picking it. Moreover, their knowledge of delicate ecosystems is often greater than that of the country dwellers, and a passion for wilderness preservation has replaced the more dilletantish nineteenth-century attitudes toward landscape as "picturesque."

Nevertheless, there is still a fundamental difference between *inhabiting* a landscape and coming to it as a visitor. In the Escalante country, the main hiking season begins in April and extends through October— from spring's high waters through the dry heat and sudden thunderstorms of summer to the long, mellow autumn. Few outsiders experience the Escalante winter, bleak and lonely and subject to bone-chilling cold spells that have been known to freeze the culinary water line solid. Visitors bring equipment and supplies from outside—come, in effect, securely wrapped in an insulative shell that will surround them throughout their time in the wilderness and go with them when they leave. And their stay is likely to be brief. After an exhilarating and testing and renewing encounter with nature, most visitors go back to suburbia and the convenience of supermarkets, freeways, shopping malls, and good jobs.

Not all visitors to the Escalante country fit this pattern, of course. Some, in the tradition of Everett Ruess, are wilderness bohemians, people who have temporarily or permanently dropped out of the mainstream and spend nearly all their time in or near the wilderness. Some of them are as migratory as geese, returning to southern Utah regularly or irregularly in the course of their cyclic wanderings. A few remain year-round, having found no place they would rather be. These are often the most passionately protective, anxious to preserve the unique qualities that attracted them to the region. But even for them, Escalante remains a place they have chosen, and there is always the possibility of choosing otherwise.

To be a native of a place like Escalante is a kind of fate, unchosen, inescapable. The scene of one's first consciousness—the shape of the horizon, the quality of the light, the taste of the air—forms the baseline of reality. This is especially true when one's native place is relatively isolated and self-contained. A town like Escalante is a little world, a congeries of accumulated artifacts and human types that is yet comprehensible in a way a larger city is not. It is rather like a big family or a tribe, capable of inspiring intense attachment and loyalty, but also rivalry, resentment, and a desire for escape. In Escalante, after a hundred years of solitude, the actual kinship ties are intricate and extensive, and a certain clannishness is inevitable. The basketball teams from other small southern Utah high schools are said to dread their trips to Escalante because the competitive spirit has been known to spill over from the playing floor, and the visitors have sometimes felt lucky to get out of town in one piece afterward.

These tribal bonds are deeply involved with the landscape. Escalanteans know that their forebears chose this place when no one else valued it, and they live among the accumulated signs of the long struggle to secure a foothold and wrest a living from a difficult land. They feel, further, that outsiders do not really understand the country. The old cowmen who have spent their lives in the desert canyons are scornful of the REI-equipped backpackers. Inevitably, Escalanteans feel that this wide and broken landscape rightfully belongs to them, and that the government agencies that hold titular control are somehow intruders, like an army of occupation. Environmental activists provoke much the same feelings as northern carpetbaggers in the post-Civil War

172

South. The very disadvantages of the place—the long struggle to make a living, the awareness of having less money, fewer and poorer public services, scantier opportunities for growth than other places—only pull the bonds of attachment tighter. And for many of the many who leave, life elsewhere is a kind of exile.

Beyond the simple dichotomy of native-born and outsider, however, there is the conflict between two deeply held but fundamentally different visions of the human relationship to the earth: the wilderness ethic and the developmental ethic. Both visions rest on partly illusory foundations. Both are highly appealing in their more idealistic manifestations, but both are also susceptible to abuse.

The wilderness ethic has its roots in a love for the earth and a desire that some part of it, at least, may be preserved in an unspoiled natural state. This basic view is expressed, with variations, in the writings that have assumed virtual scriptural status within the movement—Thoreau, Muir, Burroughs, et al.—but nowhere more succinctly than in the passionate plea that concludes Gerard Manley Hopkins's poem "Inversnaid":

What would the world be once bereft
Of wet and of wildness? Let them be left,
O let them be left, wildness and wet;
Long live the weeds and the wilderness yet![38]

Or, in the words of the late crotchety guru of wilderness, Edward Abbey, "Perhaps a few places are best left forever unexplored, seen from a distance but never entered, never walked upon."[39]

There is something fundamentally right about the wilderness ethic. When you contemplate the wholesale damage to the environment that mankind has wrought—the desertification of marginal lands, destruction of rainforests, atmospheric pollution, extinction of species, and all the other environmental sins we must collectively bear upon our consciences as the price of exponential population growth and an exploitative life-style—surely when so much of nature has been sacrificed to human convenience, some of the little that remains relatively unspoiled ought to be preserved so that future generations might know what the world once was, to say nothing of more utilitarian needs to preserve gene pools of various organisms. At the same time, however, it is important to recognize that the wilderness ethic, in its usual manifestations in our society, rests on a Romantic nature myth and is susceptible to certain illusions. Perhaps the first illusion is in even thinking there is such

173

a thing as pristine wilderness. Except for the areas of the globe that are absolutely uninhabitable—the Antarctic ice cap, for example—no place has escaped being affected by human activity. And, of course, atmospheric pollution has affected every part of the earth without exception. Moreover, the human impact on the environment is by no means a recent development. Indeed, without the destruction of wilderness human civilization could not have come into being.

Even in the most remote parts of southern Utah, the assault on the wilderness began long before the coming of the Mormon settlers, the stockmen, or the miners. The Anasazi, at their peak, were extremely hard on the environment, so much so that they had to move their habitations every few years. They were also addicted to graffiti—though the passage of time has invested their rock art with an aura of value that sets it apart from more recent human markings upon the land. The "Moqui" remains, as they are called in southern Utah, now seem to be a part of the wilderness itself and are usually included in the proposals for wilderness protection. But there is more than a little irony in the reflection that they once represented an exploitative intrusion of human civilization into the wilderness.

It is customary in our time to associate the love of the earth exclusively with the wilderness ethic, but it is important to remember that it can take other forms, including the developmental ethic. If the wilderness ethic rests upon the myth of a pristine natural order in which civilized man is an intruder, the developmental ethic has its roots in the myth of the Garden of Eden. In this view, the earth was not originally wilderness but rather a garden: an environment created for mankind in which all things were adapted to human need and delight. With the Fall, the garden was supplanted by wilderness—that which is alien and inimical to the human—and the imperative then becomes to restore the paradisal condition by reclaiming the wilderness and making it a garden once more.

The garden myth is of course anthropocentric, and many of the abuses of the developmental ethic can be traced to its privileging of human values—and particularly economic values—over all other considerations. But the wilderness ethic has an equally dangerous tendency toward elitism and even misanthropy. Wilderness advocates deny this, maintaining that their ranks are open to anyone converted to their cause. But "conversion" is precisely the point. A frequently recurring element in modern nature writing is a patronizing or openly hostile attitude toward the intrusion into the wilderness of the non-elect.

No matter which ethic we may profess, we are all susceptible to a

174

common though not very admirable human tendency: a desire to possess absolutely and to the exclusion of others the things we value most. For example, in 1987, during a tense stage of the battle between wilderness groups and Garfield County officials over the improvement of the Burr Trail, the Bureau of Land Management accused a prominent wilderness activist of building a home on public land that had been set aside for possible wilderness designation. The "trespass" was apparently not intentional but resulted from inaccurate surveys. However, there is something profoundly ironic in the picture of a wilderness advocate fighting to keep his own development in the wilderness while at the same time trying to prevent other developments. A further ironic twist can be found in the fact that the structure in question was not built from native materials but from recycled rock hauled more than a hundred miles from Sanpete Valley.

Another example of the same kind of inconsistency appears in a 1977 *Harper's* essay by Edward Abbey recounting a visit to the Escalante Canyons. Like many other wilderness advocates, Abbey bitterly opposed the construction of the Glen Canyon Dam. He refers to Lake Powell as a "National Recreational Slum" and with characteristic scorn declares, "There is no lower form of life known to zoological science than the motorboat fisherman, the speedboat sightseer."[40] However, since the lake offered the most convenient access to the area Abbey and his party wished to visit, they also traveled by motorboat. He complains about the litter on the beaches and the impossibility of finding a decent campsite near the lake, but he goes on to describe with relish the way he and his friends rolled rocks off the rims and enjoyed the noise and dust they made as they fell into the canyons. To be sure, the campsite litter of beer cans and toilet paper is probably more offensive than the moving of a few rocks in a land of rocks. But a case can easily be made that Abbey and his friends were also exploiting the land for their own pleasure.

It is a mistake to set the developmental ethic in direct opposition to the wilderness ethic. Both are complex in their manifestations. People who favor development do not necessarily favor all development or development at all costs. Wilderness lovers also come in many shapes—including Escalante ranchers who have spent their lives in this dramatic landscape because there is nowhere else they would rather be, and who are likely to confide, once they feel they can trust you, that they know the location of numerous rock arches and other natural wonders no outsider has ever seen. The very existence of the community of Escalante has unquestionably done some damage to the natural environment over the last hundred years. But the town itself has become part of the environment. The grovelike village and its patchwork of cultivated fields winding down the canyon floors and spreading southward under the massive wall of Fifty Mile Mountain are remarkably harmonious with their setting and at the same time contribute another element of difference to a landscape whose chief excellence is its contrasts.

At the same time, Escalante also represents an ideal of human community. Its origins partook of the utopian dream of equality and abundance, as manifest in the equal distribution of land and water rights among the first settlers. That ideal failed at Escalante, as it has failed elsewhere, in the face of the hard facts of human nature, but its heritage lives on in a genuine community, where people know and are known, where individuality—even of the maverick variety—is valued yet at the same time balanced with an imperfectly realized yet still enduring commitment to the common good. These values are not highly self-conscious. Indeed, many local residents are more aware of the internal divisions in the community than of its larger harmonies—just as in a large family disputes are magnified while the fundamental fact of relatedness is taken for granted. The "we" feeling Lowry Nelson found in Escalante in 1923—and that he saw as declining a quarter of a century later—is still there, and so are the deep bonds to place that only a small town can inspire.

But the essential qualities of a place like Escalante are not always apparent to the casual observer. To see Escalante whole, you have to take in more than the "front" view. You have to go around to the back, to the barnyards and orchards and backhouses. You have to perceive these elements in time as well as in space—the gradual accumulation of a community, generation by generation—and you have to be sensitive to the symbols in the landscape. The black locusts are such a symbol: trees not native to the region but well adapted for survival, with deep roots, and small leaves to minimize evaporation, and thick bark to keep the living tissue deeply protected from heat and cold and wind. The backhouses are also symbolic: functional, unpretentious, easily overlooked, but solidly built and enduring. Seeking a way to live on the margins of the wilderness, the Escalante pioneers dug down into the earth for shelter from summer heat and winter cold. As they altered the landscape to make possible the kind of community life they envisioned, they came out of the ground to build plain, dignified houses of brick that matched the colors of the rock around them. They planted lilacs in the dooryard to fill the desert air with a fragrance foreign to but capable of blending with sage and cliffrose and oose. They moved out of the dugout but never entirely abandoned it. Under the backhouse, it is still there, a link to the earth itself and a symbol of the human presence in a beautiful but hard land.

10

A WOMAN AND
SOME COWS

T he decade of the 1870s began inauspiciously for John Doyle Lee.
Brigham Young, faced with charges from the Godbeite faction
and their *Utah Magazine* that he was protecting those responsible
for the 1857 Mountain Meadows massacre, first sent Lee to the remote
settlement of Skutumpah, under the southern rim of the Paunsagunt
Plateau, and then, in October 1870, excommunicated him from the
Mormon church.[1] When Lee petitioned for a rehearing, he received an
unsigned note that read,

> If you will consult your own safety & that [of] others, you will not press
> yourself nor an investigation on others at this time least [sic] you cause
> others to become accessory with you & thereby force them to inform upon
> you or to suffer. Our advice is, Trust no one. Make yourself scarce & keep
> out of the way.[2]

In November 1871, Jacob Hamblin, probably at the behest of Mormon
church leaders, advised Lee to move to the remote crossing of the Colorado at the mouth of the Paria River, telling him that it was "a good
place for settlement & you are invited to take it up & occupy it with as
Many good Ranches as you want & can secure. . . . So if you have a
woman that has Faith enough to go with you, take her along & some
cows."[3]

The mouth of the Paria was the only place on the Colorado accessible to wagons in the four hundred miles between Spanish Valley, in
eastern Utah, and the Grand Wash near the Nevada border. The river
emerges from Glen Canyon through the abrupt uplift of the Echo Cliffs
and runs past the Paria delta before entering the chasm of Marble
Canyon. The place had a prehistory written in numerous Anasazi relics
and a history dating to 1776, when the Dominguez-Escalante party
found themselves bottled up there on their return trip to Santa Fe. The
river was too deep and the current too swift to ford, and the cliffs

177

seemed to allow no egress. They named their camp San Benito Salisipuedes—"get out if you can!"[4] They eventually got out by scrambling up the two-thousand-foot wall of the Paria Canyon and making their way to the old Ute Ford, twenty miles upstream.

The Mormon frontiersman Jacob Hamblin first visited the site in 1858 in search of a route to the Hopi villages. On this occasion, he had no better luck in crossing the river than the Spaniards eighty-two years before, and he was compelled to follow their route to Ute Ford. Hamblin made the first recorded successful crossing on a raft in 1864 and repeated it several times in the following years.[5] Powell's first river expedition camped at the Paria delta on August 4, 1869.[6] In October of that year, the Mormons stationed guards at the crossing in an effort to halt Navajo raids on southern Utah. They erected a small stone building called Fort Meeks, and the next spring Hamblin cleared a little plot of land for farming.[7] The second Powell expedition in 1871 pulled out of the river at the Paria on October 23 and cached their boats there before proceeding to Kanab for the winter.[8]

All of these and others had visited the Paria delta before John D. Lee arrived in December 1871, but Lee was the first to establish a permanent residence, the first, also, to bring wagons to the site and thereby open the road by which Mormon settlers would enter Arizona in the late 1870s. Lee brought not just one woman but two, Rachel Woolsey and Emma Batchelder, wives number six and seventeen.[9] Rachel arrived first and had a big pot of stew on the fire when the others pulled in on the evening of December 23. The next morning, Emma surveyed the ragged cliffs surrounding the little valley and exclaimed, "Oh, what a lonely dell!"[10] Lonely Dell was the name by which the Lees knew the place thereafter.

In May, Lee moved Rachel to Houserock Valley to secure a claim to the water of Jacob's Pools. He quickly threw up a shelter of willows and brush before starting construction of a substantial stone house. But it was the willow shanty, not the house, that was to have the greater symbolic permanence. On June 2, 1872, Powell's photographer, E. O. Beaman, took a picture of Lee and three of his children standing beside the shanty. The print sold widely in stereoscopic form as a vivid representation of primitive living conditions in the West.[11]

Lee's Ferry is today part of the Glen Canyon National Recreation Area. The hike through the Paria Gorge is a sought-after challenge among more adventurous backpackers, though few of them could imagine driving a herd of cattle down the gorge as John D. Lee did in 1871. The surviving buildings at Lonely Dell Ranch, including a cabin and blacksmith shop built of flood logs salvaged from the Colorado and dating to Lee's time, are protected as a historical monument, and the National Park Service has planted an orchard in an effort to restore the ranch's oasis character. The Colorado still flows swiftly past the ferry site, but only fifteen river miles below Glen Canyon Dam it is cold and clear, free from the red silt that gave it its name. Though the ferry operation was abandoned after an accident in June 1928 (the nearby Marble Canyon Bridge was completed in January 1929),[12] the riverbank is still busy as the entry point for float trips through the Grand Canyon. This is Mile Zero, the arbitrary dividing point between the upper and lower Colorado basins and the point from which all distances on the river are measured. On the south bank, the precipitous Shinarump ledge known as Lee's Backbone rises against the Echo Cliffs.

It is difficult to imagine Lee's Backbone as a road, but thousands of vehicles passed over it. The route to Lee's Ferry from the Utah settlements was bad enough, with its long waterless stretches, its deep sand that clung to the wagon wheels and forced the draft animals to strain in the desert heat, its impassable washes during rainy weather. And the ferry crossing was no picnic, with the swift current, makeshift equipment, and Marble Canyon yawning below. But it was the Backbone that stuck most vividly in the memories of many who followed this route.

Two of my great-grandfathers came this way in the early 1880s, one of them moving his young family to the Mormon colony of St. Johns, the other driving a herd of cattle in quest of new range. Felt Acord, the cattleman, was bred on the Iowa frontier, had lived with the Sioux and driven freight teams to the Montana mines. But Lee's Backbone was more than he could handle. His eldest daughter recounted,

> I was driving a hack and a span of horses. One of our herders came to me and said, "Your father says you must come back and drive the ox team."
>
> I went up to Father, he sat with his hat over his eyes, as it made him sea sick to look down over that high precipice we were driving over. I don't know the height now. But the river was 360 yards across, and from the top of the Back Bone it looked like a narrow ribbon. Well I drove the family over. I was but nineteen. The oxen had been taught to be driven by motion, not by voice. If I wanted the oxen to "gee," I motioned the rod from me. If to "haw" I would bring the stick toward me, and if we went down a steep place and wanted the wagon let down carefully, I tapped lightly on the nigh ox's horn. Sometimes there would be a drop of eight or ten inches, and so rocky, with no sign of a rut. We were hours and hours going over that miserable road. I, with my first long dress, had a time keep-

ing it out of the way of my feet. When we got down to the foot of it we camped for two days.[13]

John D. Lee actually resided at Lee's Ferry for only a few months. Pressures from the law drove him southward in 1873, and he established another ranch at Moenave, near the Hopi villages. Emma Lee, however, remained at Lonely Dell for almost five years after her husband's arrest in November 1874 and two years after his execution by firing squad at Mountain Meadows on March 23, 1877. While first James Jackson and then Warren M. Johnson were hired to operate the ferry, Emma herself is said to have been capable of handling the long sweep oars.[14] In 1879 the LDS church purchased her property and ferry rights and assigned Johnson to manage the ferry and Lonely Dell ranch. He erected a Mormon-style two-story house made of planks, where he lived until 1895, despite the loss of four of his children during a three-week period in 1891 to diphtheria contracted from a family that had passed through.[15] In later years, members of the Johnson family once again operated Lee's Ferry, and Warren Johnson's grandson Adolf was among the three men drowned during the ferry's disastrous final run on June 7, 1928.

Many political boundaries in the western United States consist of arbitrary lines drawn on a map with little relation to either natural or social divisions. To be sure, there are some exceptions. The border between Montana and Idaho follows the Continental Divide. The Columbia River forms the boundary between Washington and Oregon, and the Colorado River separates California from Arizona. But the states of Wyoming, Colorado, and Utah have no natural borders at all, and New Mexico has only a twenty-mile stretch of the Rio Grande. Nowhere is the arbitrariness of political boundaries more apparent than on the border between Utah and Arizona, a ruler-straight line stretching east and west along the thirty-seventh degree of north latitude. The same line extends six hundred miles farther east to divide Colorado from New Mexico and Kansas from Oklahoma. But the Utah-Arizona border is the most perversely arbitrary because it bisects one of the greatest natural barriers in North America, the canyons of the Colorado River.

The portion of Arizona north of the Grand Canyon has long been called the Arizona Strip. In area it is comparable to Massachusetts, but until very recent years it supported a population of fewer than a thousand, or roughly one person for every ten square miles. Culturally, it is an extension of Utah, and its only real towns, Fredonia and Colorado City, have close ties to neighboring communities on the Utah side of the border. Popular Western novelist Zane Grey reflects the traditional view in a remark he puts into the mouth of the rugged cattleman August Naab as he introduces young greenhorn John Hare to the landscape of the Strip: "'If not overstocked, this range is the best in Utah,' said Naab. 'I say Utah, but it's really Arizona. The Grand Cañon seems to us Mormons to mark the line.'"[16] Sharlot Hall, who visited the Strip in 1911 in her official capacity as Arizona Territorial Historian, observed of the region, "Geographically it is part of the great tangle of plateaus and valleys, cliff-walled canyons and vast and fantastically eroded mountain ranges which include southeastern Utah and make up a wonderland unsurpassed upon earth, though still almost unknown except to a handful of people."[17]

The landscape of the Arizona Strip is remarkably open, even for plateau country, and favors long vistas. From the Vermillion Cliffs at the base of the Terrace Plateaus, the earth rises gradually toward the south in a broad uplift that is bisected near its crest by the Grand Canyon. The phenomenon of the Colorado cutting through the highest portion of the uplift instead of following an easier course to the north or south was taken by John Wesley Powell as evidence for his theory that the major streamcourses are older than the mountains. Powell proposed that the Grand Canyon was formed not by the river cutting down into the earth but by the earth slowly rising across the river's path. From Lee's Ferry to Grand Wash, the Colorado River falls about two thousand feet, but the Grand Canyon is a mile deep.

While the river chasm winds through the uplift on a roughly east-west course, a series of faults slice it from north to south, dividing it into several distinct units with different elevations. Lee's Ferry is situated in the angle where the Vermillion Cliffs turn sharply to the south and become the Echo Cliffs. To the west, the Paria Plateau dips southward from Utah, overlooking House Rock Valley and the Marble Canyon Platform. The highest table on the Strip, the Kaibab Plateau, is bounded by the East Kaibab Monocline and the West Kaibab Fault. From the West Kaibab Fault to the Toroweap lies the Kanab Plateau, cut by the canyon of Kanab Creek, which flows south against the general trend of the land (yet another evidence to Powell that the rivers are older than the uplifts). West of the Toroweap, the Uinkaret Plateau, crowned by the volcanic cones of Mount Trumbull, extends to the massive fault line of the Hurricane Cliffs. Between the Hurricane Cliffs and Grand Wash lies the Shivwits Plateau, and beyond Grand Wash the rugged area known locally as the Pakoon stretches west into Nevada.

Jacob Hamblin's advice to John D. Lee to take a woman and some cows to the Arizona Strip proved to be prophetic. Stockraising has been the economic backbone of the region for most of its history, and the two towns on the strip, Fredonia and Colorado City, are monuments to the practice of polygynous marriage. Because of its political separation from Utah and its physical separation from the rest of Arizona, the Strip for much of its history was a legal no-man's-land. The portion east of Kanab Creek belongs to Coconino County, whose administrative and population center is at Flagstaff, two hundred highway miles from Fredonia. The western Strip is part of Mohave County, and the shortest route from Kingman, the county seat, to Colorado City requires traveling through three states.

Fredonia, its name probably signifying "free women," was established just across the border from Kanab during the period of the Raid as a place where Mormon plural wives could escape the jurisdiction of Utah territorial officials. With the end of church-sanctioned polygamy, the village's proximity to the border came to have other uses. The Strip storyteller Rowland Rider tells of the legendary "roll away saloon," designed to allay the thirst of the local cowboys:

> So they built this little saloon and it was right on the Arizona-Utah line four miles south of Kanab and four miles north of Fredonia about seven or eight rods to the west of the present highway. It was just a kind of two-room affair, with a bar at one end and the barkeeper's bedroom at the other end. It wasn't very large, maybe twelve by eighteen feet, but it created quite a bit of disturbance among the Mormon housewives of Fredonia and Kanab because their men would come staggering up home on their horses, too late for dinner, unable to take their saddles off. So the men of these towns, fearing their women, built this saloon on rollers, log rollers that went clear under the joist.

When "the women in the Relief Society up to Kanab" formed themselves into a posse to destroy the offending establishment, the saloonkeeper got out his crowbar and pried the building across the border into Arizona. Then when the Fredonia women came after him, he rolled the saloon back into Utah.[18]

Sharlot Hall described Fredonia in 1911 as "the greenest, cleanest, quaintest little village of about thirty families."[19] Today the town is larger but less picturesque, with little but its name to commemorate its colorful origins. Two elements do appear somewhat out of place: the headquarters of the U.S. Forest Service North Kaibab Ranger District, complete with a large fleet of green vehicles, and, at the southern edge of town, the sprawling lumber mill of Kaibab Industries. Strange presences, these, in a vast, treeless landscape, but the explanation lies on the distant blue dome that closes off the view to the south and east and is, with the exception of the Grand Canyon itself, the most remarkable natural feature of the Arizona Strip.

The Kaibab Plateau is a southern extension of the High Plateaus of Utah, a rounded mass rising gradually from the base of the Vermillion Cliffs and bisected at its crest by the Grand Canyon. Though its summit rises beyond nine thousand feet, there is little sense of elevation on the Kaibab, except at the rim of the Grand Canyon, where almost six thousand feet of vertical distance suddenly yawns beneath your feet. Known to early southern Utah settlers as Buckskin Mountain by virtue of its large deer herd, the Kaibab, like so many other landforms in southern Utah and northern Arizona, received its present name from the Powell surveys. Kaibab is supposedly a Paiute name signifying "Mountain Lying Down," and that is as good a characterization as any. Sharlot Hall compared it to "a big land tortoise with a shell of steel gray limestone."[20] Highway 89A from Fredonia climbs almost imperceptibly from a sagebrush plain to the pinyon-juniper belt then winds up a short dugway and almost without transition into a forest of massive ponderosa pines.

The Kaibab Forest is large by Plateau Region standards, extending some forty miles from north to south and about thirty-five from east to west to encompass more than a thousand square miles of wooded area. The ponderosa-pine belt, narrow in the northern High Plateaus, is dominant here, though at the higher and moister elevations it merges into spruce-fir-aspen forest. Because the Kaibab is separated from other wooded regions by miles of desert and by the virtually impassable Colorado gorge, its islandlike character is even more pronounced than that of the High Plateaus of Utah. In this isolation, distinctive subspecies such as the white-tailed squirrel have developed. However, the Kaibab's biotic kinship with the High Plateaus is reflected in its general range of plant and animal varieties, including the largest stands of spruce and fir in Arizona, bracken among the aspens, gambel oak, snowberry, New Mexican locust, manzanita, sagebrush, and wildflowers including lupines, bluebell, asters, columbine, and yarrow. The animals, too, are those of the High Plateaus, except for the presence of a large wild turkey population and the absence of those species that depend on a riverine environment.

Deer in Kaibab Forest, from 1929 Utah Parks travel brochure. Photo courtesy Union Pacific Railroad.

For despite its extent, elevation, and an annual precipitation comparable to the High Plateaus of Utah, the Kaibab does not have a single living stream upon its surface. The porous limestone permits the water to percolate to deeper formations where it emerges from springs inside the Grand Canyon. The water supply for the creatures of the forest comes from a few springs whose waters quickly sink into the earth, and from numerous small pools, mostly sinkholes whose outlets have become clogged, causing them to hold the rainwater.

U.S. Highway 89A penetrates the Kaibab Forest only as far as Jacob Lake before turning eastward toward House Rock Valley. Arizona Highway 67, running forty-five miles from Jacob Lake to the North Rim, is rightly considered one of the most beautiful drives in the West. It follows a string of open parks that extend from north to south through the middle of the forest, remnants of an ancient drainage system probably formed before the plateau was uplifted. The most interesting approach to the Kaibab, however, is not by way of these major highways but by a secondary road designed for logging traffic, branching off from Highway 89A just east of Fredonia.

This road approximates the route taken by Clarence E. Dutton on his first visit to the Kaibab. In his book on the High Plateaus, Dutton described the Arizona Strip as viewed from the Kolob Terraces as "blank, lifeless, and glowing with torrid heat."[21] When he actually experienced the Strip, however, he came to appreciate the beauties of the arid plains and canyons he had earlier contemplated with a shudder of dread, and his *Tertiary History of the Grand Cañon District* is generally regarded as his finest work. Stegner calls Dutton "almost as much the *genius loci* of the Grand Canyon as Muir is of Yosemite."[22]

In his account of a journey from Kanab to the Kaibab, Dutton, with his usual perceptiveness, identifies the fundamental cause of the region's great sense of openness:

> The desert before us is really no more uneven than the rolling prairie of Iowa, but the range of vision is vastly greater. The reason is soon explained. In the prairie the curvature of the earth soon carries the surface out of sight. In the Kanab Desert we are constantly looking across a very wide but shallow depression of the surface. . . . In a word, the earth's surface is here slightly concave instead of convex, and the radius vector of the concavity has a length varying from 15 to 30 miles. Anywhere within the depression, therefore, the prospect is a very wide one. The general impression conveyed is that of a gently undulating plain of immense extent.[23]

Fifteen miles from Fredonia, near the site of the old copper mine called Ryan, the road enters Nail Canyon, a long, north-south trending depression that drains the west side of the Kaibab Plateau. A gentle ascent of nine miles brings us to Big Spring, which cascades down the canyon wall and forms a half-acre pool in a meadow of deep grass. Dutton noted that "a stream of that size anywhere else in the Plateau Country would ordinarily run eight or ten miles, and in a moist country would run much further."[24] But here the stream sinks into the porous soil after a few yards.

Dutton remarks of his journey to Big Spring, "In some way, without knowing exactly when and where, we seem to have gotten into the Kaibab."[25] Indeed, the approach is just that gradual, and the transformation to a mountain landscape seems almost miraculous. As a general rule, Dutton notes, a traveler in the Plateau Country will prefer to climb directly up a mountainside than struggle up a ravine "obstructed by fallen fragments and thickly set with scrub, its bottom scoured into rough gullies by the sudden floods." But the ravines and canyons of the Kaibab are different:

> Like the paths trodden by the pilgrims in the Delectable Mountains, "their ways are pleasantness and all their paths are peace." The ravine we enter is

but a fair specimen of a vast number of them which cover the whole broad surface of the plateau with an infinite network of ramifications. Its bottom is covered with a carpet of grass and flowers growing rankly in a smooth firm soil free from rocks and undergrowth. Here and there a clump of aspens or noble pines grow in the way, but offer no obstacles to progress. It is like riding through a well-kept park or an avenue shaded by ancient trees.[26]

Dutton locates some of the Kaibab's charm in its climate—Powell declared that it has "four months of the sweetest summer man has ever known"[27]—and some in "the contrast of the desert, with its fatigue, its numberless discomforts and privations." The unique combination of massive yet open woods has to be another element of the appeal. Because of the broad, gently undulating character of the plateau top and the absence of rocky promontories that allow for long views, the Kaibab Forest is that rarity of the plateau region, a place where one feels it would be possible to get lost. Dutton reports, "Even the Indians who live and hunt there during the summer and autumn have sad tales about comrades lost when the snows came early and buried the trails so that they could not be followed." And yet, he declares, "the riddle of the Kaibab is soon solved, and, once read, all danger is over." The key is to be found in the chain of open parks running north and south in the middle of the plateau. All of the major ravines "head upon the summit which looks down into the park."[28]

Her journey from Fredonia to the Kaibab in 1911 made Sharlot Hall realize "more than ever the bigness and wildness of this country." By that time, the plain had been "sheeped to death" and the bunchgrass replaced by sagebrush. Inspired by the dryfarm boom, several squatters had staked claims and plowed the ground, and Hall confidently predicted, "Some day there will be farms over this valley and the little mesas and flats that lie in the finger-like foothills of the Buckskins."[29] The waters of Big Spring had been diverted to irrigate some cropland on the floor of Nail Canyon, "a field of alfalfa and oats a mile or two long and a hundred yards wide—like the fields of Arkansas, where the farmer carries his grub and blankets on the plow and runs a furrow down one day and back the next."[30]

With the establishment of the Kaibab National Forest, a ranger station had been built at Big Spring. Arriving at dusk, Hall camped overnight there and woke to the exquisite beauty of the spring itself:

All night between the fall of rain on the tent and the roar of wind in the pines I heard the running of water. This morning it seemed as much overhead as the clouds up the cliff; back of the house ran a carpet of green like a velvet curtain led down from the white lime cliff of the canyon rim and the gurgle and rush of water came down muffled in the dense thicket of stinging nettles tipped with purple blossoms like baby cat-tails, the hop vines clambering over tall wild rose bushes and mingling their pale green clusters of hops with the glossy red rose haws, and the blackberry runners woven in and out like barbed wire.

Perhaps a hundred feet up this green-draped cliff a regular halfgrown river of crystal-clear, icy water bursts out in jets and gurgling streams and leaps down a wooden sluice with such force that when I put my hand in the spray flew up and gave me a second face washing for nothing.[31]

Like Dutton before her, Hall was impressed by the gradual ascent to the Kaibab platform. Though cattle had by this time grazed the forest for several decades, the landscape had not lost its lush abundance. Hall writes,

I walked all the morning far ahead of the wagon, alone with the mountain; when I grew tired I lay down in the grass and rested, and thought that it would be lovely to be buried in such a serene and yet majestic spot, the flowers dancing above and the quakenasp leaves tinkling like little silver bells.

Never have I seen a more exquisite bit of earth than the upper miles of Nail Canyon, park and trees and low-rounded hillsides. The great quakenasps were all scarred by the names of cowboys and with cattle brands of the ranches that used to be here long ago, cut deeply with pocket knives into the bark. It seemed sad, the poor names that mean nothing now—yet each seeking brief record of its owner.[32]

In the spruce/fir zone, Hall found "dainty baby trees two and three feet tall," wild roses, and an extensive growth of bracken fern. In the cabin of the famous government hunter James T. Owens, she saw a "border of paws and skulls" of the mountain lions he had killed. She writes,

This Kaibab Plateau was so full of lions and wolves when the Old Hunter came seven years ago that the stockmen had given up trying to raise horses and even lost grown stock as well as colts and calves. Owens had killed a hundred and eighty-four and trapped and roped a dozen or more alive and they were thinning out.

She continues, "the good of the lion killing showed today when we saw little fawns in groups like calves among the bracken ferns and does sniffed at us and bounded away on 'rubber-tired legs.'"[33]

187

"Thirty Thousand Deer Roam Unmolested in Kaibab National Forest," from 1929 Utah National Parks travel brochure. Photo courtesy Union Pacific Railroad.

What Hall was actually observing, without realizing it, was a disaster in the making, one of the greatest fiascos in the history of wildlife management. The Kaibab had always been known for its deer. The early settlers in Kanab reported ceremonial hunts by the Paiutes and Navajos during which a thousand carcasses might be seen in one camp.[34] This hunting activity, plus the coyotes and mountain lions, kept the deer population in balance with the available summer and winter range. Then in 1906 President Theodore Roosevelt declared the Kaibab Forest a national game preserve. All deer hunting was prohibited, and a systematic elimination of predators was begun. Between 1907 and 1919, Uncle Jim Owens by his own claim killed more than six hundred mountain lions.[35] Thus protected, the Kaibab deer multiplied rapidly, increasing at least tenfold, from an estimated three thousand in 1906 to thirty thousand in the early 1920s. Thirty thousand, indeed, was the conservative estimate of the game managers. Estimates by local stockmen ran as high as one hundred thousand.

In an effort to save the deer range, the forest managers reduced the domestic livestock permits from fifteen thousand head of cattle and five thousand sheep in 1913 to about five thousand cattle and twenty-five hundred sheep by the mid-1920s. The Grand Canyon Cattle Company conducted its last roundup on the Kaibab in 1924 and moved its herd to

Mexico. Beginning in 1926, government hunters went after the wild horses that roamed the region, killing more than a thousand over a five-year period. And still the range deteriorated. A group of Flagstaff citizens financed a massive project to drive Kaibab deer across the Grand Canyon and relocate them elsewhere in Arizona. An army of herders moved across the plateau from South Canyon to Saddle Canyon, ringing cowbells as they went. As Walter G. Mann laconically reports, "At Saddle Canyon there were no deer in front of the men but thousands of deer behind them, and the drive was abandoned as impossible."[36] Efforts to trap mature deer for relocation and to capture fawns to be reared by local ranchers were equally ineffective.

Despite warnings from wildlife biologists that "Wherever herbivores are protected and their natural enemies removed, they will destroy themselves by overstocking the range,"[37] strong political forces resisted efforts to reduce deer numbers by hunting. Until the late 1920s, tourism promotional materials continued to boast of the tameness and abundance of the Kaibab deer. For example, a brochure published by the Union Pacific Railroad declared,

> Afternoon and morning [the parks] are the gathering places of many of the 30,000 black-tail mule deer that range unfrightened through the forest. They do not require patient stalking to be seen; crossing the forest one may usually count several hundred haughty bucks, solicitous does, and adorable prancing fawns of exquisite grace.

Without recognizing the implications of the conditions described, the brochure also praised the exceptional cleanliness of the forest: "Beneath its stately trees the grassy forest floor is free from underbrush and fallen timber, as clean as if raked daily by ten thousand foresters."[38]

And indeed the forest was swept daily, not by ten thousand foresters, but by thirty thousand or a hundred thousand deer anxious to scavenge anything edible. On the favored west-side winter range, hungry deer browsed the bitter brush and cliffrose back to the stalks then turned to the less palatable Brigham tea and sagebrush, even eating juniper and pinyon pine as they grew more desperate. They almost entirely eliminated the willows and wild raspberries, the bracken and other undergrowth in the spruce/fir forest. They clipped aspen sprouts to the ground and devoured the lower limbs of mature trees as high as they could reach. They ate the terminal buds of ponderosa-pine seedlings, effectively halting all timber renewal.

And then they starved. Reports of the U.S. Biological Survey indicate that as much as forty percent of the deer herd died during the winter of 1924–25 and that most of the survivors "were in such poor physical condition that the outlines of the ribs, ilia and scapulae could plainly be seen through the skin."[39] Beginning in 1924, limited deer hunting was allowed in the Kaibab Forest, but massive winterkills continued throughout the 1920s. Desperate to bring the population into balance with the feed supply, forest managers obtained a Supreme Court ruling in 1926 permitting a slaughter by government hunters. In ten days in December, more than a thousand deer were killed; does were particularly targeted in order to reduce the breeding population. Several hundred of the carcasses were in such poor condition that they were left to rot where they fell. The others were delivered to Indian schools or given to residents of neighboring towns.[40]

By 1931 there were some signs of recovery in the range. Still, many of the browse plants had been killed out entirely, and an investigative committee estimated that "the Kaibab area is not now producing more than 10% of the available and nutritious forage that this range once produced."[41] Range recovery had progressed far enough that the deer herd survived the exceptionally dry season of 1934 without substantial losses, and by the end of the decade an enlightened management plan had stabilized the herd at about ten thousand. In his 1941 update of the 1931 monograph on the Kaibab deer, forest supervisor Walter G. Mann philosophically observed that while the range was making a good recovery, "It will require several years for the area to come back to as good condition as it once was. The plant cover may not be exactly the same because many of the plants were killed; and, since the rule of nature is change, the new forage plants may be of different percentage composition."[42]

No doubt the plant life of the Kaibab Forest is different today from what Clarence E. Dutton found in 1880. As compared with the High Plateaus in Utah, there is a relative scarcity of undergrowth, but this may be attributed in part to the essential character of Ponderosa pine woods. In any event, it is a characteristic Dutton remarked upon:

> Instead of dense thickets, where we are shut in by impenetrable foliage, we can look far beyond and see the tree trunks vanishing away like an infinite colonnade. The ground is unobstructed and inviting. There is a constant succession of parks and glades—dreamy avenues of grass and flowers winding between sylvan walls, or spreading out in open meadows.[43]

Despite more than a century of grazing and logging, of wildlife management and mismanagement, of increasingly heavy tourism, the Kaibab still retains much of its freshness and its mystery. "It is difficult," Dutton writes, "to say precisely wherein the charm of the sylvan scenery of the Kaibab consists. We who through successive summers have wandered through its forests and parks, have come to regard it as the most enchanting region it has ever been our privilege to visit."[44] The appeal of the Kaibab is no more accessible to analysis now than it was in 1880, but it is still there to be experienced.

John Wesley Powell found three Paiute bands inhabiting the Arizona Strip in 1870. In the west were the Shivwits, or "people of the springs"; the Uinkarets, or "people of the pine mountains," lived amid the volcanic domes of Mount Trumbull and Mount Logan; and the Unkakaniguts, or "people of the red lands," made their home at the base of the Vermillion Cliffs.[45] They hunted the Kaibab deer, organized rabbit drives on the wide bunchgrass plains, gathered pine nuts and grass seed on the higher portions of the Uinkaret and Shivwits plateaus, and did a little farming at the few surface springs and even in the depths of the Grand Canyon.[46] The Havasupais on the south side of the Grand Canyon and the Hopis, long established in their mesa-top villages to the southeast, seem not to have ventured north of the Colorado, and the Navajos, whose reservation today reaches the boundary of the Strip, are relative latecomers, having moved westward from the mountains of New Mexico in the mid-nineteenth century.

Powell was struck by the primitive condition of the Paiutes at the beginning of the 1870s, but he recorded their own sense of the good life on the Arizona Strip in his translation of the speech of a Shivwits headman:

We love our country; we know not other lands. We hear that other lands are better; we do not know. The pines sing and we are glad. Our children play in the warm sand; we hear them sing and are glad. The seeds ripen and we have to eat and we are glad. We do not want their good lands; we want our rocks and the great mountains where our fathers lived.[47]

Twenty years later, after the white man's sheep and cattle had displaced the Shivwits' game and destroyed the grass seed that formed a dietary staple, St. George stockmen offered to trade land along the Santa Clara River for their territorial claims on the Shivwits Plateau.[48] Most of the band evidently relocated at that time, though a few continued to cling to the rocks of their fathers until well into the twentieth century. The band Powell called the Unkakaniguts were given a reservation south of the Vermillion Cliffs and a share of the water of Moccasin Spring and came to be known as the Kaibabs. It is not clear what happened to the Uinkarets; most likely they merged with one or both of the other bands.

The Mormons entered the Arizona Strip rather tentatively from their southern Utah settlements. The vast area of grasslands made the Strip inviting ranching country, but water was in short supply. The only perennial stream is Kanab Creek, which runs in a deep canyon for much of its course. A few springs emerge from the base of the Vermillion Cliffs and the slopes of Mount Trumbull and Mount Logan and the Kaibab. But for hundreds of square miles the only available water is the rainfall held in natural tanks on the surface. Whoever controlled the waterholes controlled the range. That is why John D. Lee was anxious to secure a claim to Jacob's Pools and why, almost a decade earlier, William Maxwell established ranching operations at Short Creek and Moccasin and James M. Whitmore sought title to Pipe Spring.[49]

Whitmore and his brother-in-law Robert McIntyre were killed by Indians in January 1866, apparently while attempting to recover stolen cattle. This event and the general Indian unrest that characterized the years of the Black Hawk War inhibited further development of the Strip until 1870, when Brigham Young organized the Canaan Cooperative Stock Company. Under the management of Anson P. Winsor, this ranching operation, made up of church tithing cattle and some privately owned animals, was designed to control the range from bases at Canaan Spring, northwest of Short Creek, and Pipe Spring. To provide a safe refuge for herdsmen plus a fortified way station on the road between St. George and Kanab, Young directed Winsor to build the rock fort that became known as "Winsor Castle," now the centerpiece of Pipe Spring National Monument.

The cooperative ranching operation went through several reorganizations and name changes before it was taken over by the Orderville United Order in 1884. During the period of the "Raid" in the late 1880s, property held by church cooperatives was transferred to private individuals to avoid seizure by federal officials enforcing the antipolygamy laws. Even before this time, stockmen based in St. George and other Virgin River Valley towns had begun to move their herds into the western portion of the Arizona Strip. The region was all open range, and few ranchers troubled themselves with obtaining legal title to the land, merely asserting rights of prior use to the springs and pools. This informal approach changed with the arrival of Preston Nutter in 1893.

192

Nutter was a tall Virginian who had come west in 1863, at the age of thirteen. (He memorialized the year of his hegira by the "63" brand he used throughout his life for his horses and mules.) He worked for a time in the Nevada mines then moved to San Francisco, where he worked at the Cliff House and took courses at a business college. In 1873 he joined the rush to the new ore strikes in the San Juan Mountains of Colorado, and in passing through Provo fell in with a party of prospectors led by Alferd Packer. When the party reached Chief Ouray's winter camp on the Gunnison River, Nutter heeded the Ute chief's advice to stay out of the mountains until spring, thus escaping the fate of the five men who went on with Packer and eventually became provender for the notorious "man-eater."

Nutter, who had a good head for business, soon discovered that there was better money to be made in transporting ore and supplies than in prospecting. He invested his profits in cattle and by 1886 accumulated a large herd that he ran on the East Tavaputs Plateau, north of Thompson Springs. Nutter was to make the Tavaputs country his home base, eventually establishing a headquarters ranch in Nine Mile Canyon.[50] But the Arizona Strip also appealed to him for its relatively mild winters, and he was determined to develop a breeding operation there.

When he brought almost five thousand head of Arizona cattle across the Colorado at Scanlon's Ferry, he immediately ran into opposition from local ranchers, who refused to allow access to their water holes. An account coauthored by Nutter's daughter declares,

> Outsiders were not accepted, and the men who used the Strip backed up their claims with the theory that "might makes right." However, Nutter was not easily discouraged. He developed water holes of his own, and then took necessary steps to acquire legal titles on some of the land and springs, using preferred Indian scrip that he bought in Washington, D. C., at a premium price. This required a lot of time, effort, and money; and since he had no support from local St. George authorities, he was forced to hire Texas cowhands and deputize them to protect his cattle and springs.[51]

Not surprisingly, a local history takes a somewhat different view, quoting Strip rancher Reed Mathis:

> It was highway robbery the way Nutter got hold of those springs out on the Strip. He had push enough and foresight enough and was ruthless enough to get control of all that permanent water. He had Black Rock; he had

Wolfhole; he had Rock Canyon; he had Big Spring; he had Ivinpatch, New Spring, Whitmore, Hidden, Andrus Spring, Green, and Penn's Pockets. And he got everything by putting "script" on everything. That was the legal way to do it. . . . Foremaster had developed New Spring and Poverty Spring, digging it out of the ground. Then Nutter put "script" on it, with a "NO TRESPASSING" sign, warning everyone to stay off. Al Foremaster is said to have carried a gun for some time, hunting for Nutter. It was ruthless, taking what a man had developed like that.[52]

Nutter averted a range war by buying out several of his rivals, and the Nutter Livestock Company dominated the western portion of the Arizona Strip until Nutter's death in 1936. But he found the region to be "lawless, rugged country that continued to plague him to the end."[53]

In the eastern portion of the Strip, the highly desirable grazing drift between the Kaibab Plateau and the winter range of House Rock Valley was first exploited on a significant scale by the Orderville United Order, which ran two thousand head of cattle there in 1885 and 1886. The Order sold its interests to a pair of easterners named Thompson and Van Slack, who established the VT brand. The VT Ranch then passed through a series of Salt Lake City-based owners before being acquired by the Grand Canyon Cattle Company, which ran the Bar-Z brand. The range on the west side of the Kaibab and the Kanab Plateau was opened up by John C. Naegle of Toquerville and later grazed by the herds of several small ranchers based in the Kanab region.[54]

By the turn of the century, an estimated twenty thousand head of cattle and two hundred thousand sheep were grazing the eastern Strip with probably at least as many on the west, where in 1917 a quarter of a million sheep were sheared at Gould's pens.[55] These numbers far exceeded the permanent carrying capacity of the range and contributed to the desertification of what had been a prairielike landscape. But the destruction of the grasslands was a complicated matter, involving climatic cycles as well as overgrazing. Describing the view from Pipe Spring in 1880, Clarence E. Dutton wrote,

Ten years ago the desert spaces outspreading to the southward were covered with abundant grasses, affording rich pasturage to horses and cattle. Today hardly a blade of grass is to be found within ten miles of the spring, unless upon the crags and mesas of the Vermillion Cliffs behind it. The horses and cattle have disappeared, and the bones of many of the latter are bleached upon the plains in front of it. The cause of the failure of pasturage is twofold. There is little doubt that during the last ten or twelve

194

years the climate of the surrounding country has grown more arid. The occasional summer showers which kept the grasses alive seldom come now, and through the long summer and autumn droughts the grasses perished even to their roots before they had time to seed. All of them belong to varieties which reproduce from seed, and whose roots live but three or four years. Even if there had been no drought the feeding of cattle would have impoverished and perhaps wholly destroyed the grass by cropping it clean before the seeds were mature, as has been the case very generally throughout Utah and Nevada.[56]

Yet grazing continued to increase on the Arizona Strip for two decades after Dutton pronounced the death of the range. The area around Pipe Spring had probably been more heavily grazed than most portions of the Strip, but clearly there had to be considerable grass still available somewhere to encourage the tremendous growth in livestock numbers during the 1880s and 1890s. Rowland Rider, who worked for the Grand Canyon Cattle Company in the early years of the twentieth century, claims the grass was "stirrup high" in House Rock Valley when the cattle were brought down from the Kaibab in the fall of 1909.[57] The traveler who crosses the bare soil of the valley today on U.S. Highway 89A would find it difficult to imagine it as a sea of tall grass.

The Grand Canyon Cattle Company ran into conflict with James Emett, a big, rugged frontiersman who had taken over Lee's Ferry in 1895 and who ran cattle in the eastern portion of House Rock Valley. In 1906, the company filed a criminal complaint against Emett, charging him with cattle rustling. Among the spectators at the trial in Flagstaff in 1907 was a consumptive young man from Ohio who had been sent west by his family to regain his health or die. His name was Zane Grey, and he saw in Emett the very type of the virile Western hero. After Emett's acquittal, he invited the young man to accompany him to Lee's Ferry. Grey thought it "the strangest and most wonderful place in the world,"[58] and the novel that established his successful Western formula, *The Heritage of the Desert*, grew directly out of his experience with Jim Emett on the Arizona Strip.

The Arizona Strip provides a good example of the way in which multiple meanings can be inscribed upon a landscape as if by a succession of overlays. Mormon frontiersmen were community oriented. Even Jacob Hamblin, in all his travels, ventured out from and returned to established homes at Santa Clara and Kanab. The dominant Mormon mode of occupation was the village, not the isolated ranch, and ranchers usually maintained a "town place" where their families could spend the winter months with access to church, school, and community activities. When Emma Lee called the Paria delta a "lonely dell," she would have been responding less to the ruggedness and inhospitableness of the place than to its extreme isolation, several days' hard travel from the closest Mormon settlements at Johnson and Kanab. She was no stranger to hardship, having crossed the Plains with the ill-fated Martin handcart company and participated in the settling of the "ragged edge" villages of Harmony and Skutumpah. After leaving Lee's Ferry, she spent her remaining years in the rough frontier towns along the Little Colorado. But in all of these places, no matter how small or poor, there were neighbors, friends, social activities. Lee's Ferry was an outpost, not a community, and Emma must have always been lonely there.

In contrast to the Mormon preference for community life, Zane Grey's romantic Western myth valued the isolated ranch over the town, the rugged individual over society. Upon the barren text of Emma Lee's Lonely Dell, Grey superimposed an Edenic image. August Naab rescues the sickly greenhorn John Hare in the desert and brings him to a secret valley called the Garden of Eschtah:

> "We'll look over my farm," said August. . . . He led Hare through fields of alfalfa, in all stages of growth, explaining that it yielded six crops a year. Into one ten-acre plot pigs and cows had been turned to feed at will. Everywhere the ground was soggy; little streams of water trickled down ditches. Next to the fields was an orchard, where cherries were ripe, apricots already large, plum-trees shedding their blossoms, and apple-trees just opening into bloom. Naab explained that the products of his oasis were abnormal; the ground was exceedingly rich and could be kept always wet; the reflection of the sun from the walls robbed even winter of any rigor, and the spring, summer, and autumn were tropical. He pointed to grape-vines as large as a man's thigh and told of bunches of grapes four feet long; he showed sprouting plants on which watermelons and pumpkins would grow so large that one man could not lift them; he told of one pumpkin that held a record of taking two men to roll it.
>
> "I can raise any kind of fruit in such abundance that it can't be used. My garden is prodigal. But we get little benefit, except for our own use, for we cannot transport things across the desert."[59]

In the black-and-white universe of the popular Western, the competition for grazing lands and water on the Arizona Strip becomes a monumental struggle between good and evil. August Naab stands for the independence and integrity of the small rancher, fighting to maintain his rights against the sinister Holderness, who secretly employs the outlaw gang led by the violent Dene in his attempt to gain control of the entire range. In the context of this struggle, John Hare will recover his health in the bracing desert air, prove his manhood in single combat with Holderness, and gain his reward in the form of the beautiful, half-Navajo Mescal. The novel's landscape is drawn from the actual terrain of the eastern Strip. The village of White Sage is modeled on either Kanab or Fredonia. The Kaibab is called Coconina, and the mesa where John Hare regains his strength approximates the Paria Plateau. August Naab is modeled on Jim Emett, and John Hare is Grey's heroic projection of himself. Mescal, of course, is pure wish-fulfillment fantasy.

B. F. Saunders's Grand Canyon Cattle Company is presumably the model for the Holderness empire, but Grey's representation of the big outfit as an evil force that drives the small ranchers from their range was by no means shared by all of the local people. Rowland Rider, who claimed to have had a role in the negotiations that led to Saunders's purchase of Emett's ranch in 1909, characterized the company as a responsible operation and suggested that there were good grounds for the charge that Emett was rustling Bar-Z cattle.[60]

The gesture of resistance that led to the founding of Fredonia was repeated forty years later and thirty miles farther west. The isolation of the Arizona Strip had made it a refuge for those who refused to give up the practice of plural marriage after the Woodruff Manifesto of 1890, including a group of Warren Johnson's descendants at Lee's Ferry. Wallace Stegner reports that "Governor Hunt of Arizona went through the town once and somebody told him the farmers there were polygamists and ought to be prosecuted. The Governor took one look around and said, 'Hell, if I had to live in this place I'd want more than one wife myself.'"[61]

In the mid-1930s, Price and Elmer Johnson, Carling Spencer, Edner Allred, and Cleveland LeBaron moved their families from Lee's Ferry to the hamlet of Short Creek. They soon attracted other adherents of "the Principle" and of nineteenth-century communitarian ideals, including John Y. Barlow from Salt Lake City, who became the ideological leader of the group. The version of the United Order they established to control the property and share the wealth of the community had considerable appeal in the middle of the Great Depression, and despite the isolation and bad roads there was an influx of settlers to what was promoted as the "Millennial City." Unfortunately, there was not much wealth to share. Most of the water and agricultural land was controlled by an earlier settler who refused to join the movement, and most of the converts brought little with them except wives and children.

Nevertheless, the expansion of the shanty town alarmed officials down in Kingman, who feared Short Creek might grow big enough to tilt the balance of political power in Mohave County. Late in the summer of 1936, the sheriff and the county attorney made the long journey to the Strip, which before the completion of Hoover Dam required traveling southwest to Needles, California, then north to Las Vegas, northeast to St. George and Hurricane, then southeast on a rutted dirt road to the Arizona border. When they arrived at Short Creek, there ensued a series of charges, dismissals, flights from prosecution, and changes of venue before Price Johnson and Carling Spencer were sentenced to two years in the Arizona Penitentiary.

Writing a few years after these events, Wallace Stegner portrayed the 1936 raid as the beginning of the end for the Short Creek experiment.[62] But he underestimated the staying power of fundamentalist zeal. The community did not prosper, but it hung on through the 1940s, supported by funds from underground polygamous groups in Utah and California. The FBI conducted a raid in 1944, and by the early 1950s apprehensions were once again rising in Kingman. Though there were fewer than fifty male heads of families in Short Creek, the numerous women and children made it the second largest town in Mohave County. But because most of the property was held by a "charitable philanthropic trust" called the United Effort Plan, it produced almost no property-tax revenues. At the same time, the large families placed a disproportionate burden on state and county school and welfare funds.

Probably motivated as much by these fiscal considerations as by moral outrage at the marrying of young girls to older men, Arizona officials, prodded by Mohave County Superior Court Judge J. W. Faulkner, decided to make another attempt at destroying the community.[63] To fund the operation, Governor Howard Pyle pushed a secret appropriation through the legislature labeled as being for "grasshopper control." There was, however, one sticky problem. While Arizona law prohibited plural marriage, it did not stipulate a penalty. The attorney general finally got around this difficulty by charging the United Effort Plan and its members with being engaged in a conspiracy and in "a state of insurrection."

On Saturday, July 25, 1953, a strike force consisting of most of the Arizona State Highway Patrol plus thirty deputy sheriffs, twelve liquor-control officers, and a contingent of the Arizona National Guard assembled in Williams. In an effort to keep the operation secret, officials had informed the police officers that they would be attending a "traffic school." The efforts at secrecy did not, however, extend to concealing plans from the press, and a large group of reporters were included in the party. The caravan pulled out after dark, dividing into two units, one to travel by way of Marble Canyon Bridge and come at Short Creek from the east, the other to make the swing through Nevada and Utah and approach the village from the north.

Seldom has an operation been more overplanned for the task. When the invaders, bouncing along the rutted desert roads with their lights out, finally entered Short Creek in the predawn darkness, they found the residents, who had known about the impending raid for some time, assembled in front of the schoolhouse singing patriotic songs. Even though the Short Creekers were within a few yards of their homes, many of them stocked with bottled fruit and other supplies, the National Guard set up a field kitchen and fed the residents as though they were refugees. The men were arrested and hauled to Kingman for processing. After a few days, the women and children were taken to Phoenix—the children as wards of the state, the women because nobody knew what to do with them. The press gave the raid extravagant play, with newsreel and television clips and stories in several national magazines. *Time* labeled it "The Great Love-nest Raid," and *Life* ran a photo spread. Both *Colliers* and *True* published "as told to" stories by polygamous men.[64]

The disruption of the Short Creek community was dramatic but not permanent. Some women and children who had escaped the dragnet took refuge with other fundamentalist groups. Several men were put on trial, but when it came to the point the state was unable to bring very serious charges against them. Despite talk of permanently removing the children from an unwholesome environment, most of the families had more or less reassembled within a year. Perhaps in an effort to escape the publicity occasioned by the raid, or perhaps to project an identity more in keeping with their aspirations, the town elders changed the name from Short Creek to Colorado City, and the community continued its dogged growth.

Though it has now attained a population of several thousand, Colorado City is still a town without visible means of support. Despite a dramatic setting at the base of the Towers of Short Creek and on the most direct route from Interstate 15 to the North Rim of the Grand Canyon, the town resolutely turns its back on the tourist trade, with not so much as a single convenience store facing the highway. There is scarcely a commercial district, only a cooperative store and a few small businesses scattered among the residential lots, and the tiny industrial park on the Utah side of the state line could not provide jobs for more than a miniscule fraction of the town's labor force. The nearest significant source of employment is St. George, forty miles away, and the nearest major market, Las Vegas, is almost a hundred and fifty miles—a long commute even for the West.

At first glance, Colorado City looks like a newly opened desert subdivision, with scores of houses rising from the red sand. A closer inspection reveals that these "new" houses have plywood sheathing bleached and weathered by many years' exposure to sun and wind. As you drive along the dusty streets, it becomes apparent that nearly every house is in some state of incompletion, even in the upper part of town, where mature trees and shrubbery speak of long establishment. But though unfinished, the houses are not unoccupied. There are curtains in the windows, cars parked in the front yard, women in long drab dresses chatting at corners, children everywhere. The big yards, the absence of any apparent vestige of zoning, the general air of spaciousness and clutter are reminiscent of Utah farm villages, but the scale here is entirely different. Unlike the "hope houses" that were a common sight in Utah towns a generation back—occupied basements constructed in hope the family could someday afford to add the main floor—these are by no means modest dwellings. Massive pillared porticos stand in bold contrast to unfinished walls, as though a southern mansion under construction had been lifted from its foundation in a Dallas suburb and plumped down in this unlikely setting. Large two- and three-story houses boast even larger skeletal wings of unsheathed framing.

A sprawling school on the Arizona side of town and a smaller one on the Utah side (which is called Hildale) emphasize the fact that the community's major product, today as in earlier stages of its development, is children. A large building evidently serves as a combination churchhouse and offices for the United Effort Plan—for despite the town's general air of unregulated individualism, title to the land is still held by this trust, firmly controlled by the fundamentalist elders. A good share of the community's unwanted publicity in recent years has come from the efforts of disaffected residents to retain possession of their houses in the face of eviction notices from the Plan.

There have been other overlays of human dreams and aspirations on the wide landscape of the Arizona Strip. A brief and unproductive gold rush brought prospectors to the Colorado River sandbars in the 1870s, and there have been sporadic mining activities ever since. Also during the 1870s, the search for timber to build the St. George Temple led to the ponderosa-pine forests of Mount Trumbull. A steam-powered sawmill was established at Nixon Spring, and hundreds of wagon loads of lumber made the dusty sixty-mile trip to Utah. The more extensive Kaibab Forest was later in being exploited but now supplies the major industry of the Strip.

Unpromising as it appears for agriculture, the Strip was promoted for a time as having a suitable climate for dryfarming. Sharlot Hall, anxious to stimulate her fellow Arizonians' interest in the region, predicted in 1911 that "within another quarter of a century this unknown part of Arizona will rival the richest of the central valleys in population and products."[65] In 1916 Abraham Bundy, a Mormon convert from Nebraska who had been flooded out of Beaver Dam Wash in the 1890s and driven from Mexico by the revolution of 1910, rode over a ridge and viewed the expanse of tall grass on the Cactus Flats, west of the Hurricane Cliffs. With his Plains background, Bundy figured anyplace that grew grass would grow grain. The homestead laws had been amended to permit desert entries of 640 acres instead of the original 160 acres, so Bundy and several family members and friends staked out their square miles, erected lumber shacks, and set about placing their own overlay on the landscape.

The post office carried the name Mount Trumbull, but everyone called the settlement Bundyville. It was never a village, merely a one-room schoolhouse (for a time two of them, the "little school" and the "big school"), a store attached to Roy Bundy's house, and homesteads spread up and down the valley, but it achieved a population of almost two hundred during the 1920s. In good years, the farms yielded wheat and barley and even Mexican corn and beans, and the young men found employment as cowboys and sheepherders. The settlement never had a water supply except for what could be captured in earthen tanks or hauled in barrels from distant springs.[66] During the terrible "Winter of the Blue Snow" that began with a blizzard on Christmas Day, 1936, Bundyville was cut off from the rest of the world for almost three months, and cattle and sheep perished by the hundreds. One ranch woman kept her stock alive by baking bread and feeding it to the animals one slice at a time.[67] Writing in Colliers in 1952, Maurine Whipple declared,

The Bundys have the tenacity of the ant, the industry of the bee, the strength of the eagle. They are rooted not to pavement but to earth, and the fertility of earth flows in their veins. It is startling in these days of small families to meet a woman like Chloe, who has given birth to 14 children and at the age of sixty-three has 50 grandchildren and great-grandchildren; or her daughter Genevieve, who has borne 16 children, and still has all her teeth. Moreover, only eight of these 30 children were delivered by a doctor in a hospital. And the Bundy youngsters are all beautiful, healthy and intelligent, with not a deformity or subnormality in the lot.[68]

Despite their extreme isolation and the difficulty of wringing a living from the reluctant land, the last inhabitants of Bundyville held out until the late 1960s before abandoning their homes to the arid Strip wind.

In sharp contrast to the waterless plains of Bundyville is the oasis valley of Moccasin, whose history is also closely tied to a single family. The side road that leads from Highway 389 to Pipe Spring continues northward across a juniper-covered ridge to the dwellings and community hall of the Kaibab Paiutes. Then the landscape suddenly opens on another of those secret valleys that characterize the southern portion of the high plateaus region. The village of Moccasin nestles in a cove of the Vermillion Cliffs, its massive cottonwoods and spring-fed fields a vivid contrast to the red tones of the rocks. This delightful valley was once part of the far-flung holdings of the Orderville United Order. Upon the breakup of the Order, the land and most of the water of the springs (a portion was reserved for the Paiutes) fell into the hands of Jonathan Heaton, who kept one family there and another at Alton, in the upper valley of Kanab Creek. The village of Moccasin is still largely peopled by Heaton's descendants, who have quietly cultivated their small fields, run their livestock on the wide ranges of the Strip, and nurtured their family life through a century of change in the outside world.[69]

11

THE CAMPS

When I was growing up in Huntington, the only radio station we could get clearly during daylight hours was KEUB (the call letters were later changed to KOAL). The studios were located alongside the highway between Price and Helper, and the announcers with scrupulous impartiality gave the location as "Price-Helper" at one station call and "Helper-Price" at the next. On this station, we listened to the adventures of Tom Mix, Gabriel Heatter and the News, the baseball Game of the Day, and every afternoon the Request Hour. I can still hear, in my mind's ear, the announcer's nasal tones as he worked his way through names alien to my own Anglo-Saxon and Scandinavian heritage: "'Ave Maria,' requested by Rose Andreini for Mary Tallerico; also by Catherine Spigarelli for Teresa Fazzio." "'The Bluebird of Happiness,' requested by Helen Flemetakis for Sophie Protopappas." "'Happy Birthday,' requested for Angelo Douros by his mother; also for Louis Demczak by Mary Bezyack." And the names went on and on: Kaminsky, Karasevich, Karchich, Kochevar, Kokal, Konakis, Koncher, Kosec, Kourianos, Kraync, Kutkas; Madrigal, Magliocco, Mahleres, Majnik, Manzanares, Marakis, Marchello, Marinoni, Marvidikis, Mascaro, Matekovic, Mele, Migliore, Milano, Montoya, Moynier; Sacco, Saccomanno, Salazar, Sampinos, Sandoval, Sanfelice, Scartezina, Seppi, Silvagni, Skriner, Slavensky, Stamatakis, Svetich.

It was a long time before I learned to attach particular names to particular national origins. To my perceptions, they were all simply "foreign," calling to mind images of the dark-eyed women with scarves on their heads who crowded Price's Main Street on Saturdays after the mine paydays, or the old men in black suits who loitered in groups at the doors of coffeehouses on Carbon Avenue, conversing in an incomprehensible tongue over newspapers covered with indecipherable markings. Sometimes, on the other hand, I identified people by nationality alone. I never knew the name of the family that came down from Hiawatha each spring to gather dandelion greens on our farm. They were simply "the Greeks." We didn't begrudge them their harvest but found it hard to conceive of going to all that trouble to eat weeds.

Like most residents of the Mormon villages of Emery County, I had a kind of love-hate relationship with Price. We bought our school clothes at J. C. Penney and Price Trading and Boyacks, and our farm supplies at Price Commission. We drove Nash cars from Kraync Motors and Chevrolets from Redd's and Dodges from Bunnell's, and aspired to high-tailed Cadillacs from Standard Motors. As teenagers we often sought out the Saturday night action on Price's brightly lighted Main Street, gazed in fascination at the smartly dressed couples coming and going at the lounges and honkytonks, and drove slowly past reputed red-light hotels. But we resented the intrusions of Price boys on our own turf. Cautionary tales were told at family and church gatherings about the dangers of dating outside the faith, and many a high school dance at Huntington or Ferron was interrupted by the crowd streaming out of the gym to watch some local hero defend the honor of Emery County against a Carbon County invader.

These mixed reactions go back a long way. Ferron-bred Lowry Nelson recounts in his memoirs the experience of going to Price in 1912 to attend the newly opened Carbon High School, where he found the faculty well qualified and the townspeople supportive. Upon graduation, he took a summer job as night clerk at the new Savoy Hotel before going to Logan in the fall to attend Utah State Agricultural College. Working at the Savoy, Nelson became acquainted with "the other side of the Price community":

> Although there were only some fifteen or sixteen hundred people in Price, there was about one saloon for every hundred. These sixteen liquor places usually had a gambling room in the back, and sometimes rooms for the "girls" upstairs. It was a "wide-open" town with a large floating population of drunks and gamblers that occupied the place after dark and bore no relation to the sober, upright population that went about its activities during the day.[1]

The development of Carbon County as a multiethnic industrial society in a region otherwise dominated by agrarian Mormon villages was largely the result of historical accident. By the late 1870s, Castle Valley, a triangular expanse bounded by the Wasatch Plateau on the west, the Tavaputs Plateau on the north, and the San Rafael Swell on the southeast, was one of the largest and most eligible regions for settlement remaining in Utah. The first colonists on the Price River differed little from those elsewhere in Castle Valley. Emery County, divided off from Sanpete County in 1880, took in the entire valley until 1894, when Carbon County was carved out of its northern portion. The ecclesiastical ties lasted even longer, with Carbon County remaining a part of the LDS Emery Stake until 1910.

If the Rio Grande Western Railway had been completed along the originally intended Spanish Trail route, the history of Castle Valley—and indeed of much of southern Utah—might have been very different. Castle Dale would in all likelihood have become the dominant town in the region, rather than Price, which would probably have remained as it began, a Mormon farm village. The coal camps would have been established in the canyons of the Huntington, Cottonwood, Ferron, and Muddy creeks. But when the railroad chose the Soldier Summit route, the northern part of Castle Valley was destined to an industrial future while the southern part retained its original Mormon village culture, though influenced by the nearness of the mines. Cleveland, for example, was settled by people from Scofield and sustained by income from the mines until the long canal could be completed and the land brought into production. Even then many families continued to divide their time between the camps and the farm villages, or the men would go to the mines in the winter while the women and children remained on the farm to care for the stock. With the coming of automobiles and improved roads, scores of men from the Emery County towns commuted daily to the mines. Nevertheless, the towns themselves remained essentially farm villages with a homogeneous Mormon population.

The road from Zion to Babylon led across the blue hills of the Washboard Flat. We caught our first sight of the Price River Valley from the crest of Four Mile Hill, with the town nestled up against the benchlands beyond the creek. We drove up Carbon Avenue past the decayed railroad hotels, the Greek coffeehouses, and the tavern popularly known as the Bucket of Blood. At the end of the street, the white pillars of Carbon High School appeared to be holding up a big water tank (actually situated on a shelf of the hill behind the building). Above the tank, a large block C had been painted in blue and white on the cliff face. Price had the rectangular grid and wide streets of its Mormon origins, but its hybrid character was apparent not only in the business district but in the four major religious structures: the Catholic parish church of Notre Dame de Lourdes on North Carbon Avenue, its name reflecting the prominence of French Basque families such as the Dusserres, Moyniers, and Jeanselmes; the white brick Carbon LDS Stake Tabernacle and the Community Methodist Church a block apart on East

Main Street; and the Byzantine dome of the Hellenic Orthodox Church of the Assumption at Second East and First South, reputedly the oldest continuously occupied Greek church in the United States.

If we were making our once- or twice-a-year trip to Salt Lake City, the route led west on Main Street and through a narrow underpass, then turned north and ran alongside the railroad tracks, past the low white building that housed the KEUB studios (you could sometimes hear the rumble of passing trains on the radio) and on to the narrows called the Blue Cut, where a mossy concrete dam diverted the water of the river into the irrigation canal. Beyond the Blue Cut, the river valley opened up again to form the cove where Spring Glen was located, then narrowed toward the mouth of Price Canyon. Here, at the base of Steamboat Mountain, filling the narrow river valley and climbing up the benches on both sides, lay the railroad town of Helper, the true heart of the coal country. Radiating out from Helper like the spokes of a wheel, up Price Canyon and Spring Canyon and extending west and south and east along the base of the Wasatch Plateau and the Book Cliffs, were the coal camps whose names were recited over the radio station each day in the litany of the "Mine Report":

> This is the Mine Report. Mines working tomorrow, Thursday, include Castle Gate, Rains, Royal, Latuda, Hiawatha, Consumers, Sweets, Sunnyside, Columbia, and the Geneva Mine at Horse Canyon. Kenilworth, Spring Canyon, Peerless, Standard, and Wattis will be idle.

The term *camp*, though often used by residents and non-residents alike, was negatively charged, suggesting something *ad hoc* and transitory, less than a town or even a village. And indeed, some of the coal camps consisted of merely a few grimy houses huddled around the tipple. But others were well planned and solidly constructed, with a reasonable share of civic amenities, including parks, baseball diamonds, churches, and amusement halls. The larger camps, Castle Gate, Hiawatha, and Sunnyside, were substantial towns, with peak populations of more than a thousand. Kenilworth and Columbia, somewhat smaller, were attractive communities with tree-lined streets and well-maintained homes. Storrs, later renamed Spring Canyon, had houses built of stone that gave it an illusory air of permanence. Yet because the camps depended for their existence on a finite block of coal reserves, they were all temporary. What A. Philip Cederlof, once general manager of the Peerless Coal Company, said about coal mines can also be applied to the camps. Each of them "has not only a story but also a distinct personality. It is discovered, is born, lives, and dies."[2]

206

Though their history is relatively brief, the geologic foundations of the coal camps go back more than a hundred million years to the Cretaceous period, when an ocean covered all of eastern Utah and sediments washed down from the highlands to the west settled in thick marine deposits on the seabed. The thickest of all was the blue-gray Mancos shale that now covers the valley floors and forms the lower slopes of the Wasatch Plateau. On top of this soft siltstone was deposited the cliff-forming Star Point sandstone. As the sea shifted eastward, lowland swamps and forests developed on the delta plains, with sequoia, palm, fig, cypress, and magnolia trees rising above a dense mat of ferns and mosses. The accumulating deposits of organic matter were intermittently buried by new layers of sediment as the shoreline rose and fell. Thus was created the 1200-foot thick Blackhawk formation, which is the chief source of coal in eastern Utah. Sometimes a dinosaur would wander across a peat bed, leaving imprints of its three-toed feet to be filled with sand and thereby preserved to stimulate wonder in the miners who discovered the huge tracks overhead when they removed the coal.[3]

Near the end of the Cretaceous period, the seas withdrew as the entire western portion of North America began to rise in an uplift that continued into the Tertiary period. The great mountain-building episode known as the Laramide Orogeny thrust up the Uinta Mountains, the San Rafael Swell, and the Circle Cliffs uplift. What is now the Wasatch Plateau was covered by the waters of Lake Flagstaff, filling a depression between highlands to the east and west. Streams flowing into the lake deposited the rounded riverbed stones that seem so strangely out of place on the high flat surface of North Horn Mountain, while the shells and skeletons of lake animals settled to the bottom to form the hard white Flagstaff limestone that now caps the Wasatch Plateau.[4]

The final uplifting of the High Plateaus and the relative subsiding of the Great Basin did not occur until late Tertiary and early Quaternary times, perhaps five million years ago, after the great lakes that covered much of eastern Utah had drained away through the ancestor of the Colorado River. The upwarp bent the formations on the west side of the Wasatch Plateau into an immense monocline, but the thick marine and lacustrine deposits retained their horizontal position throughout most of the plateau, though displaced up and down by numerous faults that were later to complicate the mining of coal. Erosion created the distinctive eastern escarpment of layered vertical cliffs and steep shale slopes, with pediment foothills.[5] Prominent among the cliffs is the white-tinged Star

Winter Quarters, 1900. G. E. Anderson photo, courtesy Utah State Historical Society.

Point sandstone, and coal developers learned early that the best coal seams were likely to be located just above the Star Point formation, in the lower levels of the Blackhawk.

From the earliest years of Anglo-European settlement in Utah, a concern about exhausting scarce timber resources for fuel spurred the search for coal. In 1850, coal and iron ore were discovered near Cedar City and were used in an unsuccessful attempt to make iron, but these deposits were too remote to supply fuel to the Wasatch Front. In 1854, a Ute named Tabby appeared at a Mormon church conference in Ephraim and presented Brigham Young with a lump of coal. At Brigham's insistence, Tabby led John Rees and John Price, immigrants from the coalfields of South Wales, to a canyon in the Gunnison Plateau that forms the western boundary of Sanpete Valley. These deposits were mined for several decades, but the coal seams were thin and mixed with a good deal of rock (or "boney" as the miners call it). In 1858 coal was discovered in Chalk Creek Canyon, only fifty miles east of Salt Lake City, and for some years this district near the town of Coalville provided much of the city's fuel supply.

With the coming of the railroad in the 1860s, the Union Pacific developed the coal deposits at Rock Springs, Wyoming, to fuel its locomotives and began to ship to the Utah market. The UP, however, took advantage of its monopoly position to charge outrageous prices, so there was still plenty of incentive to search for other supplies. The first coal mine on the Wasatch Plateau was opened by a group of Fairview men in 1874 at Connellsville, in the upper reaches of Huntington Canyon, but the difficulty of transportation over the skyline ridge and down the steep canyons to Sanpete Valley limited the possibilities of development.

Pleasant Valley, just over Trough Springs Ridge from Huntington Canyon but at a lower elevation, offered easier accessibility to the growing population of the Wasatch Front. In 1875 the newly organized Pleasant Valley Coal Company sent John Nelson and Abram Taylor into the area to secure the company's claims. The two men spent the winter holed up in what was then called Grizzly Gulch, and one story has it that the canyon was named Winter Quarters to commemorate this event. In the spring of 1877, a party of miners under the direction of Peter Moran opened the Winter Quarters mine. They had intended to work into the fall and then withdraw to the lower valleys, but an early snow trapped them in the mountains. Finally, in February, their supplies exhausted, the party made their way through the snow to Utah Valley.[6] It is possible that this episode, rather than the earlier vigil of Nelson and Taylor, was the source of the Winter Quarters name.

To get the coal to market, the Pleasant Valley Coal Company, whose chief investor was a Springville merchant named Milan Packard, undertook the construction of the narrow-gauge Utah and Pleasant Valley Railroad. The project was carried out with limited capital, and the construction workers were paid in part with merchandise from Packard's store, including fabric—hence the popular name of the Calico Road.[7] From a connection with the Utah Southern at Springville, the Calico Road went up Spanish Fork and Soldier Creek canyons to a sawmill settlement called Clear Creek, later renamed Tucker, situated at the confluence of the three main branches of Soldier Creek. The railroad then ascended the South Fork, crossed a high ridge, and followed a curving path down the sagebrush slopes into Pleasant Valley. Because of the steepness of the grade, trains on the Calico were limited to twelve small cars, and the schedule was erratic. The miners learned to expect the train at any hour of the day or night and were often rousted out of bed to load the cars.

Before the completion of the Calico Road in 1878, Packard and his associates sold out to a syndicate under the direction of C. U. Scofield. The Scofield group in turn sold the railroad and the mining company to William Jackson Palmer's Rio Grande Western Railway in 1881. It was said of Palmer that "if a farmer had a wagon load of pumpkins on the other side of the mountain . . . Palmer . . . at once would throw a pair of narrow gauge rails in that direction to pick up the cargo."[8] Because the Union Pacific controlled the east-west through traffic, the Rio Grande had to generate its income along its own lines, and it had already laced the Colorado Rockies with spurs to the mining camps there. Among the attractions of the Soldier Summit route over the earlier-contemplated Salina Canyon route were the already existing rails from Springville to Tucker and the proximity to the Pleasant Valley coalfield. The Western as finally completed connected with the parent Denver and Rio Grande at the Colorado state line, followed a route along the base of the Book Cliffs to Gunnison's Crossing on the Green River, skirted the northern edge of the San Rafael Swell, ascended the Price River Canyon to Soldier Summit, and descended the East Fork of Soldier Creek to the connection with the Calico line at Tucker. From the Calico terminus at Springville, the Western extended its rails to Salt Lake City and Ogden. Because the Union Pacific refused to allow the Rio Grande Western to share its connection with the Central Pacific at Ogden, the final segment of rails was laid secretly at night, in order to present the UP with a *fait accompli*.

In 1884, the Western built a new spur into Pleasant Valley by way of Fish Creek Canyon, and the excessively steep route up the South Fork of Soldier Creek was abandoned. Though Soldier Summit was a lower pass than the South Fork route, the seven-mile ascent from Tucker to the summit still had an average grade of four percent, requiring extra engines to be attached to trains at Tucker for the hard pull to the top. By the turn of the century, engine sheds, switching tracks, water towers, boardinghouses, and shops crowded the narrow canyon floor, and the town had a population of about five hundred.

The location that made Tucker a vital point on the railway eventually doomed the town. In 1913, the Rio Grande undertook a major construction project to reduce the Soldier Summit grade from four percent to two percent.[9] This required beginning the ascent three miles below Tucker and proceeding up the mountainside by a long switchback. With the completion of this new route, the railroad operations were moved fifteen miles down the canyon to Thistle; Tucker, now two hundred feet below the tracks, was abandoned. My first memories of Tucker date to

210

Patriotic assembly, Scofield school, about 1900. G. E. Anderson photo, courtesy Brigham Young University photo archives.

the mid-1940s, when the place consisted of a single roadside store and filling station, with a few seldom-occupied tourist cabins under trees still grimy from coal smoke. Now almost all traces of the town have been obliterated, and the site is a pleasant rest stop alongside U.S. Highway 6, with a grassy plot under the narrowleaf cottonwoods and a footbridge leading across Clear Creek from the parking lot to the restrooms.

The town of Scofield is situated on high ground two miles south of the reservoir of the same name, the oldest and largest of the major impoundments on the Wasatch Plateau. Once the most populous community in Carbon County, Scofield had shrunk to only a few dozen residents when I first visited it around 1950. What then seemed to be a drift toward abandonment was slowed in the following years by outsiders who began buying the old houses as summer vacation homes. Now with new mines developed in the canyons to the south, Scofield has a small core of year-round residents, but it retains the atmosphere of a ghost town. The old brick school stands empty at the upper end of town, and there are abandoned buildings scattered through what was once the business district. Only the cemetery on a hill to the east suggests that this was once a community of some size. And visitors to the cemetery quickly be-

Caskets at Wasatch Store, Winter Quarters, May 1900. G. E. Anderson photo, courtesy Utah State Historical Society.

come aware of something peculiar, row upon row of gravestones that all record a single death date: May 1, 1900.

Unlike the rather barren landscape surrounding Scofield Reservoir, the southern portion of Pleasant Valley is indeed pleasant, with water meadows along Mud Creek and spruce-fir groves on the north-facing slopes. On the outskirts of Scofield, cattle graze in a pasture at the mouth of Winter Quarters Canyon, and a ranch house sits peacefully in a landscape that seems perfectly bucolic, except that it is possible to trace the line of an abandoned railroad grade curving across the pasture. The road into the canyon is a mere dirt track resembling scores of similar tracks on the Wasatch Plateau, used by stockmen in the summer and deer hunters in the fall. Beaver dams form a series of pools and waterfalls along the creek, and if you walk up the road in June, as I did, the sound of falling water mingles with the bright mountain sunlight and the fir-scented air to create a feeling of peace and pleasant solitude. Then, as you clear a rise, you suddenly catch sight of two tall stone walls against the forest background, an anomalous but emphatic intrusion on the unpeopled landscape.

These are the ruins of the Wasatch Store, the company store of the Pleasant Valley Coal Company. As you draw closer you come upon scat-

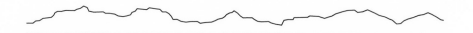

tered foundation stones, then a strip of concrete sidewalk and the foundation of what must have been a church or a boardinghouse, then the remains of the school, a concrete floor slab with front steps still in place, the upper structure entirely vanished except for a few scattered bricks. Farther up the canyon, thick concrete piers mark the location of the tipple and mine tram. These scattered traces are all that remain of the first major coal camp on the Wasatch Plateau.

Most of the first miners at Winter Quarters were Mormon converts from the coal districts of Wales, England, and Scotland. One of them, David Williams, leased the Winter Quarters Mine from the Pleasant Valley Coal Company from 1880 to 1885, operating it in the dual capacity of mine manager and bishop of the local LDS ward. When the Rio Grande Western acquired the coal company, they undertook the development of a new mine on Mud Creek, a mile from Winter Quarters, much to the chagrin of Williams, who protested that the new mine infringed on his lease. Because Bishop Williams controlled the Mormon miners, the Pleasant Valley Coal Company brought in Chinese laborers to work the Mud Creek mine.

The Chinese made excellent miners. Later observers remarked on the beautiful workmanship of the mine's arched entryway, constructed entirely by pick work, but so fine that it appeared to have been chiseled into the rock.[10] But the 1880s were a period of strong nativist opposition to Chinese labor, culminating in the Rock Springs riots of 1885. The Pleasant Valley expression of this resentment came when the nativist Winter Quarters miners (most of whom were in fact immigrants from the British Isles) herded the Chinese into a box car, bolted the door, and sent the car freewheeling down the tracks. Fortunately, the car did not leave the rails, but it must have been a terrifying ride through Pleasant Valley and down the narrow Fish Creek pass, until a slight upgrade near the junction with the main line at Colton brought the car to a halt. Apparently no one was injured. Local traditions give no indication of who released the Chinese from the car or where they went, but they did not return to Pleasant Valley.[11]

The second group of non-English-speaking immigrants to find their way to the Pleasant Valley mines were the Finns. Rural poverty and government oppression in Russian-ruled Finland had led thousands of its people to emigrate to America, most of them settling in the upper Midwest. Some, however, drifted west to the Wyoming coal mines.

213

From Wyoming they came to Pleasant Valley, where they found employment at Winter Quarters and at the new camp at Clear Creek being developed six miles to the south by the Utah Fuel Company, another Rio Grande subsidiary. The long mountain winters were probably nothing new for the Finns, and perhaps the white-barked aspen groves reminded them of their native birch forests. Unlike the Italians and Greeks and South Slavs who came later, the Finns tended to remain in the isolated mountain camps, where they built "Finn Halls" and saunas and carried on their own culture largely apart from the other miners.

Underground mining has always been a hard and dangerous labor, and it was especially so under the conditions that prevailed in the nineteenth century. Workers were attracted to the mines despite their dangers because it was possible to earn higher wages there than at most other forms of manual labor. It seems clear that many of the early Utah miners saw mine employment as a temporary condition, a chance to build a financial stake in order to acquire land or otherwise establish themselves. Some succeeded in making this transition. Others were partly successful, in that they acquired farms and homes away from the coal camps but continued to work in the mines during the winters in order to supplement their farm income.

This widespread view of the coal camps as only a temporary home, added to the laissez faire attitudes of management, made for harsh working and living conditions. At an elevation of eight thousand feet, Pleasant Valley enjoys sunny days and cool nights during the summer, but winters are long and dreary, with deep snow that makes all movement difficult. Photographs of Winter Quarters at the turn of the century show large families living in two- or three-room wooden shacks, where cabin fever must have been endemic. Scofield, a mile to the east, had some civic amenities, including lodge halls and other buildings that could be used for the musical activities so loved by the Welsh, but the homes were no less cramped.

While there were independent merchants in Scofield, most of the Winter Quarters miners' trade was with the company-owned Wasatch Store. The company store was a profitable operation for the coal company, and in some camps miners were required to shop there as a condition of employment, or were paid part of their wages in scrip good only at the company store. Even without such coercive measures, however, the company store got most of the camp trade by allowing miners and their families to charge purchases against current wages. At the end of the month, the store bill was deducted from the miner's pay and only the remainder actually paid out in cash.

Ostensibly, miners were not employees of the company but independent contractors. They owned their own tools, provided their own blasting powder and lamp oil, and were paid on the basis of the tonnage of coal mined. Such necessary "dead work" as timbering the rooms and clearing haulageways was uncompensated. In reality, the miners were in a kind of bondage to the company. They were at the mercy of bosses in the assignment of working areas, which could make the difference between a good income and starvation wages. They also depended on the bosses and mule drivers to supply the cars that carried the coal from the mine, and on the company weighmaster to give them honest credit for their coal at the tipple. Many companies operated on a dual weight system, in which the customer's ton was the normal two thousand pounds but the miner's ton was several hundred pounds heavier, supposedly to compensate for "boney." Even when this factor was taken into account, however, miners often felt that they were "short-weighted" at the tipple. One of the first demands they made when they began organizing was for the right to hire a "checkweighman" at their own expense to keep an eye on the company weighmaster.[12]

At Winter Quarters, as in most coal mines during the nineteenth century, it was common to have boys as young as age ten working underground as furnace tenders, doorkeepers, or general "gofers" for the older miners. A single family might have several members working in the mine, the father and older sons as full-fledged miners, the younger sons in these attendant jobs until they were strong enough for pick-and-shovel work.

The first miners in the Utah coalfields brought with them the techniques they were accustomed to in British mines. Working usually in two-man teams, they performed every operation necessary to extract the coal.[13] The most strenuous and painful labor was the pickwork required for undercutting. In order to prevent the explosive charges from pulverizing the coal or fracturing the roof of the mine, it was necessary to provide a space at the bottom of the coal seam to receive the force of the blast. Lying in a prone position, often in mud and water, the miner would pick out an opening about a foot high and as deep as he could dig. This work placed tremendous strain on the arm muscles, for there was no way to put the strength of the shoulders or back into the pick strokes.

After the coal was undercut, the next operation was drilling. This, too, was done with hand tools, normally a breast auger with a long hardened steel bit that would drill a hole an inch or so in diameter and several feet deep. Blasting powder was then inserted into this hole. A. C. Watts, who had spent most of his life in the Utah coalfields, wrote in

1948 that miners in the early days would purchase black powder in kegs and carry it to their working area in the mine. They would punch a hole in the end of the powder keg with the point of a pick and pour powder into cartridges made from old newspapers. All the while, Watts recalled, they would be working by the light of oil lamps attached to their caps and often with lighted pipes in their mouths, even though the slightest spark could ignite the powder.[14]

Two or three pounds of black powder normally constituted a charge. After filling their cartridges, the miners would plug the hole in the powder keg with a wad of paper, push the explosive cartridges into the drill holes, then pack the holes with a mixture of mud and coal dust around a thin copper tube. When the tube was withdrawn, it left a narrow tunnel leading to the powder charge. The miners would then light a "squib"—similar to a bottle rocket—that would shoot through this tunnel and ignite the blasting powder. Black powder was a dangerous explosive to use in a mine. It could not only be ignited by a spark from the lamp or by concussion, but it also produced a lot of flame. If a "shot" were too big, or if the plug blew out of the drill hole, the danger of a dust or gas explosion or a coal fire was very real.

A well-placed and properly detonated charge would blow the coal downward and shatter it into workable sizes. Because large lumps were more valuable than smaller pieces, the goal was to break the coal up but not pulverize it. After the dust had settled, the miners would return to the working face and load the coal onto mule cars. In order to get as much coal on a car as possible, they would first load the biggest lumps (using a sledgehammer to break up lumps too heavy for two men to heft), then fill in the spaces around the lumps with smaller coal. When they reached the top of the car sides, they continued to load, carefully building a structure of lumps several feet above the sides of the car. A skilled miner who was on good terms with the bosses and the mule drivers could load in a day a good deal more than the "sixteen tons" of the old Tennessee Ernie Ford song.

In order to make good wages, however, and stay in the bosses' favor, miners had to work long shifts, typically twelve hours or more. Moreover, they labored in cramped conditions, in total darkness except for the poor light given by the oil lamps on their caps, and in a polluted atmosphere of dust and smoke. Before the advent of electric ventilating fans, the usual means of bringing fresh air into a mine was the "stack and furnace" method. An exhaust tunnel would be dug to an outlet on the mountainside higher than the mine portals. A fire was kept burning at the bottom of this "chimney," and as the heated air was exhausted fresh air was drawn in through the portal. Air flow was further regulated by doors inside the mine that could close off unused side tunnels and direct the air to where the miners were working. The rate of air exchange by this method was not high enough, however, to keep the mines clear of smoke—or of explosive or poisonous gasses. In some mines, methane gas could seep from the coal and accumulate in explosive concentrations in the poorly ventilated tunnels, ready to be ignited by the open flame of the miners' lamps. Or "black damp"—compounded of carbon monoxide and other poisonous gases—could come upon them without warning. It was a common practice to bring caged canaries into gassy mines, since they were affected by poison gas more rapidly than humans.

Thus the miners worked under threat of numerous hazards. The roof of the mine might collapse on them, either in a random rockfall that might crush only two or three miners, or in a "bounce" that could trap entire crews. Some Pleasant Valley mines were in coal seams as thick as thirty feet, compared to the seams of four feet or less that many European miners were accustomed to. But such thick seams were a mixed blessing. While they enabled the miners to work in more spacious conditions and usually allowed for greater productivity, the high roofs were much more difficult to timber safely, and even a small rock falling that distance could kill or seriously injure a miner. If a miner escaped all of these dangers, there was still the slow deteriorating effect of dust and bad air on his lungs. Even at the mid-twentieth century, it was unusual for a coal miner to reach the age of fifty without being disabled by mine injuries or "black lung."

From the standpoint of current expectations about safety, working conditions, and compensation, the conditions of coal miners at the turn of the century seem incredibly bad. But laborers in other fields were also subjected to harsh conditions, and coal miners, then as now, were among the highest paid of industrial workers. The miners at Winter Quarters probably did not regard themselves as having an intolerably bad way of life. While employment and pay rates fluctuated with the market, the demand for coal had been steady enough between 1885 and 1900 to justify the opening of several additional mines in the Pleasant Valley district. By 1900 there were four mines at Winter Quarters, and the haulage tunnels were fairly extensive.

May 1, 1900, had been designated as Dewey Day in honor of the hero of the Battle of Manila the previous year. A dance was scheduled at the

Odd Fellows' Hall in Scofield in the evening, and there must have been at least something of a holiday mood among the men and boys as they trekked toward the mine that morning. A few weeks earlier there had been an explosion in the Castle Gate mine when the blasting powder ignited methane, which in turn ignited the coal dust. No one had been injured in this explosion because a different procedure was employed for blasting. Because Castle Gate was a gassy mine, individual miners were not allowed to do their own blasting. Instead, they drilled their shot holes and prepared their charges with electrical fuses at the end of the shift. Then after all the miners had left the mine, the charges were detonated from a single switch by a "fire boss." The older, individualized system was still in use at Winter Quarters because the coal seam there was free from methane, and conventional wisdom of the period held that coal dust by itself was not explosive.

A few minutes after ten o'clock, a loud detonation rumbled through Pleasant Valley. Several Scofield residents later recalled that they had first thought someone was celebrating Dewey Day by setting off explosives.[15] But the camp grapevine quickly spread the dread news of "something wrong at the mine," sending women running up Winter Quarters Canyon to where smoke and dust were pouring from the portal of Number Four.

The state mine inspector later concluded that either there had been a "bad shot" (which could occur when too heavy a charge of powder was placed in the drill hole or when the hole was inadequately packed, allowing flame to shoot out rather than directing the force of the explosion into the coal) or powder stored in the mine had accidentally been ignited. The initial explosion of black powder had ignited the coal dust in the poorly ventilated tunnel. The superheated wind produced by this combustion had roared through the mine, fueling itself as it went by stirring up and simultaneously consuming more coal dust, and finally issuing from the portal with enough force to blow John Wilson more than eight hundred feet across the canyon. Wilson was critically injured but recovered. James Naylor, who was also working near the portal, was blown two hundred feet without serious injury and was able to take part in the first rescue attempts.

With these two exceptions, the miners working in Number Four were killed almost instantaneously by the force and extreme heat of the explosion. More than two hundred miners were working in Number One, which was connected with Number Four. Many of these men escaped, but more than a hundred died because they either delayed their flight or attempted to leave the mine through the Number Four entry rather than take the longer route to Number One portal. They thus ran

Removing bodies from the mines, Winter Quarters, May 1900. G. E. Anderson photo, courtesy Utah State Historical Society.

directly into the afterdamp, the carbon monoxide that filled the tunnels after the explosion. Some miners were overcome so quickly by the afterdamp that they were discovered in the posture of lighting a pipe or eating a sandwich. Fifteen-year-old Thomas Pugh, who was working alongside his father in Number One, immediately covered his nostrils when he felt the explosion and put his hat between his teeth in an attempt to filter the air. He ran the mile and a half to the portal in total darkness and fell unconscious just outside the mine. His father did not escape.

T. J. Parmley, who was both superintendent of the mine and bishop of the local LDS ward, led the first rescue party into the mine within minutes of the explosion. However, the afterdamp was still so strong that two members of the party lost consciousness and had to be carried from the mine. In addition to the gas, the mine was now filled with the stench of burned flesh. The explosion had also caused rockfalls that blocked off portions of the mine and made other areas unsafe. Nevertheless, the surviving miners, who were neighbors and friends of the victims, labored desperately in the tunnels until they were finally ordered out of the mine at two o'clock the next morning, after sixteen hours of exhausting struggle.

Early on May 2, crews began arriving from Clear Creek, Castle Gate, and Sunnyside, and organized recovery work went on in shifts

Luoma residence, Winter Quarters, May 1900. G. E. Anderson photo, courtesy Utah State Historical Society.

until May 6. The official death toll announced by company and state officials was two hundred, including twenty young boys, but unofficial accounts suggested that the dead were far more numerous. The miners who had counted the bodies as they were brought from the mine in coal cars had reported a total of 246 dead, and stories persisted in Pleasant Valley for many years that there were still unrecovered bodies deep inside Number Four.

It is difficult to imagine how there could be such uncertainty, but at the time of the Winter Quarters explosion there was no way of keeping track of which miners were inside the mine. Partly as a result of this disaster, a system of miner checks was instituted. A board in the mine office had a hook for each miner and a brass tag with an identifying number stamped on it. On his way into the mine, each man was required to remove his tag from the board and carry it with him. At the end of his shift, he would replace the tag on the board. This meant that the timekeeper could tell which men were inside the mine merely by glancing at the board, and in case of mutilating accidents the tags enabled miners' bodies to be identified.

Because no such system was employed at Winter Quarters in 1900, no one knew exactly how many men were inside the mine at the time of the explosion. Officials had to depend on reports from family members and on the difficult process of identifying bodies as they were brought from the mine. With some of the badly burned or mutilated bodies, identification was little more than guesswork. While many of the miners were family men, others were unattached and had no one to report them as missing.

Almost a third of those killed at Winter Quarters were Finns. As was common among industrial immigrants, many of them were single men who were either sending money back to their families in Finland or were hoping to save enough themselves to return and buy land. But some entire families had emigrated. For example, seven Louma brothers had made their way to the Pleasant Valley coalfields. Just a few months before the Winter Quarters disaster, the brothers had sent to Finland for their aged parents. One of the photographs taken in the aftermath of the disaster shows the old couple sitting in front of a small frame house in Winter Quarters, flanked by their one surviving son and his wife. The other six sons and three grandsons all died in the explosion.

The Finns maintained that several of their countrymen had not been recovered from the mine or listed in the official body count. On the other hand, the English and Welsh miners complained that the Finns, with one exception, had refused to participate in the recovery work. Some attributed this to their "superstitions," but others expressed open resentment at what they viewed as an unwillingness to assume their share of the burden. Perhaps as a result of this general wave of resentment, rumors spread that Finnish miners had been the cause of the explosion. Allegedly they had stored excessively large supplies of powder in their working areas and had overcharged their drill holes in hopes of loosening more coal and thereby increasing their income.

Whatever the truth or falsity of these accusations, the animosity toward the Finns in the weeks and months that followed was a black spot on an otherwise heroic story of sacrifice and compassion. The scale of the disaster brought immediate national and international attention and stimulated many charitable acts. The millers of Salt Lake and Ogden shipped carloads of flour to the bereaved community. Florists sent their entire stock of cut flowers for the mass funerals. A large crew came from Provo to assist in digging almost a hundred and fifty graves in the Scofield cemetery (the remaining victims were buried elsewhere). Bishop Lawrence Scanlon of the Salt Lake Catholic diocese offered to accommodate orphaned children in the church's St. Anne's orphanage. A total of more than two hundred thousand dollars was contributed by communities from Utah and throughout the nation for the relief of the widows and orphans—a sum that represented considerably more than a year's wages for each of the dead miners.

The response of the Pleasant Valley Coal Company was also regarded as generous by the prevailing standards of that laissez-faire era. The company supplied burial clothes and coffins for all of the dead and donated five hundred dollars to each family that had lost one or more of its members. In addition, it canceled the debts at the company store, which amounted to some eight thousand dollars, thereby enabling the families to draw the entire amount of the miners' earnings for the month of April without deductions. This immediate relief was all most families were to receive, however, since there was no such thing as industrial insurance at that period and few of the miners would have carried life insurance. Still, the survivors received much more than they would have done if the men had been killed in separate accidents. (More than twenty years later, the widow of a man killed in the Rolapp mine was visited a few hours after her husband's death by the company superintendent, who presented her with fifty dollars as a "gift" and told her to be out of the company house within a week.)

On May 28, just four weeks after the disaster in Number Four, coal mining resumed at Winter Quarters. While some of those who had escaped the explosion left the area for other work, many others returned to the mines. The dead were soon replaced, though production evidently suffered somewhat from the loss of the more experienced miners. Some changes in procedure were made, including the check system and a state-enforced practice of spraying the mine with water to keep the coal dust down. Within a few years, black powder had been replaced by flameless powder or dynamite as the blasting medium, and electric fans replaced the old stack-and-furnace ventilating system. Despite declining profitability, the Winter Quarters mines continued to operate until the 1930s. The tipple and other large structures were dismantled for their salvage value during the early years of the Second World War; the school, the LDS chapel, and the boardinghouse were leveled; and the houses were torn down or moved away. Now only two stone walls of the Wasatch Store remain standing on the site, and the fir-scented breeze sweeps down Winter Quarters Canyon as naturally as if the human drama of life and death had never been enacted there.

Scofield, sustained by several mines in Pleasant Valley, was still the largest town in Carbon County in 1915, when its citizens made an attempt to have the county seat moved to their community from Price. By the 1920s, however, the coal industry in Pleasant Valley was clearly in decline. Clear Creek, established in 1887, the most remote and at 8,300 feet the highest of all Carbon County coal camps, reached its peak population of about six hundred around 1920, with a substantial Finnish population and distinctive saltbox-shaped houses that perhaps reflected an old-country influence.[16] While Clear Creek residents enjoyed a beautiful natural setting, their isolation made them especially vulnerable to exploitation by the company store monopoly.

A few houses remain at Clear Creek, enough to suggest that it was a very liveable community, and the names on the landscape—Finn Canyon, Boardinghouse Canyon—tell of its history, but it requires an act of the imagination now to picture the miners trooping to work through the grimy snow in the winter predawn, the wives visiting back and forth between their snug, identical houses, and the warm glow of the Finn Hall in the evening.

This is not to say that coal mining is dead in Pleasant Valley. New mines were opened in Mud Creek and Eccles canyons during the early 1980s. Their state-of-the-art loading facilities tower above the subalpine forest, and long unit trains carry Pleasant Valley coal to the West Coast for transhipment to Asia. But a coal mine no longer means a coal camp. Except for a few who make their homes in Scofield, the mine work force now commutes from the lower valleys.

Near the mouth of Price Canyon, the coal-bearing Blackhawk formation dips to ground level, capped by the cliff-forming Price River formation, whose most striking landmark is the narrow sandstone wall known as Castle Gate. When the Rio Grande Western was being built through the canyon in 1882, roadbed cuts revealed coal veins, but it was not until 1888 that the railroad, through its Pleasant Valley Coal Company subsidiary, began to develop the Castle Gate mines. The coal from Winter Quarters was not suitable for making coke, then much in demand by the burgeoning smelting industry of the Salt Lake Valley. Though Castle Gate coal was of only marginal coking quality, some two hundred coke ovens were in operation in the narrow canyon by the turn of the century. Better coking coal was discovered in the Book Cliffs, twenty miles east of Price, and the Utah Fuel Company's Sunnyside mines became the main supplier of coke from 1900 onward.

The expansion of the mines during the 1890s brought on a labor shortage. The preference of many Mormons to mine in the winter and farm in the summer had not posed a serious difficulty when the coal was used primarily for home heating purposes, since demand was highest in the winter. But industry required a year-round supply. The coal companies began recruiting Italian and "Austrian" immigrants at Ellis Island. (Most of those labeled as Austrians were actually Slovenes, Croats, and other South Slavic peoples then ruled by the Austro-Hungarian Empire.)

Immigrants from northern Italy tended to be craftsmen or industrial laborers with experience as migratory workers in Europe. They also possessed a political awareness that led them to be active in the labor movement. The more numerous immigrants from the Mezzogiorno, the impoverished South, were mostly farmers who "had never traveled beyond their village."[17] Most South Slavs similarly came from rural backgrounds. Immigrants came initially as unmarried men or left their wives and children at home, in the established pattern of migratory labor. Their goal in many cases was to earn enough money in the mines to enable them to return to their native villages as men of substance. In these aspirations they did not differ greatly from the Mormon miners who endured life in the camps in hope of eventually establishing themselves in a preferred agrarian life-style. This similarity of motives, however, was largely unrecognized, even many years later. In 1976, a former miner explained why he left the Carbon County camps to return to the limited economic opportunities of his native Sanpete Valley in these terms:

> Two of my kids were old enough to start school and I wanted to get away from all that nationality. They had everything, Italians, Greeks, Japs and Chinamen over in that county. They are good people and I have got nothing against them. But I thought I would rather educate my people around their own nationality than I would all different nationalities.[18]

It is not hard to imagine a former Italian miner back home in Calabria explaining his reasons to his neighbors in very similar terms.

For some, then, the coal camps were indeed camps, a temporary condition. But for others the hoped-for escape from industrial labor never came. Mormon miners came to realize that they would never be able to maintain their families on the limited agricultural resources of Castle Valley. Non-Mormon immigrants were often obligated to send their surplus earnings to the old country to provide dowries for sisters or pay mortgages on family land. Gradually, as more and more of them recognized that they were not likely to find better opportunities elsewhere, the Slavs and Italians began to bring brides from their homelands to the developing multiethnic communities of the coal camps. By 1903, a majority of the miners employed at Castle Gate, 356 of 473, were Italians. At Sunnyside, there were 358 English-speaking miners, 246 Italians, and 222 "Austrians." Clear Creek had 172 Italians, 128 Finns, and 95 English, while Winter Quarters had 181 English, 126 Finns, and seventy-four Italians.[19]

With expectations of permanence came a desire for improved work-ing and living conditions. A brief walkout by Winter Quarters miners in 1901—in some respects a result of the 1900 explosion—was followed by a longer strike beginning in the fall of 1903 and affecting all of the Car-bon County mines. The main issue in this strike was union recognition. The United Mine Workers of America sent a charismatic organizer named Charles Demolli, who quickly galvanized the political sensibili-ties of the Italian miners. Legend has it that Demolli slipped past the Utah Fuel Company guards at Sunnyside by hiding in a load of hay,[20] and entered Scofield concealed in a bread box.[21] With the support of the Italian fraternal lodges, Demolli organized union locals at Sunny-side, Castle Gate, and Scofield, and by November 21 had succeeded in shutting down the Castle Gate mines.[22]

The coal companies retaliated by cutting off credit at the company stores and threatening strikers with eviction from company housing. They also set about recruiting strikebreakers and hired armed guards to protect company property. Along with these actions came an intensive media campaign portraying the strike as the work of "the worst sort of foreigners" and resulting in the mobilizing of the Utah National Guard on November 23. While the strike had support among miners from all ethnic backgrounds at the outset, it was increasingly portrayed in the media as being caused by the Italians, who were characterized as refusing "to amalgamate with Americans or learn the English language" and as having "the intention of getting out of this country all they could and then returning to their native land of olives and dirt."[23] Leaders of the LDS church spoke out in support of the coal companies and encouraged church members to take strikebreaking jobs at the mines. This not only increased tensions between Mormon and non-Mormon residents of the region, but also between old-time Welsh and English Mormon miners and their antiunion coreligionists.

A crucial turning point occurred on December 21, when the Castle Gate mine, the only one shut down by the strike, resumed operations with a small work force. By this time, numerous strikers had been evicted from homes on company property in Sunnyside and Castle Gate (despite the fact that many of the houses at Castle Gate had actually been built by the miners). The homeless Italians gathered in tent com-munities on the Whitmore ranch near Sunnyside and around the "Half Way House" of Paul and Caterina Pessetto, located beside the Price River midway between Castle Gate and Helper. While it was obvious to most people by this time that the strike would not achieve its objec-tives, the Italian strikers, in particular, continued to hold out.

225

In addition to Charles Demolli, another legendary figure in American labor history became involved in the Carbon County strike in April 1904, when the crusty socialist organizer "Mother" Mary Jones, a seventy-three-year-old woman of Irish birth and obscure history (her detractors claimed that she had operated a brothel in Denver), arrived in Helper with her usual flair for the dramatic gesture:

> She walked to the best hotel and announced who she was. Later she entered the dining room and sat down to dinner. At the close of her meal the waitress placed a finger bowl before her. "Take it away my girl," she said in a voice that could be heard all over the dining room, as was doubtless intended, "such things are not for me, they only give some poor overworked girl extra work at washing dishes."[24]

Because Mother Jones had met with a strike leader who was under smallpox quarantine, local officials attempted to confine her to a quarantine hut, but strikers set the hut on fire, damaging it beyond use. Mother Jones found refuge at the Half Way House, and when a sheriff's deputy attempted to arrest her he was driven away by armed strikers who had taken up positions at the house and behind rocks on the nearby hills. On Sunday, April 24, Carbon County Sheriff Hyrum Wilcox led a posse of forty-five men (many of them coal company guards) down the canyon from Castle Gate. Mother Jones claimed in her memoirs that she had received advance notice of the raid and in order to prevent violence had persuaded the strikers to hide their guns among the rocks on the mountainside. She gave the following account of the raid:

> Between 4:30 and 5 o'clock in the morning I heard the tramp of feet on the road. I looked out my smallpox window and saw about forty-five deputies. They descended upon the sleeping tent colony, dragged the miners out of their beds. They did not allow them to put on their clothing. The miners begged to be allowed to put on their clothes, for at that early hour the mountain range is the coldest. Shaking with cold, followed by the shrieks and wails of their wives, and children, beaten along the road by guns, they were driven like cattle to Helper. In the evening they were packed in a box car and run down to Price, the county seat and put in jail.[25]

The *Deseret News* account of the raid claimed that while many strikers were "hustled out of bed in their night clothes," they "were allowed to return and dress." The *News* added,

When the officers were taking the strikers away the women were very abusive in their language and some threats were made. The men were very peaceable and made no resistance. As the strikers were being marched to the train, their wives and children who had followed them down to Helper, were weeping as they said good-bye. The scene will not be forgotten soon by those who witnessed it."[26]

Because the county jail was too small to hold such a large group of prisoners, they were placed under guard in a "bull-pen" outside of Price to await trial. Several of the arrested men were brought to trial on various charges and with varying results, but the expense of the legal proceedings and of feeding the prisoners, combined with a rising tide of public sympathy for the strikers and their wives, led to a release of prisoners on May 13. In July, the United Mine Workers gave up the unionizing effort and discontinued financial support of the strikers. In November the union sent seven thousand dollars to Carbon County to pay the railroad fares of strikers who wished to leave the area. Many did, but many others remained. Some found employment with the railroad. Others acquired farms or went into business in Helper or Price. One result of the strike, then, was that the Italians, who had formerly viewed themselves as a temporary labor force, began to acquire a permanent stake in the region. Another effect was to stimulate the growth of Helper, where housing was not subject to the uncertainties of the company town.

While the coal companies blamed the 1903 strike on "foreigners," they did not hesitate to bring in additional immigrants to replace the striking miners. The first Greeks entered the Utah coalfields when Salt Lake City-based labor agent Leonidas G. Skliris, known as the "Czar of the Greeks," sent some twenty-five strikebreakers to Castle Gate.[27] Their numbers were augmented in the following years, especially after 1907, when the failure of the currant crop deprived Greece of its chief agricultural export and increased the distress of the already impoverished countryside.

The Greeks were perhaps the most intensely nationalistic of all immigrants, rivaled only by the Japanese. Helen Z. Papanikolas, second-generation chronicler of the Greek experience in Utah, writes of the first immigrants:

Any life outside *patridha*, "the fatherland," was exile. Not knowing what the three *Moiroi*, "the Fates," had decided for them during their first three days of life, many brought a bit of earth in an amulet or small bottle. If their destiny was death in American exile, a priest would have a pinch of Greek earth to sprinkle over them as they lay in their caskets.[28]

227

Like other immigrant peoples, they came first as young single men—most still in their teens—truly in exile from their patriarchal culture that required the services of women to prepare feasts for the men's name days and the ritual foods for the Orthodox religious services.[29] Gradually, however, the Greeks transplanted their cultural traditions to the new land. First came the coffeehouse—sometimes nothing more than a tin shack near the mines—as a place to socialize after work. Then the Hellenic Orthodox Church began sending priests to bury and marry and otherwise enable the exiled Greeks to maintain their ties to the fatherland and the national faith. (Because it was difficult to get priests to come to such a remote place, the early priests were sometimes only partially qualified, in effect "battlefield commissions."[30])

Especially after the completion of a church in Price in 1916, the Greek men began sending home for "picture brides." For the most part, these were dowryless women who had no chance for marriage in the old country. The families would arrange an exchange of photographs between marriageable young women and the overseas workers. While they often came from the same villages, the men in most cases had emigrated several years earlier, when the women were still young children, so they were in effect strangers to each other. His selection made, the man would remit money to pay for his bride's passage. Imagine the situation of a young woman who had scarcely ventured beyond the boundaries of her native village in Crete or the Balkan Peninsula, and who spoke nothing but the local dialect, setting out for what must have seemed the ends of the earth. With a tag pinned to her clothing listing her destination and the name of her intended, she had somehow to complete the steerage passage across the Atlantic, to endure the confusion and humiliations of Ellis Island and the several stages of the railway journey west, only to be set down perhaps in the middle of a sagebrush flat, miles from any town, there to be met by a stranger who would take her and her baggage to the section gang or sheep camp where her husband-to-be was employed. Some women came in groups that provided some mutual support. Sometimes agents were appointed to help get them through Immigration and onto the right train in New York City. Sometimes a group of men would contribute money to enable one of their number to travel to Greece and escort the women to America. This procedure, however, tended to raise suspicions of white slavery among Immigration officials.

A marriage and a life in an alien land begun in such a way must have been very difficult at best. Sometimes, however, the situation was further complicated by deception on one side or the other. Helen Papanikolas remembers the gossip that passed among second-generation Greek girls about the marriages of their elders:

> The girls giggled about Tsikouris who had been shown a plump, pretty woman for his approval, but when she lifted her veil at the conclusion of the wedding ceremony, her dark, oily skinned sister had been substituted instead. And there was Monoyios who gaped when his ugly picture bride stepped off the D&RGW, then ran to one sheep camp after the other, chased by her brother who caught him and begged him not to destroy his family's *filotimo*, its self-respect, by refusing his sister who would then be left forever unmarried. Mrs. Papakostis, distracted, had stepped off the train and realized that the thin, hook-nosed man approaching her was not the man whose picture she held in her hand. Papakostis had sent his handsome brother's picture instead of his own. The bride turned to get back on the train, but she had nowhere to go.[31]

Despite the difficulties of adjustment, both cultural and personal, and despite the fact that some Greeks preserved for decades the idea of someday returning home, they also were gaining a stake in the new land and imprinting their own meanings upon it. The High Plateaus reminded at least some of the men of their homeland.[32] There were plenty of rocks and not too much green, and sheep and goats could graze here. The coal camps clinging to the slopes of the Wasatch Plateau even bore a slight resemblance in situation to the mountain villages of Crete. Several Greeks left the mines or the railroad and became sheepmen. Others began by establishing coffeehouses or boardinghouses or bootlegging operations in the camps, and eventually expanded into other businesses in Helper and Price. Those who remained in industrial occupations tried to recreate at least a part of their native village cultures. They built chicken coops and rabbit hutches and traditional domed mud ovens. They planted gardens in their backyards or on whatever scraps of irrigable land they could find on the outskirts of the camps. The women marveled at Mormon-style irrigation that brought streams of water right to the dooryard garden. In the old country, they had sometimes been forced to carry water from distant wells or streams.

The Rio Grande Western Railway's monopoly position in the Carbon County coal industry ended in 1906 with the opening of the first major independent mine at Kenilworth, high on the Tavaputs foothills east of

Sunnyside coke ovens under construction, 1902. G. E. Anderson photo, courtesy Utah State Historical Society.

Helper. The next fifteen years brought the establishment of Cameron (later renamed Rolapp, then Royal) and Heiner, in Price Canyon above and below Castle Gate; Mohrland, Black Hawk, Hiawatha, and Wattis along the base of the Wasatch Plateau south and west of Price; and a whole string of camps in Spring Canyon, west of Helper: Peerless, Storrs, Standardville, Latuda, Rains, and Mutual. In 1922, the Columbia Steel Company developed a mine in the Book Cliffs near Sunnyside to supply coke to its Ironton plant, located between Springville and Provo. Consumers, National, and Sweet's were established on the North Fork of Gordon Creek in the early 1920s, together with the intended residential and commercial community of Coal City, which never had more than a hundred residents but enjoyed its day in the national spotlight when heavyweight boxing champion Jack Dempsey chose it as a training site in 1923.

A coal camp typically started with the most rudimentary kind of housing near the mine: tents, lumber shacks, shelters built of empty blasting powder boxes. When more permanent houses were built, they were likely to be assigned first to "American" miners, while the immigrants continued to live in "Ragtown" for some time. Even in the uniformity of the fully developed camp, there were distinctions based on job status or ethnicity. The bosses lived on "Silk Stocking Row" in

Company houses at Sunnyside about 1900. G. E. Anderson photo, courtesy Utah State Historical Society.

larger and better-appointed houses than those assigned to the laborers. Ethnic groups tended to congregate, partly by preference, partly as a management strategy to prevent unifying labor movements, in "Greek Town" and "Bohunk Town" and "Little Italy." And there would be someplace on the fringe of the community for whichever group occupied the bottom of the social scale—first the Japanese (who in the early days were often denied the use of the company shower facilities), later the blacks (never very numerous in the Utah coalfields) or the Hispanics (again, with only a small population until World War II, when larger numbers moved in from New Mexico and southern Colorado).

The efforts of immigrants to preserve European peasant traditions intensified social divisions in the camps. Lucile Richins, who grew up in Sunnyside, recalled being "raised with a whole-hearted contempt for Greeks, Italians, and other southern Europeans who lived there":

> At one time, about 1915, when Sunnyside was booming in its greatest, a few of these southern European immigrants lived in New Town next door to us. They hollowed out one side of the foundation of their house and installed several hogs. The smell was awful. Complaining neighbors were responsible for them being ordered to get rid of them. They butchered them on the kitchen floor, and when the lady of the house decided to clean the

entrails to stuff them with sausage, she tied one end of them securely to the faucet of the only water hydrant in the neighborhood and turned on the water. The odors from this and the entire family nearly drove the Americans out of the neighborhood. . . .

When Standardville was built, the Standard Coal Company built a very modern town. Every house had its bathroom. Within two years they had to remove most of the bathtubs from houses, and from all the houses they rented to these immigrants. They clogged up the plumbing by using the bathtubs to scald their hogs at butchering time.[33]

It is interesting to reflect how important a little distance can be. The southern European tradition of keeping farm animals in or near the farmhouse offended the sensibilities of the Anglo-Americans in the coal camps. Yet the Mormon farm villages that were often part of their own tradition were also characterized by the keeping of livestock, with their attendant odors, near the homes. Clearly, however, a pigpen in the barnyard seemed to be a very different thing from a pigpen attached to the house.

Whether from a spirit of benevolent paternalism or from a desire to attract and keep the best workers, some companies not only provided well-built houses at a modest rent but also a fairly extensive range of community facilities. For example, Kenilworth boasted a school, a hospital, tennis courts, a barbecue pit, and "a large auditorium that housed a movie theater, dance hall, library, pool hall, and miscellaneous meeting rooms."[34] A 1925–26 report from the Utah State Industrial Commission portrayed the United States Fuel Company town of Hiawatha as a model industrial community:

At Hiawatha, modern cottages are furnished for the miners, electric-lighted and supplied with water from mountain springs. Homes of mine officials are steam-heated. An up-to-date store and butcher shop with refrigerating plant makes house-to-house deliveries. Many of the miners own automobiles and are provided with beautiful fireproof garages. The public school building is comparable to any in the large cities of Utah, and an attractive dormitory has been built to invite desirable teachers to the school. Several miles of concrete sidewalk have been laid and the streets are well lighted with powerful electric lights.[35]

In addition to the company store, recreation hall, confectionery, barber shop, and laundry, the company established a dairy to supply fresh milk to the community and built two churches, one for the Mormons, the other to be shared by other denominations.

Even Peerless, a shoestring operation supported by a thin coal seam, where the mine mechanics sometimes had to labor through the night to mend the machinery so the miners could work the next day, was not without some community amenities. General Manager A. P. Cederlof recalled,

> A nice part of life at Peerless in our time were the dances. The employees fixed up an old stone building near the highway that had been the camp store. The company supplied the material. A new hardwood floor was put in, among other improvements. We found a good used jukebox, and records were provided by the mine employees. Polka music was often played. The favorite dance tunes were recordings by Frankie Yankovic and his orchestra. The most popular tune was "Charlie Was a Boxer." Other favorites were "Just Because" and "You'll Be Sorry from Now on." Louis [mine superintendent] and Zelpha Vuksinick joined in the dances and other camp activities and events.[36]

Every camp that could provide a scrap of level ground had a baseball field. The baseball team was a source of pride to miners and bosses alike, and a good player could always find employment. On Sunday afternoons throughout the summer, the camp teams played a schedule of games against one another and teams from the Emery County farm towns. Helper had a real ballpark with a grandstand and sodded field, and supported a semi-pro team that competed in the old Utah Industrial League.

The houses in the coal camps were typically four-room frame structures in a pyramid-cottage or bungalow style, sometimes with screened porches at the rear. Clear Creek and Sunnyside had more distinctive story-and-a-half saltboxes. Homes on "Silk Stocking Row" might have a couple of extra rooms but otherwise did not differ greatly from the laborers' housing in design or construction. In the better camps the houses were well built, well maintained, and freshly painted at regular intervals. Indeed, many camp houses have outlasted the camps to which they originally belonged. Old-timers in the valley towns can still point out transplanted Mohrland houses, Hiawatha houses, Castle Gate houses in their communities. On the other hand, some of the apparently more "permanent" buildings constructed of stone by craftsmen from the Italian Tyrol have fallen into decay or been demolished.

Despite the reasonably good housing and community facilities, life was not easy in the coal camps. When the market was slow, mines frequently went on short weeks, with miners sometimes getting only two or three days' work or being laid off altogether. Wages were quickly reduced when the price of coal fell but recovered more gradually when prices improved. While housing was cheap, there was the constant threat of eviction should a miner go on strike or be incapacitated.

A major strike in 1922 produced several violent confrontations between strikers and company guards, and two men were killed, a striker shot by a deputy sheriff on the outskirts of Helper on May 14, and a company guard shot while taking a trainload of strikebreakers into Spring Canyon on June 14.[37] In another strike in 1933, the conflict between miners and the coal companies was overshadowed by the fierce competition between the United Mine Workers of America and the radical National Miners Union. On September 11, some four hundred NMU supporters from that union's strongholds in the Spring Canyon and Gordon Creek districts marched down Price's Main Street to protest the arrest of two of their leaders. They were met by a force of seventy-five deputy sheriffs and state highway patrolmen, who threw tear-gas grenades and directed high-pressure water hoses indiscriminately at men, women, and children.[38]

The second-greatest disaster in the Utah coalfields occurred on March 8, 1924, when the Castle Gate Number Two mine blew up, killing 171 men and leaving 415 widows and dependent children.[39] But death and serious injury were threats hanging over the miners at all times. Between 1910 and 1915, an average of fifteen men were killed each year in the Carbon County mines. By the decade of the 1940s, despite numerous improvements in coal mining methods, the average was still about ten per year.[40] Coal camp women lived in dread of the whistle that signalled "something wrong at the mine." J. Eldon Dorman, hired as a young camp doctor at Consumers in 1937, recalled that "the men wanted someone at the portals when they were hurt."

> I had a mine telephone in my office and in my home. If an accident happened at the mine I was notified by phone and was frequently requested to meet the more seriously injured at the portal of the mine. It was quite an uphill walk, so I started driving my car. No road existed but I could drive almost to the mine entrance. The entrance, however, stood in view of the entire town and every woman in camp recognized my car. Soon each was standing on her front or back porch, wringing her hands on her apron and wondering if her husband or son was hurt or killed. I only drove up there twice. The ever-present fear of death in mine accidents, explosions, or afterdamp already haunted the families enough.[41]

Consumers was far from being a model camp. At an elevation of 7,600

Main Street, Consumers, 1936. Dorothea Lange photo, Library of Congress USF34-9037-E.

feet, it had a harsh climate, poor housing, and a history of labor-management tensions. During the 1933 strike, supporters of the National Miners Union, mostly South Slavs, actually seized control of the town until a National Guard detachment broke the blockade. During this episode, mine superintendent David Parmley, who was also chairman of the Carbon County Commission, was according to his own report assaulted by "6 big Austrian women," who "threw me down, took my revolver, threw my shells away and held me down and peed on me."[42]

In 1936, photographer Dorothea Lange made Consumers her first stop in a Farm Security Administration-sponsored study of rural poverty in Utah. In a strong ideological indictment of the exploitation of workers by "absentee capital," Lange shot photos of hard-faced men carrying their lunchbuckets to work, of rutted streets, open sewers, and houses that were little more than shacks strewn helter-skelter along the canyon.[43] One picture showed children beside a dilapidated outhouse. Perhaps as a response to this image, the Civilian Conservation Corps came to town a short time later and erected a row of toilets behind the shacks. Dr. Dorman recalls that these were the only structures in the camp arranged in a straight line. When the property at Consumers was later being dismantled for its salvage value, several of these well-built toilets ended up out back of houses in rural areas of the valley.[44]

Every community has its own life and vitality, often imperceptible to outsiders. Dr. Dorman, who arrived in Consumers only a year after Lange's visit, says little in his memoir about the bad housing or the dreariness of the setting. Despite having wrecked his car on the way and being compelled to finish the journey in the back of a coal truck, he has pleasant memories of his first day in the coal camp:

> I found patients waiting for me. I saw several sick people and handled some injuries. Before midnight I delivered a baby boy. I received the surprise of my life when the father pressed a twenty dollar bill in my hand shortly after I severed the umbilical cord. Never in my previous practice had I been paid so promptly. I had learned to settle many of my bills by barter—a sack of spuds, a box of apples, or perhaps some eggs, butter, or chickens. That crisp new bill in my otherwise empty pocket made me think I had come to the right place, and indeed I had. I spent three of the most pleasant and enjoyable years of my life in the coal camps of Carbon County.[45]

The workers and coal companies of the three Gordon Creek camps, Consumers, Sweet's, and National, had jointly organized a medical association and built a well-equipped clinic and five-bed hospital. For a fee of $1.50 a month, a miner and his family had access to the physician and clinical facilities for all office and house calls and medications. Dorman soon developed "a personal respect for the old-time Austrian, Italian, Greek, or Welsh coal miner" who asked for nothing more than "a chance to work—to dig the coal to pay off his debts, feed and clothe his family, and perhaps send his son to school."[46] However, Dorman does not gloss over the seamy side of coal-camp life, including the bullies who terrorized their neighbors, the prevalence of venereal diseases (by tracing their spread, the camp doctor was generally well aware of "who was doing what and to whom"), and the wild barroom brawls on Saturday nights. He tells of being summoned to the beer parlor at Sweet's to patch up a man whose throat had been slit from ear to ear. Dorman laid the man on the pool table and sewed up the wound under the eyes of a "helpful and sometimes critical audience." "The thump of the juke box never died and the drinking, smoking, and revelry only paused momentarily to inspect my stitches." Then he learned that the bar's patrons had smashed thirteen beer bottles on the assailant's head in an unsuccessful effort to subdue him. "I found Sam at the bunkhouse squatting in a galvanized tub of water and holding a bloody washcloth to his bleeding, macerated scalp. I asked him how he felt. He looked up and said: 'I feel pretty good, but I do got a leetle bit headache!'"[47]

Coal-camp doctors were typically young men just out of medical school, trying to pay off school debts or accumulate a financial stake that would enable them to develop a practice somewhere else. Some, however, like Dorman, became so attached to the people of the coal camps that they made their permanent homes in the area. Claude Mc-Dermid, for example, came to Sunnyside in 1911 with the intention of staying only long enough to buy a new blue serge suit. He remained in the camps for twenty-eight years, becoming not only a trusted physician but also a vigorous defender of the miners' interests. When a new manager at Castle Gate threatened to cut off electricity to the miners' homes, an enraged McDermid knocked him to the floor.[48]

In a not uncommon pattern, my father's elder sister, Fawn, brought up in the farm town of Huntington, found her first job after college teaching school in the camps. There she met and married Ray McCandless, a man of many talents ranging from mine mechanics to meat cutting. Among my earliest memories was watching my cousins piling into their car for the trip back to Spring Canyon after a Sunday visit at my grandparents' place. They must have moved to Rolapp a short time later, for another early memory is of Uncle Ray lifting a toy dump truck from a high shelf at the company store there and presenting it to me. I knew Sunnyside first by the red glow of the coke ovens at night and the cloud of smoke that hung by day over the Book Cliffs horizon. Hiawatha and Wattis were clusters of lights against the mountain, visible at night when we were traveling to or from Price.

My mother's brother Uncle Leon Ungerman and his family lived in Hiawatha for a time, and I remember visiting them there. The houses seemed very close to each other, compared to the spacious layout of our farm village, and I had the feeling that it would be a rather dull place to live, without a barnyard or an irrigation ditch to play in or fields to roam. On the other hand, though, the cliffs were invitingly near. (Indeed, many children died over the years in falls from ledges near the coal camps.) I remember walking with a cousin along a sidewalk several feet above the level of the street, past the schoolhouse and the clanging, dusty tipple that dominated the town, to a confectionery and soda fountain in the basement of what must have been the recreation hall. I recall a cavelike place, cool and filled with such good smells that for a moment I wished we could live in the camps.

During the Second World War, my schoolteacher father took a summer job as a bookkeeper at the Horse Canyon Mine, then being developed to supply coal to the new Geneva Steel Plant. Horse Canyon was more than forty miles from Huntington, so Dad had a long daily commute to work. He took me with him a couple of times, and I played around the office while he worked, or went outside to view the mile-long conveyor belt that was used in place of a tramway to carry coal from mine to tipple. Dad had an opportunity for permanent employment at a better salary than he earned teaching school, and for a time my parents seriously considered the possibility of moving to the new town of Dragerton. I remember a Sunday afternoon when we walked through some of the houses under construction, imagining what it would be like to live there. Dragerton was the last of the Carbon County coal camps to be established, though really it was not a coal camp in the usual sense. Built by the government on a bench below Sunnyside, Dragerton was several miles away from the mine it served. It resembled other government towns built during that period and later at Los Alamos, New Mexico, Hanford, Washington, and Page, Arizona—neatly arranged but bland and undistinguished, pure "project towns."

When Dad eventually left schoolteaching it was to go to work as a salesman for Nabisco. His territory took in a large swath across central Utah, and much of my early acquaintance with areas outside our own neighborhood came from traveling with him during the summers. He worked on a basic two-week rotation. One week he was on the road, staying Monday night in Nephi, Tuesday in Delta, Wednesday in Salina, and Thursday in Ephraim (unless he managed to compress two days' work into one and make it back home Thursday night). The next week, he serviced the stores in Carbon and Emery counties and was able to come home each night.

Traveling with Dad, I visited nearly all of the coal camps and their company stores, even remote Scofield and Clear Creek. The Spring Canyon district by this time was in its last days, its economically recoverable coal reserves almost exhausted, and the decaying camps seemed to me like the ruins of an ancient civilization, though in fact they were less than forty years old. Castle Gate, though older, was still active, with houses crowded close in the main canyon and extending up Willow Creek. The store stood near the old rock mine office where Butch Cassidy had pulled off his famous payroll robbery in 1897. The company store at Kenilworth was managed by an Emery County native named Cal Jewkes, a friend of my father's, so we usually spent extra time there.

238

Cal Jewkes was a storekeeper by day but better known for his mellow trombone and rich baritone voice, frequently heard at dances throughout the valley.

I liked Kenilworth for its tree-lined streets and well-kept houses and for the wide veranda in front of the company store, which served as a kind of community center where off-duty miners loitered in conversation and olive-skinned women came and went with dark-eyed children in tow. Columbia, neatly tucked away in its rocky canyon, was another of my favorites. But any coal camp was an interesting place to be when a loaded trip was coming down the tramway from the mine portal, or when a steam engine was shunting railroad cars at the tipple.

The heyday of the camps was the period from about 1915 to 1930, when coal production in the Carbon County mines averaged between four and five million tons a year. During the depression of the 1930s, production dropped to just over two million tons. It soared to a peak of more than seven million tons during the Second World War, then began a long decline to three million tons per year by the late 1960s.[49] There was a resurgence in the coal industry during the energy crisis of the late 1970s, leading to the development of new mines in Pleasant Valley and farther south along the Wasatch Plateau in Emery County, where two large electrical generating plants were built to convert coal to a more marketable form of energy. But even though production has risen to new highs during the last decade, employment is far below the peak of the 1920s. Coal mining has become a highly mechanized operation, with huge long-wall mining machines that can strip the coal from an entire face, automated conveyors to carry it to the surface, and loading equipment that can fill a train in less than an hour—a far cry from the days of the pick and shovel, the hand drill, the mule car, and the sixteen-ton shift.

By the middle of the twentieth century, the paternalistic company town was an anachronism. Most workers preferred to commute to the mines from Price or Helper, where they could own their homes and have better access to stores and schools, outside the control of the company. So little now remains of some coal camps that they scarcely qualify even as ghost towns. Of Rolapp, whose tramway once bridged the highway and whose buildings crowded the floor of Price Canyon, nothing is left but a few ruined houses in a small side canyon. The historic camp of Castle Gate was demolished in 1974 so that improved loading facilities could be constructed on its site. The last residents were resettled in a Helper subdivision that extends a short distance up Spring Canyon. Except for these homes at the canyon's mouth, Spring Canyon, once home to several thousand people, is now entirely abandoned. The same fate has befallen the Gordon Creek camps, though coal is still mined there. A few residents remain in Hiawatha and Kenilworth, and there is a fair-sized community at Dragerton, which has annexed Columbia and renamed itself East Carbon City.

With the abandonment of the surrounding camps, Helper fell upon hard times, losing population and the commercial vitality that had once made it a rival to Price. Price grew as former camp-dwellers relocated there during the 1950s and '60s, but also experienced a business decline as the population of Carbon County fell from twenty-five thousand in 1950 to fifteen thousand in the early 1970s.

In 1950, my father left Nabisco and began teaching at Carbon College (later renamed the College of Eastern Utah) in Price. The main attraction of the job was that it enabled him to indulge his passion for the theater, but among other duties he also served for several years as the college public-relations director, working with civic organizations and traveling throughout eastern Utah to recruit students. Not long after he joined the faculty, the college faced a major crisis as Governor J. Bracken Lee, himself a Price native, proposed to get the State of Utah out of the junior college business by shutting down Carbon and giving Weber, Snow, and Dixie back to the LDS church, which had operated them until the 1930s. While engaged in an intensive campaign to avert the threatened closing, Dad developed a wide acquaintance with and a high regard for the ethnically diverse people of Carbon County. But I'm not sure he ever entirely learned to read the complicated interactions among the different groups, which included rivalries between northern and southern Italians and between mainland Greeks and Cretans. The second- and third-generation young people he worked with were of course thoroughly Americanized, but the rhetoric of ethnicity was still prevalent. On one occasion, for example, when a student of Greek ancestry had made a successful presentation in a speech class, another student called out, "Good job! Come on over and sit with the white people." Upon which someone else with a Greek name shouted, "Who says a Cretan is white?" Dad was frozen with dismay until he realized that he was the only one in the room who had taken the banter seriously.

I had my own discoveries to make when I began attending Carbon College in 1956. By this time my earlier sense of Carbonites as generic "foreigners" had been replaced by more particular distinctions. I knew that Greek names usually ended in s and that musical names like Tallerico, Giacolleto, and Spigarelli were likely to be Italian. I was not yet conscious of the Slavs as a distinct group, even though such names as Bosco, Majnik, and Kosec were hard to assimilate to my sense of either Italian or Greek. Nor did I then realize that the prominent Howa and Sheya families were descended from Lebanese peddlers who had hawked their wares in the coal camps. At the college I discovered that my classmates with strange-sounding names were often very bright indeed. Many of them went on to make distinguished academic and professional careers. Under the guidance of other students, I learned which of the local taverns and lounges did not inquire too closely into their patrons' ages. I learned, too, that you never called these establishments by the name above the door but instead referred familiarly to "Gus's Place" or "Sam's." It was like a revelation when a friend took me into one of the alien cafes on South Carbon Avenue, where the white-aproned proprietor greeted us in scarcely understandable English but served up an exceedingly tasty lamb stew.

While I got to know my way around Price to some extent, Helper remained terra incognita. With its narrow, crowded Main Street and small huddled blocks, Helper bore no resemblance whatever to a Mormon town—even though, interestingly enough, the first settler on the site had been Teancum Pratt, a son of the early Mormon Apostle Parley P. Pratt.

By his own account, Teancum Pratt was a dissatisfied man. A child of Parley P. Pratt's seventh wife, he had an unhappy childhood after his father was murdered when Teancum was six years old. At the age of sixteen, he took up some land near Goshen, in southwestern Utah Valley, but abandoned it because "I felt Goshen was not good enough for me." He moved from Goshen to Salt Lake, then back to Goshen, then to Santaquin. In 1874, he joined his brother Helaman at Prattville, near Richfield, but soon moved into Richfield, then went south to the United Order community of Kingston, "where we tried the experiment of living and eating at one table. This was a failure. I was at last tired and concluded to quit and commence the old and incorrect way again of everyone for himself and the devil for all." After Kingston, Pratt tried Hillsdale, then Panguitch, then Santaquin again, then Spring Lake, where he "suffered awful poverty." In June 1880, he decided to "go out to the frontier and take up land." He first located at the mouth of Gordon Creek, but finding that "the neighbors were hunters, trappers, and bachelors, and soreheads and did not welcome any settlers," he moved farther up the Price River and established a homestead on the site of Helper.[50]

Pratt built a dugout for his first wife, Anna Mead, and a cabin a couple of miles down the river in Spring Glen for his second wife, Sarah

Ewell. He grew fruit and vegetables on small plots of ground near the creek, tried to develop a ranch on Oak Spring Bench to the west, had trouble with his wives and neighbors, was imprisoned for violating the laws against plural marriage, and found life in general to be a hard struggle. In 1886, he complained in his journal, "These have not been very happy years for me. I have lived in the wilderness with my families and had seemingly no friends and naught but poverty."[51]

Pratt had received some money from the Rio Grande Western in 1882 for a right-of-way across his homestead. In 1892, the railroad elected to establish a division point at Helper, naming it for the helper engines attached to the trains there for the pull to Soldier Summit. Anticipating prosperity at last, Pratt laid out a townsite with seven hundred lots. But early sales were slow, and he remained deeply in debt until the late 1890s, when he opened a small mine in Hardscrabble Canyon and began to supply coal to the residents of Helper. Compared to the rigors of agricultural pioneering, Pratt found mine work "pleasant and light" as well as profitable. He wrote in 1899, "I never was as happy and free from care as during this summer."[52] At the same time, however, he was troubled at the prospect of remaining with his family in "this unholy land of gentiles and apostates"[53] and formed various plans of moving to Salt Lake City or to his ranch on Oak Spring Bench. In the summer of 1900, Pratt went to Scofield and began working in the Winter Quarters mine, probably drawn by the demand for new workers after the May explosion. He had been working there for only three weeks when he was killed by a rockfall.[54]

The town he had founded, which had a population of 385 in 1900, received an influx of new residents in the aftermath of the 1903 strike, and with the development of the mines at Kenilworth and Spring Canyon became the commercial hub of the coal camps, with stores, hotels, restaurants, coffeehouses, saloons, ethnic lodges, and dancehalls crowded together along the narrow Main Street. Many of the frame structures in the business district were destroyed by a fire in 1919 and rebuilt on a larger scale in brick or stone during the 1920s, probably Helper's golden age.[55]

Teancum Pratt would probably not have approved of the development of Helper, since it was predominantly the work of "gentiles." A leading example was the career of Joseph Barboglio, who had been local treasurer for the UMWA at the time of the 1903 strike. Thrown in jail for a time with Charles Demolli by company guards at Sunnyside, Barboglio left Utah when it became apparent that the strike could not be won. He made his way to Missouri, where he married an Englishwoman named Jennie Causer and operated a bar for a time. Within a year or two, the Barboglios returned to Helper, where Joe erected a business building, casting the solid concrete blocks with his own hands. Barboglio eventually became a successful banker, mayor of Helper, and role-model for the children of industrial immigrants. When students at a Helper school were assigned to identify the greatest men in world history, one Italian-American boy listed "Jesus Christ, Napoleon, and Joe Barboglio."[56]

Among the central figures in Helper's Greek community were John Diamanti and his wife. Barba Yianni, "Uncle John," as he was commonly called, was regarded as a wise man, "a man of charisma, a folk healer, an interpreter of dreams, and a foreteller of the sex of unborn children. Each Easter he examined the shoulder blade of the paschal lamb and told what the following year would bring."[57] The role of Mrs. Diamanti, one of the first Greek women to come to Carbon County, was in some ways even more vital:

> The Greek Town children called Uncle John's wife *Thitsa* ("Little Aunt"). Their elders called her *Yiannina*, the genitive of her husband's name. She seldom smiled; the responsibilities Greek culture placed on her were enormous. No one gave her role much thought: she was merely a woman doing woman's work. The Greek bachelors were constant guests. As the matriarch she was in charge of weddings and baptisms. Each Saturday she had the Greek water boys of railroads and mines come down from their tents and shacks and line up to take their turn at having her wash their hair. No child went without shoes or food if she knew about it, and it did not matter if they were the children of immigrants or Americans. People remembered that she would set out with Uncle John's bootleg money in her purse to buy her sons clothing; it was gone by the time she reached town. On the way she saw a child with worn-out overalls, another with ripped-off shoe soles.[58]

Not until I read Helen Papanikolas's accounts of her childhood did I begin to get a sense of life in Helper. She writes of her own sense of self and the world having its first center in the row of white frame houses built by Joe Bonacci near the railroad tracks below the massive escarpment of Steamboat Mountain; of the Irish railroader's wife, "Killarney" Reynolds, who took it upon herself to advise the women of the polyglot immigrant neighborhood on American ways; "the gardens and white and dark green frame houses of Wop Town and Bohunk Town on a plateau on the other side of the river";[59] the "safety" of Greek Town, near the schoolhouse:

Clusters of houses were set here and there in the dessicated earth, each with a small garden and cascades of silver lace vines on the wooden porches. In the backyards, shiny and smooth from the lye and soap of wash waters, were wash houses, coal and wood sheds, rabbit hutches, chicken coops, pigeons, and domed earth ovens supported on wooden stilts.

The warm, yeasty scent of baking bread hovered over Greek Town, and mothers were quick to cut us large pieces and slather them with butter. The admonition we heard from our mother daily came with the offering: "Bread is holy! If you drop it, make the sign of the cross and kiss it before eating. If it can't be eaten, bring it to me to burn. Never throw bread in the garbage! Bread is holy!"[60]

Papanikolas tells of schoolyard battles fought between Mormon children on one side and the children of immigrants on the other; of the antiforeign sentiment during the 1922 strike, when a Greek name was sufficient cause to assign a child to the "Low" division of the first grade instead of the "High";[61] of the Ku Klux Klan burning crosses on one side of town while on the other side of the narrow valley the Catholics burned an answering circle affirming that the KKK was "nought." She tells, too, of how those who are struggling to make their own place in society can victimize others more marginal than themselves, as in the case of the black man who was lynched near Price for shooting a mine guard:

Not long after, while my mother visited in a Greek house and the women's voices shrieked in my ears, I turned the pages to a Greek house staple, the photograph album. There were the usual pictures of weddings, baptisms, naked boy babies propped against pillows to reveal their incipient maleness, girl babies in embroidered white dresses, picnics with men squatting to turn lambs on spits, dancing in rounds, and on the last page a black man dangling from a tree and under him men, women, children, their arms crossed, smiling for the photographer.[62]

With the disappearance of the camps, it is Helper that remains as the chief expression of the multiethnic humanscape of the coal country. This town that once contained as many as thirty-two different nationalities, with all of the attendant rivalries, has bred a strong attachment in many of its residents and former residents. Helperites still take pleasure in telling of the Italian immigrant who, after living in Helper for several years left the town for a job in central Utah. After a few homesick days, he approached the foreman to ask for his pay, declaring mournfully, "I no lika these United States. I wanna go back to Helper."[63]

12

FOR THE STRENGTH
OF THE HILLS

In 1898 a traveling photographer named George Edward Anderson was commissioned by Christian Otteson, a Huntington farmer, to take a picture of his new house. Anderson obliged him with a curious shot of the family disposed across the lawn in front of the house in stiff, erect postures like so many prairie dogs. But in addition, Anderson lugged his equipment to the top of a hill some distance to the south and produced one of the classics of nineteenth-century American landscape photography. He composed this picture with the Otteson house at the visual center but dwarfed by the surrounding natural forms. The house's truncated pyramidal shape is repeated on a vastly larger scale by the architecture of Gentry Mountain, a promontory of the Wasatch Plateau, rising in a rhythmic series of strong horizontal ledges and talus slopes to form the characteristic sharp-edged horizon of the High Plateau country. In the left foreground, an irrigation canal makes a reversed S-curve along the side of a barren Mancos shale hill. Between the canal and the cultivated fields of the river valley stretches a quarter-mile slope covered with a sparse growth of sagebrush and shadscale. To the left of the house, a granary is just visible in a grove of trees that conceals the log cabin that had been the Ottesons' former residence. Farther to the left, looking almost like a toy, are a horse and a white-topped buggy—perhaps Anderson's own traveling outfit, parked at the point where he had begun the climb up the hill.

The photograph is in the panoramic style favored by nineteenth-century landscape painters when dealing with the West. But where Bierstadt or Moran would have painted an Indian village or a mounted raiding party into the picture to introduce the human scale, Anderson has Chris Otteson's new house, its character as artifice emphasized by the absence of softening trees or shrubs, its brick walls (actually an earthy golden-buff) washed out to a glaring white in the early-morning light Anderson has chosen. The result is a scene of striking contrasts: an isolated farm laid out in geometrical fields amid a vast, rugged, seemingly

Christian Otteson farm and Gentry Mountain, 1898. G. E. Anderson photo, courtesy Brigham Young University photo archives.

barren land; a stream of water channeled into a ditch high above the creekbed from which it was diverted; and a multi-gabled pattern-book house, similar to the houses built between 1890 and 1910 in dozens of Utah towns by prosperous merchants, bankers, woolgrowers, but here apparently isolated, far from any other human habitation.

When George Edward Anderson died in 1928, his collection of more than thirty thousand glass-plate negatives was acquired by the LDS Church Historian's Office, largely because it included photographs Anderson had taken of historic Mormon sites in the eastern United States between 1907 and 1914. In the 1960s, the Historian's Office decided to dispose of most of the negatives because of their bulk. Some were destroyed, but others were salvaged by a typist in the office and ended up in the Brigham Young University library and several private collections. In 1972, Rell G. Francis, a photographer living in Anderson's hometown of Springville, first became aware of Anderson's work and devoted the next several years to cataloging and publicizing the photographs. In 1976, Francis prepared an exhibit of Anderson's photographs for the Amon Carter Museum of Western Art in Fort Worth, Texas.[1] Works from this exhibit were later included in an exhibition of nineteenth-century photography of the American West at the Smithsonian Institution in Washington, D.C.

It was in the catalog of this exhibition that I first saw the photograph of Chris Otteson's house. It hit me with a shock of recognition because I had grown up with Gentry Mountain as a prominent element of my visual horizon, had hiked many a time across the foothills to the old Otteson place, had picked apples in the orchard there, and indeed had stood on the very spot from which Anderson took the photograph. The canal, a raw intrusion on the landscape in Anderson's photo, had by the time I came along been "naturalized" with a thick growth of willows and cottonwoods. A hedge of blue spruces, newly planted in 1898 and barely visible in the photograph, had by the 1940s grown into a thick palisade that almost entirely concealed the walls of the house. The house itself was only a shell, destroyed by fire in 1939. Only the mountain, the boundary between earth and sky, appeared unchanged.

For those who arranged the Smithsonian exhibition, the Anderson photograph must have seemed an epitome of the arid West: the vast, desolate beauty of the land and the tenuousness of the human presence. But for me the photograph conjures up a vision of place and time in which landscape and humanscape are inextricably mingled. Christian Otteson was born to Danish immigrants in Fountain Green in 1861, the second year of that community's existence. He worked for local farmers from early boyhood and by age seventeen had married and saved enough money to purchase a small farm. However, because he was under legal age, his father held the deed to the land and refused to relinquish it. Being, in the words of his daughter, "very discouraged with things in Fountain Green,"[2] Chris left his bride of six months in the summer of 1879 and with his elder brother Joseph crossed the Wasatch Plateau and staked out a homestead at the mouth of Huntington Canyon.

As far as I know, there is no record of Sarah Otteson's thoughts upon coming to a log cabin beside Huntington Creek in the spring of 1880. Her elder sister Robena Collard also moved to Castle Valley that year, so Sarah was not entirely uprooted from her kin, and as a wife from Sanpete County she already knew a good deal about pioneering. Born in the village of Wales, she had gone with her family in early childhood to settle Monroe, in the Sevier Valley, only to be driven back to Sanpete by the Black Hawk War.

Most of the families that took up land along Huntington Creek built houses in town after they had proved up on their homesteads, thereafter commuting to their fields or living on "the ranch" only during the summers. Presumably the Ottesons could have done the same thing,

Otteson children with cows, Huntington, about 1900. G. E. Anderson photo, courtesy Utah State Historical Society.

if they had wished to, instead of building what was essentially a town house on the farm. However, Chris Otteson had adopted a more intensive agriculture than most of his neighbors. The riverbottom land was good, and the air circulation at the mouth of the canyon kept the spring frosts at bay, allowing the growing of fruit and berries. He grafted his own trees and in the early years kept a fish trap in the creek that provided a regular supply of trout for the table. His bees had the range of apple blossoms, raspberries, and alfalfa, plus the native flowers on the dry hills—a combination that gained his honey a prize at the St. Louis World's Fair. For Chris Otteson, it seems clear that the farm was not a lonely outpost but a garden redeemed from the wilderness, a private Eden that he had no wish to leave.

Chris and Sarah Otteson would have been in their late thirties, with six children (three others were stillborn), when they moved into the big house. Three additional children were born there, the last one when both parents were fifty. Other Anderson photos show a full-bearded Chris Otteson working with his bees and the children gathered around a favorite milk cow. Like most farm wives, Sarah made her own contribution to the family income by selling butter and in addition evidently ran a kind of farmhouse resort during the summers. A daughter remembers, "During the fruit and melon season, our yard was always full of cars, buggies, wagons and horses. It was like a celebration every Sunday. The house was full of people visiting and the yard was full of people buying, visiting and eating melons."[3] That is hardly the lonely existence one might read in the Anderson photograph. But on the other hand, there must have been times when Sarah felt the isolation, though she responded to it with the pluck of a pioneer woman:

> Father told me of an experience mother had, while they still lived in the old log cabin. Father left her there alone for a few days while he went after some freight. At a certain time, every night, the doorknob would turn, but no one ever tried to come in, or spoke. I can imagine how frightened she was, being there alone, with her neighbors miles away. This went on 3 or 4 nights, then she decided to do something about it. So, the next night she filled some pans with water and had them on the stove, to get good and hot and when the knob turned she took a pan from the stove, opened the door and let it fly. Away went an old white horse down the road. Papa said, "We found out the horse had belonged to a lady who had trained it to come to the house and turn the knob, then she'd give the horse a treat."[4]

It seems significant—though the significance can be read in different ways—that most of the Otteson children, when they grew up, also chose to make their homes some distance from town.

Some ten miles south of the Otteson farm, on one of the long pediment benches that slope up to the rugged escarpment of the Wasatch Plateau, several hundred people have assembled in a natural amphitheater on an evening in early August. The amphitheater has been fitted out with seats that face a wide earthen stage on which are arranged an open shed equipped with a blacksmith's forge, a flat-roofed rock hut, and a set representing the interior of a log cabin. In the middle background two tepees, a sheepherder's tent, and a couple of dugouts have been placed amid the pinyon pines and junipers at the base of a knoll. The farther backdrop is a sweeping panorama of Castle Valley, extending from the blue wall of the Book Cliffs, forty miles to the north, to the massive uplift of the San Rafael Swell that forms the eastern and southern horizon, a vast expanse of buttes, domes, and gorges—the "castles" that gave the valley its name from the time when the New Mexico caravans passed through the region along the Old Spanish Trail. Far to the southeast, the 11,500-foot peak of Mount Ellen, tallest of the Henrys, can be seen beyond the ridgeline of the Swell, at seventy-five miles the most distant object in view. Amid the irrigated fields in the river valley at the base of the pediment benches, clusters of dark trees mark the sites of Orangeville and Castle Dale. On the alkali flats to the south, lights flash from the three tall smokestacks of the Hunter Power Plant.

Men, women, and children in pioneer costumes move among the growing crowd, shaking hands and chatting. Against the rhythmic background thumping of the portable generators, a man dressed like an old sheepherder and speaking in a southern Utah drawl provides a running commentary on various demonstrations taking place on the stage: setting an iron tire on a wooden wagon wheel, hanging a bell, loading a pack mule, shearing sheep, milking cows. All the while, mounted horsemen ride back and forth on the stage, and wagons and buggies circle the knoll on a dirt track. The live narrative is interrupted periodically by a canned radio-baritone voice that formally welcomes the spectators on behalf of the Church of Jesus Christ of Latter-day Saints and offers nonmembers of the church a free poster of Jesus as a souvenir of the occasion.

The shadow of the high plateau deepens on the assembled crowd, while the sun's last rays cast a red glow on the castles of the San Rafael. In the fading light, a train of covered wagons appears far down the bench, making its slow way toward the knoll that will represent the valley's first settlement. The wagons disappear into the pinyon-juniper woodlands, then come into sight again, gradually drawing closer as the night falls. Just before their arrival, a flag ceremony is presented by a party of horsemen in military dress and an opening prayer is offered by one of the local Mormon leaders. Then the stage flares to brilliant life under a battery of floodlights. The wagon train comes around the knoll, and the recorded script blares from the loudspeakers and echoes among the dusty hills.

This is the annual Castle Valley Pageant, ritual folk drama of a special kind. The script focuses on four representative couples among the pioneers who came to the valley in the late 1870s in response to Brigham Young's last settlement call: Wink and Anna, John and Clara, Joe and Tilda, and Abe and Neva. Wink must take up residence on the homestead he has staked out in the new region or risk losing his land, and the pregnant Anna chooses to accompany her husband on the difficult crossing of the high plateau rather than stay in Sanpete through the winter. Clara detests the barren valley that John has brought her to and longs for the comforts of her former home. Joe and Tilda represent the humble folk who will go wherever they are "called" without questioning or calculating the costs. The young lovers Abe and Neva must find a proper balance between their love for each other and their devotion to their faith. Each summer, the spectators—many of whom return year after year—relive the birth of Anna's baby and the death of Tilda's; Clara's struggle between worldly vanities and wifely duty; and Abe and Neva's lovers' quarrels and reconciliations.

Probably in order to justify the massive undertaking each year by the local LDS stakes, involving a cast of well over a hundred plus numerous technical support people, the pioneer story is augmented by more explicit religious elements. John and Joe are called as missionaries to teach Mormon doctrine to the local Indians, thereby providing a pretext for scenes representing the birth and crucifixion of Jesus and his postmortal appearance to the Book of Mormon peoples. The final scene portrays the death of Joe and his reunion with Tilda and their baby in the spirit world. In addition, the script includes several minisermons on the theme of obedience to church leaders.

Still, the imaginative center of the pageant is in the reenactment of their ancestors' heroism by the descendants of the Castle Valley pioneers, and the celebration of a way of life. The pageant provides an occasion for the locals to show off their horses and horsemanship. The men enjoy a rousing ditchbank fight, while the children look forward each year to wallowing in a big puddle in the scene titled "Slippin' and Slidin' in the Castle Valley Mud."

The pageant script and much of the impetus for its original production were the work of a Castle Dale farmer-stockman and local historian named Montell Seely. While the production has become more institutionalized over the years, Seely remains deeply involved. He is the figure in sheepherder dress who narrates the craft demonstrations, adding to his commentary personal recollections of watching his father pack supplies for the sheep camp and repeatedly expressing the wish that he could have lived in pioneer times. Seely's riverbottom farm, located midway between Castle Dale and Orangeville, was the first homestead staked out in Castle Valley, site of a dugout dwelling built by his grandfather, Justus Wellington Seely, Jr., in 1875. For Montell Seely, the Castle Valley Pageant is obviously an act of filial piety. His sense of continuity with the past, made tangible by possession of the ancestral fields, is deep and abiding, and probably beyond the understanding of anyone who has not felt a similar attachment.

This deep sense of place, of belonging to a distinctive landscape and its history, is shared by many inhabitants of the High Plateaus region but is difficult for even sensitive outsiders to comprehend, though they may have a vivid perception of certain qualities of the landscape. E. G. Beckwith, who crossed Castle Valley in 1853 with the ill-fated Gunnison expedition, remarked on the extraordinary clarity of the atmosphere that is also apparent in George Edward Anderson's photograph of the Otteson homestead. Beckwith noted that the scenery could be viewed "with a distinctness of outline and clearness of detail, at distances difficult to be realized by persons who are only familiar with the extent, beauty, and grandeur of landscape views in the comparatively moist and clouded atmosphere of the more civilized portions of our country."[5]

For Beckwith, however, as for many other travelers since his time, the terrain seemed alien. He found Castle Valley "dreary and desolate indeed," with soil that put him in mind of "ash-heaps."[6] Gunnison himself described the view westward from the Green River as "disheartening in the extreme":

> Except three or four small cotton-wood trees in the ravine near us, there is not a tree to be seen by the unassisted eye on any part of the horizon. The plain lying between us and the Wahsatch range, a hundred miles to the west, is a series of rocky, parallel chasms, and fantastic sandstone ridges.[7]

For Clarence E. Dutton, Castle Valley represented the very type of Plateau Country desolation:

> If we stand upon the eastern verge of the Wasatch Plateau and look eastward, we shall behold one of those strange spectacles which are seen only in the Plateau Province, and which have a peculiar kind of impressiveness, and even of sublimity. From an altitude of more than 11,000 feet the eye can sweep a semicircle with a radius of more than 70 miles. It is not the wonder inspired by great mountains, for only two or three peaks of the Henry Mountains are well in view; and these, with their noble Alpine forms, seem as strangely out of place as Westminster Abbey would be among the ruins of Thebes. Nor is it the broad expanse of cheerful plains stretching their mottled surfaces beyond the visible horizon. It is a picture of desolation and decay; of a land dead and rotten, with dissolution apparent all over its face.[8]

In a similar response, the nineteenth-century English art critic and writer John Ruskin, upon viewing one of Thomas Moran's sketches of the Plateau Region, reportedly exclaimed, "What a horrible place to live in!" Moran replied, "Oh, we do not *live* there. Our country is so vast that we keep such places for scenic purposes only."[9]

Wallace Stegner, coming to the High Plateaus two-thirds of a century after Dutton, still found it to be "as terrible and beautiful a wasteland as the world can show," a place where "man is an interloper" and "everything he sees is a prophecy of his inconsequent destiny":

It is not merely the immensity and the loneliness and the emptiness of the land that bothers a man caught alone in it. The feeling is not the same that one gets on the great plains, where the sky is a bowl and the earth a disc and the eye is invited to notice the small things because the large ones are so characterless. In the Plateau Country the eye is not merely invited but compelled to notice the large things. From any point of vantage the view is likely to be open not with the twelve- or fifteen-mile radius of the plains, but with a radius that is often fifty and sometimes even seventy-five miles—and that is a long way to look, especially if there is nothing human in sight. The villages are hidden in the canyons and under the cliffs; there is nothing visible but the torn and slashed and windworn beauty of absolute wasteland. And the beauty is death. . . . The world is dead and disintegrating before your eyes.

Nowhere in the world, probably, is the transitoriness of human habitation shown so outrageously.[10]

It is interesting to superimpose upon this alienated vision the perceptions of a native. The image I have adapted for the title of this book comes from a passage in *Where Nothing Is Long Ago* where Virginia Sorensen reflects upon her own attachment to the High Plateau region while speculating on the reasons why Utah-bred sculptor Cyrus Dallin used to come back from Boston each year "to spend his summers in his old home":

His first figures had been molded of Utah clay, as had his immortal soul. He came back to renew himself with the rush of mountain water and the fruit of mountain land. Nowhere else, least of all in Boston, could one go in an hour from the tropic heat of the valley to the fragrant cool of a river running among pines. The profile of the mountains on the sky was the proper edge of his world, as of mine.[11]

My mother grew up under the escarpment of the Wasatch Plateau, not far from the likely viewpoint from which Dutton surveyed a scene of "desolation and decay." One of her earliest memories is of looking up at the irregular row of ponderosa pines silhouetted against the western sky and thinking they were Pete Joe and his cows. Peter Johansen was a neighbor who took his cattle "on the mountain" each summer. She also tells of sitting evening after evening at the kitchen window of her home on the outskirts of Castle Dale, stroking the cat in her lap and waiting expectantly for the moment when the oblique rays of the setting sun set fire to the buttes and canyons of the San Rafael Swell, transforming them into a shining city of castles more enchanted than those in storybooks.

My own first memories are charged with the mingled sense of freedom and security I derived from the wide but distinctly defined Castle Valley horizon. We lived on the western outskirts of Huntington, where the town met the irrigated fields. Beyond the fields, the Rowley Flats extended to the foothills of the high plateau, blue-gray except for the brief, glorious period when the prickly pears opened their waxy red and yellow blossoms, alive with anthills, prairie dog villages, and the lairs of badgers and coyotes. The foothills, their pediments clad in pinyon and juniper, were secret and remote, with ledges where golden eagles nested and deep washes leading to hidden glens. To the north, past Sandberg's Hill and the graveyard, lay the valley of Huntington Creek, where the ruined Otteson house stood like a lost chateau inside its palisade of tall spruces. The creek, noisy and strong above the diversion dams, was reduced to a thin stream below the dams, flowing lazily through willow thickets clotted with magpie nests, forming tepid pools where minnows darted around sluggish suckers and where I could go skinny-dipping under a canopy of garnet-studded bullberry bushes.

Having lived always at the edge of town, I grew up relishing solitude. I roamed the fields and hills, making trails, discovering secret places, founding kingdoms, or simply lying for hours at a stretch on the warm bank of an irrigation ditch, idly following the spasmodic motions of the water skaters and the slow drift of stray grains of coal in the stream: a plentiful waste of time, and the necessary laziness that fosters the imagination.

If I wanted society, there were pick-up baseball games on the dusty town square or basketball in the school gym with the Center Street Gang, snowball battles in the winter and girls' slumber parties to raid in the summer. Huntington offered all the institutions of a sizeable Mormon village: wardhouse, drugstore, post office, pool hall, honky-tonk; Twenty-fourth of July (Pioneer Day) parades, Gold and Green Balls, Relief Society parties, Old Folks parties, wedding parties, funerals; the men's glee club, acceptance into which was a major rite of passage for the boys of the town; high school basketball, track meets, debate meets, dramatics, band; fistfights outside the dance hall with the boys from Price. Then there were the people, the remarkable human variety of even an ethnically homogeneous community: ancient tottering men and women whose memories reached back to the beginning of things; the middle-aged, laboring to keep the town going; the young biding their time; cattlemen, sheepmen, lumbermen, salesmen, coal miners, merchants, teachers, millers, barbers, prospectors; seamstresses, hair-dressers, cooks, clerks, gardeners; the pious, the impious, the feeble-minded; prowlers, peeping toms, bullies, idlers, drunks, recluses.

But all of us depended, whether we were conscious of it or not, on the High Plateaus for every drop of water that came from our taps or sprinkled our lawns or irrigated our fields, for grazing land and timber land and coal, for hunting and fishing and summer campouts and pic-nics. And for giving the world its proper shape, one horizon looming high and protective, the others wide and spacious, giving tangible meaning to the hymn we often sang in the Mormon meetinghouse on Sundays:

> Thou hast led us here in safety
> Where the mountain bulwark stands
>
> For the rock and for the river,
> The valley's fertile sod,
> For the strength of the hills we bless thee,
> Our God, our fathers' God.[12]

NOTES

INTRODUCTION

1. Rowland W. Rider, *The Roll Away Saloon: Cowboy Tales of the Arizona Strip*, as told to Deirdre Murray Paulsen (Logan: Utah State University Press, 1985), 26–28.

CHAPTER 1

1. Newsletter of College of Eastern Utah Prehistoric Museum, 1989.

2. Jerry Spangler, "Researchers Unravel Mysteries of Mammoth," *Deseret News*, June 19, 1989, A1–A2.

3. "Did Now-extinct Animals Roam in Utah Mountains?" *Deseret News*, June 19, 1989, A2.

4. Spangler, "Researchers Unravel Mysteries of Mammoth," A2.

5. Wallace Stegner, *Beyond the Hundredth Meridian: John Wesley Powell and the Second Opening of the West* (Boston: Houghton Mifflin, 1954), 163.

6. C. E. Dutton, *Report on the Geology of the High Plateaus of Utah, with Atlas,* (Washington: Government Printing Office, 1880), 285.

7. Lincoln Ellison, "The Subalpine Vegetation of the Wasatch Plateau, Utah," *Ecological Monographs* 24 (April 1954): 104–5; quoted in Albert C. T. Antrei, ed., *The Other Forty-Niners: A Topical History of Sanpete County, Utah, 1849–1983* (Salt Lake City: Western Epics, 1982), 194.

8. W. H. Lever, *History of Sanpete and Emery Counties, Utah* (Ogden: Published by the author, 1898), 46–47.

9. Antrei, *The Other Forty-Niners*, 54–55.

10. U.S. Department of Agriculture, *Report on Agriculture by Irrigation in the Western Part of the United States at the Eleventh Census: 1890*, quoted in Antrei, *The Other Forty-Niners*, 59.

11. Lowry Nelson, *The Mormon Village: A Pattern and Technique of Land Settlement* (Salt Lake City: University of Utah Press, 1952), 143.

12. Glynn Bennion, "A Pioneer Cattle Venture of the Bennion Family," *Utah Historical Quarterly* 34 (Fall 1966):322; see also Charles S. Peterson, "Cowboys and Cattle Trails: A Centennial View of Emery County," in *Emery County: Reflections on Its Past and Future*, ed. Allan Kent Powell (Salt Lake City: Utah Historical Society, 1979), 79–96.

13. Montell Seely, "The Livestockmen," in *Emery County, 1880–1980* (Emery County Historical Society, 1981), 17–18.

14. Richard H. Jackson, "Utah's Harsh Lands, Hearth of Greatness," *Utah Historical Quarterly* 49 (Winter 1981):9.

15. A. H. Thompson, "Irrigable Lands of That Portion of Utah Drained by the Colorado River and Its Tributaries," in J. W. Powell, *Report of the Lands of the Arid Region of the United States, with a More Detailed Account of the Lands of Utah* (Washington: Government Printing Office, 1879), 158–59.

16. Antrei, *The Other Forty-Niners*, 273.

17. Ibid., 275.

18. The quoted phrase is from Pearle Madsen Olsen's memoir, *Nickels from a Sheep's Back* (Salt Lake City: Publisher's Press, 1976).

19. Antrei, *The Other Forty-Niners*, 276.

20. Petition from Citizens of Huntington, Cleveland, Lawrence, and Desert Lake to the Commissioner of the General Land Office, *Emery County Progress*, November 14, 1903, 4.

21. Antrei, *The Other Forty-Niners*, 196.

22. Ibid., 206.

23. Ibid., 200–201.

24. R. V. R. Reynolds, "Grazing and Floods: A Study of Conditions in the Manti National Forest, Utah," United States Forest Service Bulletin 91 (1911); Lincoln Ellison, "The Subalpine Vegetation of the Wasatch Plateau, Utah," *Ecological Monographs* 24 (April 1954); both quoted in Antrei, *The Other Forty-Niners*, 197.

25. Lever, *History of Sanpete and Emery Counties*, 68.

26. Quoted in Antrei, *The Other Forty-Niners*, 200.

27. John Petersen, "Natural Disasters Have Impacted Local Forest," *Emery County Progress*, August 1, 1991, 3.

28. Antrei, *The Other Forty-Niners*, 193.

29. Quoted in Antrei, *The Other Forty-Niners*, 206.

30. *Emery County Progress*, January 27, 1906, 1.

31. Quoted in Jay M. Haymond, "Natural Resources in Emery County," in *Emery County: Reflections on Its Past and Future*, ed. Allan Kent Powell (Salt Lake City: Utah State Historical Society, 1979), 57.

32. *Emery County Progress*, October 3, 1903, 1.

33. Antrei, *The Other Forty-Niners*, 214.

34. There is a good description of "summer dairying" in Nethella Griffin Woolsey, *The Escalante Story: A History of the Town of Escalante, and Description of the Surrounding Territory, Garfield County, Utah, 1875–1964* (Springville, Utah: Art City Publishing Company, 1964), 109–11.

35. William Lee Stokes and Robert E. Cohenour, "Geological Atlas of Utah: Emery County," *Utah Geological and Mineralogical Survey Bulletin* 52 (1956):11.

36. For a summary of the Gooseberry Valley issue from a Sanpete perspective, see Antrei, *The Other Forty-Niners*, 496–97.

37. Lowry Nelson, *In the Direction of His Dreams: Memoirs* (New York: Philosophical Library, 1985), 107.

38. Dutton, *Geology of the High Plateaus*, 284.

CHAPTER 2

1. Wallace Stegner, *Beyond the Hundredth Meridian*, 161.

2. William Lee Stokes, *Geology of Utah* (Salt Lake City: Utah Museum of Natural History and Utah Geological and Mineral Survey, 1986), 11.

3. Quoted in LeRoy R. Hafen and Ann W. Hafen, *The Old Spanish Trail: Santa Fe to Los Angeles* (Glendale: Arthur H. Clark, 1954), 112.

4. See Dale L. Morgan, *Jedediah Smith and the Opening of the West* (Cleveland: Bobbs-Merrill, 1953), 196.

5. George R. Brooks, ed., *The Southwest Expedition of Jedediah S. Smith: His Personal Account of the Journey to California, 1826–27* (Glendale: Arthur H. Clark, 1977), 11–14.

6. Ibid., 44–46n.

7. Ibid., 46.

8. John C. Frémont, "A Report of the Exploring Expedition to Oregon and North

California in the Years 1843–44," in *The Expeditions of John Charles Frémont* (3 vols., Urbana: University of Illinois Press, 1970), 1:704.

9. Brooks, 49.

10. Ibid., 47.

11. Montell Seely et al., eds., *Emery County, 1880–1980* (Castle Dale, Utah: Emery County Historical Society, 1981), 16.

12. "The Chronicles of George C. Yount," *California Historical Society Quarterly* 2.1 (April 1923):38.

13. Ibid., 39, 40.

14. Ibid.

15. Hafen, *Old Spanish Trail*, 19.

16. Ibid., 299, 308–10.

17. Ibid., 182–88.

18. Ibid., 235–39.

19. J. C. Frémont, *Report of the Exploring Expedition to the Rocky Mountains in the Year 1842, and to Oregon and North California in the Years 1843–44* (Washington: Blair and Rives, 1845), 268.

20. Ibid., 271.

21. George D. Brewerton, "A Ride with Kit Carson through the Great American Desert and the Rocky Mountains," *Harper's New Monthly Magazine*, August 1853, 306–34; quoted in Hafen, *Old Spanish Trail*, 331–32.

22. *William Clayton's Journal*, quoted in Richard H. Jackson, "Utah's Harsh Lands, Hearth of Greatness," *Utah Historical Quarterly* 49 (Winter 1981):11.

23. Journal History of the Church, December 28–29, 1849, quoted in Jackson, "Utah's Harsh Lands," 12.

24. Diary of Parley P. Pratt, March 31, 1851, quoted in Jackson, "Utah's Harsh Lands," 16.

25. Journal History of the Church, December 31, 1849, quoted in Jackson, "Utah's Harsh Lands," 17.

26. E. G. Beckwith, *Report of Exploration of a Route for the Pacific Railroad, Near the 38th and 39th Parallels of Latitude, from the Mouth of the Kansas to Sevier River, in the Great Basin* (Washington: A.O.P. Nicholson, Printer, 1855), 90.

27. Ibid., 65.

28. John C. Frémont to Thomas H. Benton, February 9, 1854, in *The Expeditions of John Charles Frémont*, ed. Mary Lee Spence (3 vols., Urbana: University of Illinois Press, 1984), 3:470.

29. For a discussion of the possible route around the San Rafael Reef, see Joseph W. Bauman, Jr., *Stone House Lands: The San Rafael Reef* (Salt Lake City: University of Utah Press, 1987), 96–105.

30. The site of the cache was identified by George Washington Bean, a resident of Beaver, who claimed to have received the information from Wakara. *Autobiography of George Washington Bean* (Salt Lake City, 1945), cited in Hafen, *Old Spanish Trail*, 300.

CHAPTER 3

1. Elizabeth Wood Kane, *Twelve Mormon Homes, Visited in Succession on a Journey Through Utah to Arizona*, ed. Everett L. Cooley (Salt Lake City: Tanner Trust Fund, University of Utah Library, 1974), 54, 61.

2. Quoted in Ward J. Roylance, ed., *Utah: A Guide to the State*, revised edition (Salt Lake City: Utah Arts Council, 1982), 525.

3. Sheldon Young's Log, in *Journals of Forty-Niners, Salt Lake to Los Angeles*, ed. LeRoy R. Hafen and Ann W. Hafen (Glendale: Arthur H. Clark, 1954), 64, 65.

4. Addison Pratt's Diary, Ibid., 73.

5. Kane, *Twelve Mormon Homes*, 62, 63. "Bishop Collister" was Thomas Callister, then president of the Millard LDS Stake.

6. Kane, *Twelve Mormon Homes*, 75, 77.

7. Stokes, *Geology of Utah*, 249.

8. S. N. Carvalho, *Incidents of Travel and Adventure in the Far West; with Col. Frémont's Last Expedition Across the Rocky Mountains: Including Three Months' Residence in Utah, and a Perilous Trip Across the Great American Desert to the Pacific* (New York: Derby and Jackson, 1860), 204.

9. Quoted in *Monuments to Courage: A History of Beaver County* (Beaver County, Utah: Daughters of Utah Pioneers, 1948), 169–70.

10. Ibid., 31–32.

11. See Linda L. Bonar, "Historic Houses in Beaver: An Introduction to Materials, Styles, and Craftsmen," *Utah Historical Quarterly* 51 (Summer 1983):212–28.

12. Kane, *Twelve Mormon Homes*, 97–98.

13. Ibid., 99–101.

14. Carvalho, *Incidents of Travel and Adventure*, 211.

15. Kane, *Twelve Morman Homes*, 103–4.

16. Ibid., 101.

17. Ibid., 108.

18. Stegner, *Beyond the Hundredth Meridian*, 161.

19. Ibid., 159.

20. Dutton, *Geology of the High Plateaus*, 189, 195.

21. *Golden Nuggets of Pioneer Days: A History of Garfield County* (Panguitch: Garfield County Chapter, Daughters of Utah Pioneers, 1949), 219.

22. Ibid., 221–22.

23. Roylance, *Utah: A Guide to the State*, 640.

24. Dutton, *Geology of the High Plateaus*, 199.

25. Ibid., 208–9.

26. Ibid., 14.

27. Clarence E. Dutton, *Tertiary History of the Grand Cañon District*, United States Geological Survey, Monographs, no. 2 (Washington, D.C.: Government Printing Office, 1882), 140.

28. Dutton, *Geology of the High Plateaus*, 8.

29. Kane, *Twelve Mormon Homes*, 123.

30. Ibid., 124.

31. Ibid., 131, 132.

32. *Journal of Discourses*, 5:222, quoted in Jackson, "Utah's Harsh Lands," 19.

33. Juanita Brooks, *On the Ragged Edge: The Life and Times of Dudley Leavitt* (Salt Lake City: Utah State Historical Society, 1973).

34. George Hicks, "Once I Lived in Cottonwood," in Thomas E. Cheney, ed., *Mormon Songs from the Rocky Mountains: A Compilation of Mormon Folksongs* (Austin: University of Texas Press, 1968), 118–20.

35. Dutton, *Tertiary History of the Grand Cañon District*, 57–60.

CHAPTER 4

1. J.W., Powell, *Exploration of the Colorado River of the West*, 92–93.

2. Frederick S. Dellenbaugh, *A Canyon Voyage: The Narrative of the Second Powell Expedition down the Green-Colorado River from Wyoming, and the Explorations on Land, in the Years 1871 and 1872* (New Haven: Yale University Press, 1926), 166–67 (originally published in 1908).

3. Wallace Stegner, "Arcadian Village," in *Mormon Country* (New York: Duell, Sloan and Pearce, 1942), 121–22.

4. Ibid., 127.

5. Dellenbaugh, *Canyon Voyage*, 262.

6. Ibid., 264.

7. Dutton, *Geology of the High Plateaus*, 226.

8. Ibid.

9. Ibid., 169, 170.

10. Ibid., 213.

11. Josiah F. Gibbs, *Marysvale Red Book: Being a Brief Synoptical Review of the Vast Resources of the Magnificent Tushar Range, Its Metal-Bearing Fissures, Great Veins and Deposits of Available Potash, with Map, and Uniquely Beautiful Illustrations of Mountain Peaks and Divides* (Marysvale, Utah: Published by the author, 1916), 3.

12. Woolsey, *Escalante Story*, 137.

13. Dean F. Herring, *From Lode to Dust: The Birth and Death of Kimberly, Utah* (Privately printed, 1989), 7.

14. Ibid., 13.

15. Ibid., 56.

16. Ed Tilton, commentary attached to Miriam Limb, *Kimberly* (Privately published, 1975), 16, 28.

17. Josephine Pace, "Kimberly as I Remember Her," *Utah Historical Quarterly* 35 (Spring 1967):119, 120.

18. For a fuller account of the Richfield Tabernacle see Pearl F. Jacobson, *Sevier County Historic Sites* (Richfield: Sevier County Historical Society, 1974).

19. *Deseret News*, October 15, 1898.

20. *Deseret News*, November 14, 1901.

21. *Richfield Reaper*, November 22, 1923.

22. Ibid., November 29, 1923.

23. A. H. Thompson places Dutton in the region of Mount Hilgard, northeast of the Fish Lake Plateau, in July 1875, "Diary of Almon Harris Thompson," *Utah Historical Quarterly* 7 (1939): 123.

24. Dutton, *Geology of the High Plateaus*, 170–71.

25. C. E. Dutton, "Church and State in Utah," *Forum* 5 (1888): 320.

26. Ibid., 320, 328, 329.

27. Ibid., 330.

28. Ibid., 322–23.

29. Ibid., 323.

30. Ibid., 324.

31. Peter S. Briggs and Brian Q. Cannon, *Life and Land: The Farm Security Administration Photographers in Utah, 1936–1941* (Logan, Utah: Nora Eccles Harrison Museum of Art, Utah State University, 1988), 5, 15–18.

32. Powell *Exploration of the Colorado River of the West*, 107, 108.

33. Roylance, *Utah: A Guide to the State*, 311–12.

34. Dutton, *Geology of the High Plateaus*, 254.

35. Ibid., 259.

36. Ibid., 262.

CHAPTER 5

1. Kathryn L. MacKay, "Indian Cultures, c. 1840," in Deon C. Greer et al., ed., *Atlas of Utah* (Provo, Utah: Brigham Young Univ. Press for Weber State College, 1981), 77. Cedar City antiquarian William R. Palmer, who cultivated a wide acquaintance among the Paiutes in the early decades of the twentieth century, claimed there were more than thirty Paiute bands with defined territories. See his "Pahute Indian Homelands," *Utah Historical Quarterly* 6.3 (1932): 88–102.

2. The standard overview is Jesse D. Jennings, *Prehistory of Utah and the Eastern*

Great Basin, University of Utah Anthropological Papers No. 98 (Salt Lake City: University of Utah Press, 1978).

3. See Pamela A. Bunte and Robert J. Franklin, *From the Sands to the Mountain: Change and Persistence in a Southern Paiute Community* (Lincoln: University of Nebraska Press, 1987), especially chapters 1 and 2.

4. Powell, *Exploration of the Colorado River*, 318–20.

5. "The Chronicles of George C. Yount," 38–39.

6. Brooks, ed., *Southwest Expedition of Jedediah Smith*, 43.

7. Ibid., 48, 49.

8. Ibid., 60–67.

9. Henry W. Bigler Journal, Charles C. Rich Diary, in Hafen, *Journals of Forty-Niners*, 153, 186.

10. John Charles Frémont, *Narratives of Exploration and Adventure*, ed. Allan Nevins (New York: Longmans, Green, 1956), 410, 411.

11. Ibid., 417.

12. Peter Gottfredson, *History of Indian Depredations in Utah* (Salt Lake City: Skelton, 1919), 74–78.

13. S. N. Carvalho, *Incidents of Travel and Adventure in the Far West; with Col. Frémont's Last Expedition Across the Rocky Mountains: Including Three Months' Residence in Utah, and a Perilous Trip Across the Great American Desert, to the Pacific* (New York: Derby and Jackson, 1860), 192, 194.

14. Ibid., 196–97.

15. Ibid., 200.

16. Powell, *Exploration of the Colorado River*, 126.

17. Ibid., 113.

18. Ibid., 115.

19. Ibid., 129.

20. Powell, *Report on the Lands of the Arid Region*, 17–18.

21. Powell, *Exploration of the Colorado River and Its Canyons*, 112–13.

22. W. W. Phelps, "O Stop and Tell Me, Red Man," in *Latter-day Saint Hymns* (Salt Lake City: Deseret Book, 1928), number 64.

23. For an argument that Mormon dealings with the Indians were relatively enlightened, see Ronald W. Walker, "Toward a Reconstruction of Mormon and Indian Relations, 1847–1877," *BYU Studies* 29.4 (Fall 1989):23–42; for the view that Mormons treated Indians about as badly as other nineteenth-century Americans did, see, for example, Howard A. Christy, "Open Hand and Mailed Fist: Mormon-Indian Relations in Utah, 1847–52," *Utah Historical Quarterly* 46 (Summer 1978):214–26, and Fred A. Conetah, *A History of the Northern Ute People*, ed. Kathryn L. MacKay and Floyd A. O'Neil (Salt Lake City: Uintah-Ouray Ute Tribe, 1982).

24. Leonard J. Arrington, *Brigham Young: American Moses* (New York: Knopf, 1985), 222.

25. Elizabeth Wood Kane, *Twelve Mormon Homes*, 64–65.

26. Ibid., 33, 40.

27. Brigham Young, "Remarks," *Deseret News*, August 16, 1866.

28. Conetah, *History of the Northern Ute People*, 37.

29. William R. Palmer, "Pahute Indian Homelands," 89.

30. Walker, "Mormon and Indian Relations," 29.

31. "A Ride with Kit Carson," quoted in Hafen, *Old Spanish Trail*, 326.

32. Antrei, *The Other Forty-Niners*, 8.

33. Conetah, *History of the Northern Ute People*, 8.

34. Gunnison wrote of "thirty sons" of "a late chief" who ruled the Utes. *The Mormons, or Latter-day Saints, in the Valley of the Great Salt Lake* (Philadelphia, 1860), 148. Conway B. Sonne gleaned from journal sources fifteen names that were described at one

time or another as brothers or half-brothers of Walker. "Royal Blood of the Utes," *Utah Historical Quarterly* 22 (July 1954): 271–76.

35. Antrei, *The Other Forty-Niners*, 130–31.

36. Ibid., 26.

37. Ibid., 135.

38. This document is reportedly held in the LDS Church Archives and is quoted in W. H. Lever, *History of Sanpete and Emery Counties* (Ogden: Published by the author, 1898), 21–22.

39. Powell, *Exploration of the Colorado River*, 311.

40. Gottfredson, *Indian Depredations in Utah*, 335–38.

41. Conetah prefers to call Black Hawk Autenquer. *History of the Northern Ute People*, 86.

42. Gottfredson, *Indian Depredations in Utah*, 130–38.

43. Ibid., 160–61.

44. Quoted in Albert Winkler, "The Circleville Massacre: A Brutal Incident in Utah's Black Hawk War," *Utah Historical Quarterly* 55 (Winter 1987): 18. Winkler's is the most comprehensive study of the Circleville massacre.

45. Ibid., 19.

46. Gottfredson, *Indian Depredations*, 203.

47. Carlton Culmsee, *Utah's Black Hawk War: Lore and Reminiscences of Participants* (Logan: Utah State University Press, 1973), 141.

48. Quoted in Gottfredson, *Indian Depredations*, 227.

49. Culmsee, *Utah's Black Hawk War*, 154.

50. Ibid.

51. Gottfredson, *Indian Depredations*, 226.

52. *Deseret News*, September 25, 1861, quoted in Charles S. Peterson, *Utah: A Bicentennial History* (New York: Norton, 1977), 137.

53. There may have been some Pahvants among the Grass Valley group. Even Conetah, writing about his own people, admits that the distinction between the Pahvants and the Sanpitches is not clear, and that "the San Pitch may have been a branch of the Pah Vant. Certainly as they acquired the horse, and as they were disrupted by white settlers, they allied themselves with the Pah Vant People." *History of the Northern Ute People*, 86.

54. Carvalho, *Incidents of Travel and Adventure*, 190.

CHAPTER 6

1. Roylance, *Utah: A Guide to the State*, 656.

2. Montell Seely, "Irrigation on Cottonwood Creek," in *Emery County— 1880–1980*, 78.

3. Ibid., 78–88.

4. Wilford Woodruff, Journal, July 24, 1847, quoted in Richard H. Jackson, "Utah's Harsh Lands," 6.

5. Thomas Bullock, Journal, July 22, 1847, quoted in Jackson, "Utah's Harsh Lands," 6–7.

6. *William Clayton's Journal*, quoted in Jackson, "Utah's Harsh Lands," 6, 7.

7. Brigham Young declared in a sermon given in Cache Valley that "the climate of these valleys has been modified and mollified" for the benefit of the Mormon settlers. *Journal of Discourses*, 16:68, quoted in Jackson, "Utah's Harsh Lands," 9. For a general treatment of nineteenth-century ideas about climate modification, see Henry Nash Smith, "Rain Follows the Plow: The Notion of Increased Rainfall for the Great Plains," *Huntington Library Quarterly* 10.2 (February 1947): 169–94.

8. J. W. Powell, *Lands of the Arid Region*, 6–7.

9. Ibid., 7–9.

10. Ibid., 10.

11. Ibid., 13.

12. Lever, *History of Sanpete and Emery Counties*, 281.

13. *Monuments to Courage*, 64.

14. James S. Brown, *Life of a Pioneer* (Salt Lake City, 1900), quoted in Hafen, *Journals of Forty-Niners*, 116.

15. G. K. Gilbert, "Water Supply," in Powell, *Lands of the Arid Region*, 57.

16. Ibid., 70.

17. Ibid., 77.

18. Thomas Hastings (1784–1872), "Hail to the Brightness of Zion's Glad Morning," *Hymns* (Salt Lake City: The Church of Jesus Christ of Latter-day Saints, 1985), 42.

19. Wallace Stegner, *The Sound of Mountain Water* (Garden City: Doubleday, 1969), 41, 42.

20. Wallace Stegner, *Mormon Country* (New York: Duell, Sloan and Pearce, 1942), 3.

21. Wallace Stegner, *Recapitulation* (Garden City: Doubleday, 1979), 193.

22. Maurine Whipple, *The Giant Joshua* (Boston: Houghton Mifflin, 1942).

23. Virginia Sorensen, *The Evening and the Morning* (New York: Harcourt, Brace, 1949), 205.

24. Virginia Sorensen, *On This Star* (New York: Reynal and Hitchcock, 1946), 12.

25. Virginia Sorensen, *Where Nothing Is Long Ago: Memories of a Mormon Childhood* (New York: Harcourt, Brace and World, 1963), 5.

26. Ibid., 7–8.

27. Ibid., 3–4.

28. Ibid., 4.

29. Ibid., 14.

30. Olive Woolley Burt, *American Murder Ballads and Their Stories* (New York: Oxford University Press, 1958), 243–44. Burt found this ballad among the papers of her mother, who had grown up in southern Utah and known the Seegmiller and Roundy families.

31. Ibid., 241–42.

32. Sorensen, *Where Nothing Is Long Ago*, 7.

33. Ibid., 6–7.

34. John Sterling Harris, "The Whittler," in *Barbed Wire* (Provo, Utah: Brigham Young University Press, 1974), 35–39.

CHAPTER 7

1. See Levi S. Peterson, *Juanita Brooks: Mormon Woman Historian* (Salt Lake City: University of Utah Press, 1988).

2. Mary W. Howard, "An Example of Women in Politics," *Improvement Era*, July 1914; reprinted in *Utah Historical Quarterly* 38 (Winter 1970):62–64.

3. Adelia B. Sidwell, "A Scrap of True History," in *Song of a Century* (Manti, Utah: Manti Centennial Committee, 1949), 35.

4. Grace Johnson, "Ephraim," in *These Our Fathers: A Centennial History of Sanpete County, 1849 to 1947* (Sanpete County Daughters of Utah Pioneers, 1947), 77.

5. James Boyd Christensen, "Function and Fun in Utah-Danish Nicknames," *Utah Historical Quarterly* 39 (Winter 1971):23–27.

6. These names are all listed in Susan Peterson, "Ephraim Stories," typescript, Folklore Archives, Harold B. Lee Library, Brigham Young University, Provo, Utah, 15–28. Other collections of Sanpete nicknames include "Ephraim's Humor," M.A. Thesis, Uni-

versity of Utah, 1950; Hector Lee with Royal Madsen, "Nicknames of the Ephraimites," *Western Humanities Review* 3 (January 1949):12–22; and James Boyd Christensen, "Function and Fun in Utah-Danish Nicknames," *Utah Historical Quarterly* 39 (Winter 1971):23–29.

7. Peterson, "Ephraim Stories," 17.

8. Antrei, *The Other Forty-Niners*, 87.

9. Woodruff C. Thomson, quoted in Peterson, "Ephraim Stories," 67.

10. Ibid., 39.

11. Ibid., 32.

12. Ibid., 34–35.

13. Ibid., 75.

14. Ibid., 43.

15. Ibid., 98.

16. Edith Christiansen, quoted in Peterson, "Ephraim Stories," 96–97.

17. Sorensen, *Where Nothing Is Long Ago*, 17–18.

18. Sorensen, *On This Star*, 20, 110.

19. Ibid., 190.

20. Virginia Sorensen, *The Evening and the Morning* (New York: Harcourt, Brace, 1949), 19, 21.

21. Ibid., 341.

22. Quoted in *Utah: A Guide to the State* (New York: Hastings House, 1941), 402.

23. Seely, et al., *Emery County*, 432.

24. This and other quotes from Mary Ann Brown are from "Personal History of Mary Ann Rowberry Brown Gordon," typescript in Special Collections, Harold B. Lee Library, Brigham Young University, Provo, Utah.

CHAPTER 8

1. John Fowles, *Daniel Martin* (New York: New American Library, 1978), 290.

2. Dutton, *Geology of the High Plateaus*, 254.

3. C. Gregory Crampton, ed., "Military Reconnaissance in Southern Utah, 1866," *Utah Historical Quarterly* 32 (1966): 145–61.

4. "The Diary of Almon Harris Thompson," *Utah Historical Quarterly* 7 (1939):83.

5. Dutton, *Geology of the High Plateaus*, 284–85.

6. *Golden Nuggets of Pioneer Days*, 146.

7. Thirza and Irene King, "Boulder, Utah," in *Heart Throbs of the West*, compiled by Kate B. Carter (Salt Lake City: Daughters of Utah Pioneers, 1943), 4: 331–32.

8. *Golden Nuggets of Pioneer Days*, 146, 147.

9. Thirza and Irene King, "Boulder, Utah," 4:331–32.

10. *Golden Nuggets of Pioneer Days*, 145.

11. Crampton, "Military Reconnaissance," 153.

12. Ibid., 156.

13. Dutton, *Geology of the High Plateaus*, 286–87.

14. Ibid., 8, 9.

15. Ibid., 19.

16. Ibid., 287, 288–90.

17. Ibid., 289.

CHAPTER 9

1. Quoted in Woolsey, *Escalante Story*, 106.

2. The fullest account of Ruess's career is W. L. Rusho, *Everett Ruess: A Vagabond for Beauty* (Salt Lake City: Peregrine Smith, 1983).

3. Ibid., 175.

4. Ibid., 178.

5. Ibid., 176.

6. Stegner, *Mormon Country*, 321, 330.

7. Rusho, *Everett Ruess*, 180.

8. Ibid., 165.

9. Ibid., 171.

10. Ibid., 178, 180, 179.

11. Ibid., Introduction, ix.

12. Woolsey, *Escalante Story*, 187.

13. "The Diary of Almon Harris Thompson," 124.

14. Lowry Nelson, *The Mormon Village: A Pattern and Technique of Land Settlement* (Salt Lake City: University of Utah Press, 1952), 83–84.

15. Dutton, *Geology of the High Plateaus*, 298.

16. Jack Breed, "First Motor Sortie into Escalante Land," *National Geographic*, September 1949, 375.

17. Woolsey, *Escalante Story*, 87.

18. Ibid., 401–2.

19. Ibid.

20. Briggs and Cannon, *Life and Land*, 5, 13–14; Nelson, *Mormon Village*.

21. Nelson, *Mormon Village*, 83.

22. Ibid., 28, 38.

23. Ibid., 85.

24. Ibid., 107.

25. Ibid., 100.

26. Ibid., 97.

27. Ibid., 107.

28. Woolsey, *Escalante Story*, 389.

29. Briggs and Cannon, *Life and Land*, 6.

30. Nelson, *Mormon Village*, 110.

31. Ibid., 115.

32. Ibid., 122–23.

33. Woolsey, *Escalante Story*, 83.

34 *Utah: A Guide to the State*, 340.

35. Nelson, *Mormon Village*, 119.

36. Woolsey, *Escalante Story*, 92.

37. Quoted in Michael Millgate, *Thomas Hardy: A Biography* (New York: Random House, 1982), 31.

38. Gerard Manley Hopkins, "Inversnaid," in *Poems and Prose of Gerard Manley Hopkins*, ed. W. H. Gardner (Harmondsworth: Penguin, 1953), 51.

39. Edward Abbey, "Last Oasis," *Harper's*, March 1977, 10.

40. Ibid., 8.

CHAPTER 10

1. Juanita Brooks, *John Doyle Lee: Zealot, Pioneer Builder, Scapegoat* (Glendale: Arthur H. Clark, 1962), 293.

2. Ibid., 296.

3. Robert Glass Cleland and Juanita Brooks, *A Mormon Chronicle: The Diaries of John D. Lee, 1848–1876*, 2 vols. (San Marino: Huntington Library, 1955), 2: 175–76.

4. W. L. Rusho and C. Gregory Crampton, *Desert River Crossing: Historic Lee's Ferry on the Colorado River* (Salt Lake City and Santa Barbara: Peregrine Smith, 1975), 11.

5. Ibid., 15, 17.

6. Powell, *Exploration of the Colorado River*, 233–34.

7. Rusho and Crampton, *Desert River Crossing*, 17–18.

8. Wallace Stegner, *Beyond the Hundredth Meridian*, 138.

9. Brooks, *John Doyle Lee*, 380, 383.

10. Ibid., 307.

11. Ibid., 311.

12. Rusho and Crampton, *Desert River Crossing*, 82–83.

13. Ida Bell Acord Jacoby, "A Brief Outline of My History as a Utah Pioneer," typescript, 1939, p. 10.

14. Rusho and Crampton, *Desert River Crossing*, 46.

15. Ibid., 54.

16. Zane Grey, *The Heritage of the Desert* (New York: Grossett and Dunlap, 1910), 43.

17. Sharlot M. Hall, *Sharlot Hall on the Arizona Strip: A Dairy of a Journey Through Northern Arizona in 1911*, ed. C. Gregory Crampton (Flagstaff: Northland Press, 1975), 87.

18. Rider, *The Roll Away Saloon*, 3–4.

19. Hall, *Arizona Strip*, 64.

20. Ibid., 60.

21. Dutton, *Geology of the High Plateaus*, 209.

22. Stegner, *Beyond the Hundredth Meridian*, 173.

23. Clarence E. Dutton, *Tertiary History of the Grand Cañon District*, 124.

24. Dutton, *Tertiary History of the Grand Cañon District*, 129.

25. Ibid., 130.

26. Ibid., 131–32.

27. Powell, *Exploration of the Colorado River*, 102.

28. Dutton, *Tertiary History of the Grand Cañon District*, 135, 136.

29. Hall, *Arizona Strip*, 66.

30. Ibid., 67.

31. Ibid., 68.

32. Ibid., 71–72.

33. Ibid., 73, 74, 75, 80, 81.

34. Walter G. Mann, *The Kaibab Deer: A Brief History and the Present Plan of Management* (Kaibab National Forest, Arizona, 1941), 7.

35. Ibid., 8.

36. Ibid., 20.

37. Ibid., 17.

38. *Zion National Park, Bryce Canyon, Cedar Breaks, Kaibab Forest, North Rim of the Grand Canyon* (Omaha: Union Pacific System, 1925), 29.

39. Mann, *The Kaibab Deer*, 15.

40. Ibid., 21.

41. Ibid., 17.

42. Ibid., 19.

43. Dutton, *Tertiary History of the Grand Cañon District*, 133.

44. Ibid., 133.

45. Powell, *Exploration of the Colorado River*, 103–4.

46. Powell reports finding a cultivated garden on the north bank of the river during his 1869 trip. *Exploration of the Colorado River*, 274–75.

47. Ibid., 323.

48. Nellie Iverson Cox and Helen Bundy Russell, *Footprints on the Arizona Strip* (Bountiful, Utah: Horizon, 1973), 10.

49. For a succinct account of the history of Pipe Spring, see David Lavender, *Pipe Spring and the Arizona Strip* (Springdale, Utah: Zion Natural History Association, 1984).

50. Virginia N. Price and John T. Darby, "Preston Nutter: Utah Cattleman, 1886–1936," *Utah Historical Quarterly* 32 (1964): 232–51.

51. Ibid., 244.

52. Cox and Russell, *Footprints on the Arizona Strip*, 13.

53. Price and Darby, "Preston Nutter," 244.

54. Mann, *The Kaibab Deer*, 8.

55. Ibid.; Cox and Russell, *Footprints on the Arizona Strip*, 15.

56. Dutton, *Tertiary History of the Grand Cañon District*, 78–79.

57. Rider, *The Roll Away Saloon*, 42.

58. Zane Grey, "The Man Who Influenced Me Most," quoted in Rusho and Crampton, *Desert River Crossing*, 58.

59. Grey, *The Heritage of the Desert*, 53–54.

60. Rider, *The Roll Away Saloon*, 42–55.

61. Wallace Stegner, "Fossil Remains of an Idea," in *Mormon Country*, 213.

62. Ibid., 209–26.

63. Wiley S. Maloney, "Arizona Raided Short Creek—Why?" *Colliers*, November 13, 1953, 27.

64. "The Great Love-Nest Raid," *Time*, August 3, 1953, 16; "The Lonely Men of Short Creek," *Life*, September 14, 1953, 35–39; Edson Jessop with Maurine Whipple, "Why I Have Five Wives," *Colliers*, November 13, 1953, 27–30; Samuel W. Taylor, "I Have Six Wives," *True*, November 1953, 22–87; see also "The Big Raid," *Newsweek*, August 3, 1953, 26; James Cary, "The Untold Story of Short Creek," *American Mercury*, May 1954, 119–23.

65. Hall, *Arizona Strip*, 17.

66. Cox and Russell, *Footprints on the Arizona Strip*.

67. Maurine Whipple, "Arizona Strip—America's Tibet," *Colliers*, May 24, 1952, 66.

68. Ibid., 67.

69. Jennie H. Brown and Nora M. Heaton, *Moccasin and Her People* (Privately published, 1983).

CHAPTER 11

1. Nelson, *In the Direction of His Dreams*, 172.

2. A. Philip Cederlof, "The Peerless Coal Mines," *Utah Historical Quarterly* 53 (Fall 1985): 336.

3. Stokes, *Geology of Utah*, 131–42.

4. Ibid., 153–54.

5. William Lee Stokes and Robert E. Cohenour, "Geologic Atlas of Utah: Emery County," *Utah Geological and Mineralogical Survey Bulletin* 52 (1956):11.

6. A. C. Watts, "Opening First Commercial Coal Mine Described," in Thursey Jessen Reynolds, et al., *Centennial Echoes from Carbon County* (Price, Utah: Carbon County Daughters of Utah Pioneers, 1948), 35.

7. Hannah M. Mendenhall, "The Calico Road," in *Heart Throbs of the West*, ed. Kate B. Carter (Salt Lake City: Daughters of Utah Pioneers, 1940), 28.

8. Robert G. Athearn, "Foreword" to O. Meredith Wilson, *The Denver and Rio Grande Project, 1870–1901: A History of the First Thirty Years of the Denver and Rio Grande Railroad* (Salt Lake City and Chicago: Howe Brothers, 1982), vii.

9. Robert G. Athearn, *Rebel of the Rockies: A History of the Denver and Rio Grande Western Railroad* (New Haven and London: Yale University Press, 1962), 219–20.

10. Watts, "Opening First Commercial Coal Mine," 37.

11. Ibid.

12. Allan Kent Powell, *The Next Time We Strike: Labor in Utah's Coal Fields, 1900–1933* (Logan: Utah State University Press, 1985), 38.

13. See Eric Margolis, "Western Coal Mining as a Way of Life: An Oral History of the Colorado Coal Mines to 1914," *Journal of the American West* 24.3 (July 1985): 5–115.

14. Watts, "Opening First Commercial Coal Mine Described."

15. For a carefully researched account of the Winter Quarters disaster, see Powell, *The Next Time We Strike*, 27–35; also see J. W. Dilley, *History of the Scofield Mine Disaster* (Provo: privately published, 1900).

16. Allan Kent Powell, "Land of Three Heritages: Mormons, Immigrants, and Miners," in *Carbon County: Eastern Utah's Industrialized Island*, ed. Philip F. Notarianni (Salt Lake City: Utah State Historical Society, 1981), 11.

17. Philip F. Notarianni, "Italianità in Utah: The Immigrant Experience," in *The Peoples of Utah*, ed. Helen Z. Papanikolas (Salt Lake City: Utah State Historical Society, 1976), 304.

18. Quoted in Allan Kent Powell, "Land of Three Heritages," 16.

19. These figures from G. W. Kramer, vice-president of the Pleasant Valley Coal Company, were published in the *Eastern Utah Advocate*, December 3, 1903; cited in Notarianni, "Italianità in Utah," 310.

20. Powell, *The Next Time We Strike*, 53.

21. Notarianni, "Italianità in Utah," 312.

22. For an account of the strike see Powell, *The Next Time We Strike*, 51–80.

23. Salt Lake City *Deseret News*, December 21, 1903; quoted in Powell, *The Next Time We Strike*, 63.

24. *Deseret News*, April 30, 1904, quoted in Powell, *The Next Time We Strike*, 71–72.

25. *Autobiography of Mother Jones*, quoted in Powell, *The Next Time We Strike*, 73.

26. *Deseret News*, April 25, 1904, quoted in Powell, *The Next Time We Strike*, 74.

27. Helen Z. Papanikolas, "The Exiled Greeks," in *The Peoples of Utah*, 411–12.

28. Ibid., 409.

29. Ibid., 417.

30. Helen Z. Papanikolas, *Emily—George* (Salt Lake City: University of Utah Press, 1987), 29.

31. Ibid., 36.

32. Helen Z. Papanikolas relayed this information to me in conversation.

33. Lucile Richins, "A Social History of Sunnyside," quoted in Powell, "Land of Three Heritages," 16–17.

34. Wayne L. Balle, "'I Owe My Soul': An Architectural and Social History of Kenilworth, Utah," *Utah Historical Quarterly* 56 (Summer 1988): 255.

35. Quoted in Powell, "Land of Three Heritages," 14.

36. Cederlof, "The Peerless Coal Mines," 353.

37. Powell, *The Next Time We Strike*, 129, 132.

38. Ibid., 182–83.

39. See Powell, *The Next Time We Strike*, 141–51; Saline Hardee Fraser, "One Long Day that Went on Forever," *Utah Historical Quarterly* 48 (Fall 1980): 379–89; Janeen Arnold Costa, "A Struggle for Survival and Identity: Families in the Aftermath of the Castle Gate Mine Disaster," *Utah Historical Quarterly* 56 (Summer 1988): 279–92.

40. Floyd A. O'Neil, "Victims of Demand: The Vagaries of the Carbon County Coal Industry," in Notarianni, *Carbon County*, 34.

41. J. Eldon Dorman, "Reminiscences of a Coal Camp Doctor," in Notarianni, *Carbon County*, 48, 49.

42. Quoted in Powell, *The Next Time We Strike*, 178.

43. Peter S. Briggs and Brian Q. Cannon, *Life and Land*, 4, 9–12.

44. Personal conversation with J. Eldon Dorman, November 6, 1991.

45. Dorman, "Coal Camp Doctor," 46–47.

46. Ibid., 48.

47. Ibid., 52–54.

48. Ibid., 59–61.

49. Floyd A. O'Neil, "Victims of Demand," 27.

50. Edna Romano, ed., "Teancum Pratt, Founder of Helper," *Utah Historical Quarterly* 48 (Fall 1980): 330–31.

51. Ibid., 338.

52. Ibid., 360.

53. Ibid., 363.

54. Ibid., 365.

55. See Philip F. Notarianni, "Helper—The Making of a Gentile Town in Zion," in *Carbon County*, 153–70.

56. Helen Z. Papanikolas, "Women in the Mining Communities of Carbon County," in Notarianni, *Carbon County*, 85.

57. Ibid., 86.

58. Ibid.

59. Papanikolas, *Emily–George*, 10.

60. Helen Papanikolas, "Growing Up Greek in Helper, Utah," *Utah Historical Quarterly* 48 (Summer 1980): 254.

61. Papanikolas, *Emily-George*, 13, 14.

62. Papanikolas, "Growing Up Greek," 259.

63. Philip F. Notarianni, "Helper," 152–53.

CHAPTER 12

1. Rell G. Francis, *The Utah Photographs of George Edward Anderson* (Lincoln: University of Nebraska Press, 1979), ix–x.

2. Elma Otteson Collard, "Christian Otteson," in *Some Early Pioneers of Huntington, Utah, and Surrounding Area*, compiled by James Albert Jones (Privately published, 1980), 219.

3. Ibid., 222.

4. Ibid., 224.

5. E. G. Beckwith, *Report of Exploration of a Route for the Pacific Railroad, Near the 38th and 39th Parallels of Latitude, from the Mouth of the Kansas to Sevier River, in the Great Basin* (Washington, D.C.: A.O.P. Nicholson, Printer, 1855), 97.

6. Ibid., 73, 95.

7. Ibid., 66.

8. Dutton, *Geology of the High Plateaus*, 19.

9. G. H. Buek, "Thomas Moran," *The American Magazine* 75 (1913):32.

10. Wallace Stegner, *Mormon Country*, 45–46.

11. Sorensen, *Where Nothing Is Long Ago*, 114–15.

12. "For the Strength of the Hills," adapted by Edward L. Sloan from Felicia D. Hemans, "Hymn of the Vaudois Mountaineers," *Hymns of the Church of Jesus Christ of Latter-day Saints* (Salt Lake City: Church of Jesus Christ of Latter-day Saints, 1985), 35.

INDEX

Abbey, Edward, 153, 173, 175
Academy Mill Reservoir, 20
Acord, Felt, 179
Adams, Ansel, 151
Allen, H. Jennings, 152
Allen, Mildred, 152
Allred, Edner, 197
Allred, William J., 100
Alton, Utah, 58, 62, 202
Alunite Ridge, 65
Anasazi Indians, 2, 84, 143, 153, 161,
    163, 174, 177
Andersen, James P., 99
Anderson, August, 142
Anderson, George Edward, 11, 16, 61, 63,
    68, 69, 102, 134, 212, 219, 220, 230,
    231, 245–49, 252
Anderson, L. R., 17
Andrew Dairy Creek, 19
Andrus, James, 80
Angle, 63, 78
Annie Laurie Mine, 66–70
Antimony, Utah, 79
Antrei, Albert C. T., 12, 16, 19
Aquarius Plateau, 2, 9–10, 27, 28, 78–81,
    83, 139–48, 149, 156, 157, 161, 169, 170
Arches National Park, 37
Arizona Strip, 1, 29, 57, 84, 177–202
Arrington, Leonard J., 92
Arropine (Seignerouch), 95–96
Arropine, Jake, 97, 99
Asay Creek, 50
Ash Creek Canyon, 32, 52
Ashley, William H., 29
Autenquer (Black Hawk), 98–103
Awapa Plateau, 28, 38, 78, 81, 139

Bacon Rind Canyon, 20, 24
Bailey, Gail, 163

Bailey, Hyme, 167
Bailey, T. C., 80
Baker, George, 142
Baker, Henry, 142
Baker Ranch, 83
Barboglio, Jenny Causer, 243
Barboglio, Joseph, 242–43
Barlow, John Y., 197
Barney Top, 161
Baseball Spring, 20
Beaman, E. O., 178
Bear Canyon, 22
Bear Peak, 45, 49
Bear River, 29, 105
Bear Valley, 34, 38, 45
Beaver City, Utah, 41, 43–44
Beaver County, Utah, 44, 110
Beaver Creek, 66
Beaver Dam Wash, 87, 201
Beaver River, 45, 84, 110
Beaver Valley, 32
Beckwith, E. G., 37, 252
Behunin, Isaac, 110
Bench, The, 157
Bennion, Israel, 13
Bennion, Samuel O., 1
Bennion family, 13
Bennion Ridge, 20
Benson, E. T., 42
Benton, Thomas H., 38
Bicknell, Utah, 82, 140, 161
Biddlecome Hollow, 20
Big Flat, 45
Big Spring, 185, 186–87
Birdseye, 21
Black Box, 38
Black Canyon, 79
Black Hawk (Autenquer), 98–103, 125
Black Hawk, Utah, 230
Blackhawk formation, 207–8, 223

Black Hawk War, 49, 72, 75, 93, 97–103, 192, 247
Blanding, Utah, 82, 161
Bluebell Flat, 16
Bluebell Knoll, 140
Blue Cut, 206
Blue Cut Canal, 106, 107
Blue Lake, 27
Blues, The, 146, 155
Boardinghouse Canyon, 20, 223
Bonacci, Joe, 243
Book Cliffs, 37, 206, 210, 223, 230, 237, 249
Boulder, Utah, 136–49, 151, 168
Boulder Creek, 143, 146
Boulder Top, 139–40, 143, 146–47
Box Canyon, 45
Boyter, Alexander, 44
Brewerton, George D., 35–36, 94
Brian Head, 48, 50
Bridger, Jim, 36
Brinkerhoff, Willard, 143
Brooks, George R., 30
Brooks, Juanita, 53, 124
Brown, Charles, 132–33
Brown, James S., 110
Brown, Mary Ann Rowberry, 132–33
Brown Cliffs, 57
Bryce Canyon National Park, 2, 47, 50, 59, 79, 80–81, 114, 139, 145–46, 151–52
Buck Basin, 20
Buckhorn Flat, 74
Buckhorn Springs, 45–46
Bulger Canyon, 24
Bullfrog Marina, 148, 149
Bull Hollow, 20
Bullion Canyon, 65
Bullion City, 65
Bullock, Thomas, 109
Bundy, Abraham, 201
Bundy, Roy, 201
Bundyville, Arizona, 201–2
Burr Trail, 148–49, 170, 175
Burrville, Utah, 78

Cactus Flats, 201
Calf Creek, 138, 139, 145
California Gulch, 65
Canaan Cooperative Stock Company, 192
Canaan Spring, 192
Candland Mountain, 20

Cannonville, Utah, 146, 161
Canyon Range, 40
Capitol Reef National Park, 2, 78, 114, 145, 149
Carbon College (College of Eastern Utah), 240–41
Carbon County, Utah, 25, 203–44
Carbon High School, 204, 205
Carson, Christopher "Kit," 35–36
Carvalho, Solomon Nunes, 42–43, 46, 88–89, 104
Cascade Falls, 50
Castle Dale, Utah, 7, 14, 17, 37, 74, 106, 131, 133–34, 205, 250, 251, 254
Castle Gate, Utah, 206, 218, 219, 223–27, 230, 233, 234, 237, 238, 239
Castle Valley, 13, 14, 15, 18, 21, 24, 29, 30, 31, 32, 74, 131–35, 204–5, 224, 247, 252–55; pageant, 249–51
Castle Valley Ridge, 31
Cathedral Valley, 83
Cedar Breaks National Monument, 2, 47, 50
Cedar City, Utah, 46–48, 62, 88, 101, 150, 160, 208
Cedar Valley, 32, 34, 84
Cederlof, A. Philip, 206, 233
Central Pacific Railroad, 210
Central Pacific Railroad Survey, 37–38
Chalk Creek (Millard County), 41
Chalk Creek (Summit County), 208–9
Chicken Creek, 39, 41, 42; peace conference, 88–89, 104
Christensen, Hyrum, 18
Christiansen, Edith, 129
Christiansen, Parley, 17
Circle Cliffs, 139, 142, 148–49, 207
Circle Valley, 38, 64, 65
Circleville, Utah, 34, 64
Circleville massacre, 100
City Creek, 105
Civilian Conservation Corps, 22, 143–45, 167–68, 235
Clark, Orange, 32, 85–86
Clayton, William, 109
Clear Creek (Carbon County), 214, 219, 222–23, 224, 233, 238
Clear Creek Canyon (Sevier County), 31, 33, 38, 70
Clear Creek Canyon (Utah County), 22, 211
Cleveland, Utah, 15, 106, 205
Cleveland Reservoir, 22

272

Clipper Canal, 107
Coal Canyon, 20
Coal City, 230
Coal Creek Canyon, 46
Coal Hollow, 20
Coalville, Utah, 209
Coconino County, Arizona, 182
Coffee Pot Spring, 20
Collard, Robena, 247
College of Eastern Utah Prehistoric Museum, 7
Colorado City, Arizona, 55, 181, 182, 197–200
Colorado Plateau, 2, 147
Colorado River, 11, 29, 32, 57, 79, 87, 141, 148, 149, 151, 153, 177–81, 191, 193, 201, 207
Colton, 16, 213
Columbia, Utah, 206, 230, 239, 240
Conetah, Fred A., 93
Conference Flat, 157
Conmarrowap, 29–30
Connellsville, 209
Consumers, 206, 230, 234–37
Cope, Maurice, 152
Corn Creek, 89, 104
Cottonwood Creek (Emery County), 17, 26, 106–7, 131, 205
Cottonwood Creek (Sanpete County), 12, 16, 22, 24
Cottonwood Creek Consolidated Irrigation Company, 107
Cove Fort, 31, 40, 41–43
Cow Fork, 20
Cowboy Creek, 20
Crooked Creek Canyon, 22
Crystal Basin, 65
Curtis, Erastus, 106

Dairy Canyon, 19
Dairy Fork, 19, 21
Dairy Point, 19
Dallin, Cyrus, 253
Dame, William H., 46, 47
Daughters of Utah Pioneers, 110
Davis, Johnny, 163
Davis County, Utah, 113
Davis Gulch, 152
Death Hollow, 143, 170
Deer Creek, 146, 148
Dellenbaugh, Frederick S., 58, 62–63
Delta, Utah, 238
Demolli, Charles, 225, 226, 242

Dempsey, Jack, 230
Denver and Rio Grande Western Railway, 21, 30, 66, 74, 205, 210, 213, 223, 229, 242
Deseret, Utah, 37
Desert Lake, Utah, 15
Diamanti, John, 243
Diamanti, "Thitsa," 243
Diamond Fork, 28
Dirty Devil River, 140, 160
Dixie College, 240
Dixie National Forest, 50
Dixon, Maynard, 151
Dog Valley, 38
Dominguez-Escalante expedition, 28–29, 32, 86, 160, 177–78
Dorman, J. Eldon, 7, 234, 235–37
Dragerton, Utah, 238, 240
Dry Creek Canyon, 22
Dry Hollow, 145
Dry Valley, 30
Duchesne River, 14, 104
Duck Creek Spring, 50
Dutton, Clarence E., 9–10, 27, 31, 48–49, 51–52, 55–56, 64–65, 75–77, 80–81, 82–83, 139, 141, 147–49, 161, 184–86, 187, 190–91, 194–95, 252, 253
Dutton's Notch, 55

East Carbon City, 240
Eccles Canyon, 20, 223
Echo Cliffs, 177, 179, 181
Electric Lake, 20, 22, 24
Elk Meadows, 45
Ellison, Lincoln, 17, 19
Elsinore, Utah, 67, 68
Emerald Lake, 27
Emerson, Ralph Waldo, 153
Emery, Utah, 38, 106
Emery County, Utah, 7, 15, 106–7, 204, 205, 233, 238, 239, 245–55
Emett, James, 195, 197
Ephraim, Utah, 12, 13, 15, 24, 110, 125, 131; Ephraim raid, 99–100, 208, 238
Ephraim Canyon, 16–17, 19, 24, 99
Ephraim Creek, 17
Escalante, Silvestre Velez de, 40, 86, 160
Escalante, Utah, 66, 137, 141, 143, 145, 146, 149, 150–76
Escalante Canyons, 138, 139, 143, 145, 147–49, 154, 175
Escalante Mountain (Table Cliff), 161

Escalante River, 140, 145, 146, 152, 160, 162
Escalante Valley, 160

Fairview, Utah, 7, 12, 15, 22, 99, 102, 123, 209
Fairview Lakes, 23
Faulkner, J. W., 198
Fayette, Utah, 12
Ferron, Utah, 204
Ferron Creek, 13, 26, 205
Ferron Reservoir, 26
Fifty Mile Mountain (Kaiparowits Plateau), 150, 151, 161, 164, 176
Fillmore, Utah, 41, 92, 101
Finn Canyon, 20, 223
Fish Creek, 20, 22, 30, 210, 213
Fish Lake, 13, 35–36, 82–83
Fish Lake High Top, 82
Fish Lake Plateau, 27, 28, 32, 34, 35, 38, 70–71, 74, 75, 78, 81, 82–83, 141
Flagstaff Peak, 27
Flat Canyon, 22, 27
Ford Stuck, 157
Forsyth Reservoir, 83
Fort Cameron, 43–44
Fort Harmony, 52, 196
Fort Meeks, 178
Fort Omni, 72
Fort Sanford, 100
Fountain Green, Utah, 12, 15, 39, 59, 102, 132, 247
Four Mile Hill, 205
Fowles, John, 136–37
Francis, Rell G., 246–47
Frazer, Thomas, 44
Fredonia, Arizona, 1, 181, 182–83, 184, 185, 186, 197
Fremont, John C., 30, 35, 36, 37–38, 42, 87–88
Fremont, Utah, 38
Fremont Indians, 2, 84
Fremont River, 38, 81–83, 140, 145
Fruita, Utah, 114

Garfield County, Utah, 63, 148, 170, 175
Gates of Monroe, 69
Geary, Edward Long, 58–59
Gentry Mountain, 10, 20, 245–47
Gibbs, Josiah F., 65
Gilbert, G. K., 111–12
Gillette, David, 5
Given, John, 99

Given massacre, 99
Glen Canyon, 162, 175, 177
Glendale, Utah, 62
Glendale Bench, 59
Glenwood, Utah, 64, 133
Gold Gulch, 65
Gold Mountain, 66
Gooseberry Valley, 22, 23, 25; Gooseberry Project, 25
Gordon Creek, 230, 234, 236, 239–40, 241
Goshen, Utah, 241
Gosiute Indians, 93
Gottfredson, Peter, 104
Grand Canyon, 47, 51, 57, 90, 151, 179, 180, 181, 183, 184, 185, 189, 191, 200
Grand Canyon Cattle Company, 188–89, 194, 195, 197
Grand Staircase, 57
Grand Wash, 177, 181
Grange, Ray, Hole, 20
Grass Valley, 34, 38, 63, 78–79, 82, 104; "squaw fight," 100
Gravelly Ford, Battle of, 100–101
Gray Cliffs, 57, 58
Great Basin, 2, 28, 35, 38, 45, 80, 114, 207
Great Basin Experiment Station, 19
Great Salt Lake, 109, 111, 112
Great Western Canal, 107
Green River, 11, 29, 32, 37, 38, 57, 210, 252
Greens, The, 157
Greenwich, Utah, 78, 104
Grey, Zane, 181, 195, 196–97
Grizzly Gulch, 209
Grover, Utah, 139, 145, 146
Gulch, The, 148
Gunnison, John W., 37, 89, 252
Gunnison, Utah, 12, 39, 75
Gunnison Crossing, 210
Gunnison Plateau, 12, 28, 29, 39, 208
Gunnison Valley, 11, 27, 32

Half Way House, 225, 226
Hall, Sharlot, 181, 182, 186–88, 201
Hall's Creek, 149
Hamblin, Jacob, 140, 146, 177, 178, 182, 195
Hardscrabble Canyon, 242
Hardy, Thomas, 171
Harris, John Sterling, 120–21
Hatch, Utah, 63

Hawley, C. M., 43–44, 57
Haws, Henry, 143
Head, F. H., 101
Heaps Slide, 157
Heaton, Jonathan, 202
Heber Valley, 101
Heiner, 230
Hell's Back Bone, 143, 144, 156
Helper, Utah, 21, 203, 206, 225, 226–27, 229, 230, 233, 234, 239, 240, 241–44
Henningson Reservoir, 27
Henrieville, Utah, 146
Henry Mountains, 26, 83, 140, 148, 149, 157, 250, 252
Herring, Dean, 66–67
Hiawatha, Utah, 206, 230, 232, 233, 237, 240
Hicks, George, 53–54
Hildale, Utah, 55, 200
Hill, Newton, 66, 70
Hillsdale, 59, 241
Hinckley, Ira N., 41
Hite, William T., 99
Hobble Creek, 110
Hogan Pass, 38, 83
Holden, Utah, 28, 41, 102
Hole-in-the-Rock, 151, 162
Holmes, W. H., 55
Home Bench, 145
Honeymoon Trail, 58
Hopkins, Gerard Manley, 173
Horn Mountain, 207
Horne, Robert H., 7
Horse Canyon, 206, 238
Horse Heaven, 20
Horseshoe Bend, 157
Horseshoe Flat, 25
Horseshoe Mountain, 9, 25
House Rock Valley, 178, 181, 184, 194, 195
Howard, Mary W., 125
Howard, William, 18
Humphrey, J. W., 17, 19
Huntington, Utah, 15, 132, 203, 238, 248, 254–55
Huntington Canyon, 22, 26, 209, 247; The Forks, 27
Huntington-Cleveland Irrigation Co., 5
Huntington Creek, 205, 247, 254
Huntington Mammoth, 5–8, 10
Huntington Plant, Utah Power and Light Co., 20, 22
Huntington Reservoir, 7, 22

Hurricane, Utah, 198
Hurricane Bench, 106
Hurricane Canal, 106
Hurricane Cliffs, 46, 52, 54, 55, 106, 181, 201
Huxley, Aldous, 154
Hyde, Orson, 133

Indianola, 21, 123
Ivie Creek, 30, 31

Jackson, James, 180
Jackson, Richard H., 14, 36, 109
Jacob Lake, 184
Jacob's Pools, 178, 192
Jensen, A. W., 17, 18
Jericho Pool, 15
Jesperson, Soren, 99
Jewkes, Cal, 238–39
Joe's Valley, 11, 23, 26, 27
Joe's Valley Reservoir, 24
Johansen, Byron, 134
Johansen, Peter, 253–54
Johns Valley, 157
Johnson, Adolf, 180
Johnson, Benjamin Franklin, 59
Johnson, Elmer, 197
Johnson, Ezekiel, 59
Johnson, George Washington, 59
Johnson, Grace, 125
Johnson, Jacob, 107
Johnson, Joel Hills, 59
Johnson, Joseph Ellis, 59
Johnson, Julia Hills, 59
Johnson, Nick, 142
Johnson, Price, 197, 198
Johnson, Warren M., 180, 197
Johnson, William Derby, 59
Johnson Canyon, 58–59, 140, 196
Jones, "Mother" Mary, 226
Jordan Canyon, 24
Juab Valley, 39
Julius Flat Reservoir, 27
Junction, Utah, 64

Kaibab Indians, 202
Kaibab Plateau, 151, 181, 183–91, 192, 194, 195, 197, 201; Kaibab deer, 187–90, 191
Kaibabits Indians, 84
Kaiparowits Peak, 81, 146
Kaiparowits Plateau, 80, 139, 140, 161, 170

Kanab, Utah, 1, 44, 54, 57–59, 62, 118–20, 125, 140, 178, 182, 185, 188, 192, 194, 196, 197
Kanab Creek, 57, 59, 181, 182, 192, 202
Kanab Plateau, 181, 194
Kanarraville, Utah, 52
Kane, Elizabeth Wood, 39–42, 45–48, 52–53, 62, 92–93
Kane, Thomas L., 39
Kanosh (Pahvant chief), 89, 94, 104
Kanosh, Utah, 40, 41, 102
Kearns, William, 99
Kenilworth, Utah, 206, 229, 232, 238–39, 240, 242
Kenner, Beauregard, 17
Kimberly, Peter L., 66, 69
Kimberly, Utah, 66–70
King, John, 142
Kingston, Utah, 64, 241
Knight, Emerson, 153
Kodachrome Flat, 161
Kolob Canyons, 52
Kolob Terraces, 28, 54, 184
Koosharem, Utah, 78, 104
Koosharem Indians, 104
Koosharem Reservoir, 78
Kuhre, Hansine, 99–100
Kuhre, Martin, 99–100
Ku Klux Klan, 244
Kumoits Indians, 84
Kwiumpats Indians, 84

Lake Bonneville, 28
Lake Canyon, 24
Lake Flagstaff, 207
Lake Fork, 21
Lake Powell, 148, 157, 170, 175
Lange, Dorothea, 78, 79, 151, 165, 235–36
Larsen, Jens, 99
Larsen, Oluf Christian, 100
LaSal Mountains, 24, 32
Last Chance Ranch, 83
Latuda, 206, 230
Lawrence, Utah, 15, 61
LeBaron, Cleveland, 197
Lee, Emma Batchelder, 178, 180, 196
Lee, J. Bracken, 240
Lee, John D., 52, 177–80, 182, 192
Lee, Rachel Woolsey, 178
Lee's Backbone, 179–80
Lee's Ferry, 177–80, 181, 195, 196, 197
Levan, Utah, 38, 39, 41, 88, 159

Lever, W. H., 17
Lime Kiln Flat, 157
Little Clear Creek, 21
Little Colorado River, 58, 77
Little Creek Peak, 45, 49
Little Pine Canyon, 22
Little Salt Lake Valley, 32, 36, 45–48, 63
Loa, Utah, 81–82, 140
Loggers Fork, 20
Lonely Dell, 178–79, 180, 196–97
Lone Peak, 25
Long Canyon, 148
Long Valley, 58, 59–62
Long Valley Divide, 29, 62
Los Angeles and Salt Lake Railroad, 47
Lost Creek, 33
Lowry, John, 97–98, 99
Lowry, Mary, 125
Ludvigsen, Peter, 99
Lund, Anthon H., 107
Lunt, Henry, 42, 88, 150
Luoma family, 220, 221
Lyman, Amasa M., 143

Madsen, David, 7
Madsen, John K., 15
Main Canyon, 157
Mammoth Canal, 107
Mammoth Creek, 50
Mammoth Reservoir, 25
Mann, Walter G., 189, 190
Manti, Utah, 11, 12, 16, 17, 18, 88, 94–96, 97–98, 115–17, 125, 131, 134
Manti Co-op, 18
Manti Creek, 17, 24, 26
Manti-LaSal National Forest, 5, 17, 24
Marble Canyon, 177, 179, 181
Marble Canyon Bridge, 198
Markagunt Plateau, 2, 28, 29, 33, 34, 45, 46, 47, 48–52, 54–56, 57, 59, 62, 63, 80
Marysvale, Utah, 21, 65–66, 164
Marysvale Canyon, 31, 65, 70
Mathis, Reed, 193–94
Maxwell, William, 192
Mayfield, Utah, 17
McCandless, Fawn Geary, 237
McCandless, Ray, 237
McDermid, Claude, 237
McElprang, Pete, Canyon, 20
McHaddon Flat, 20
McIntyre, Robert, 192
Meetinghouse Canyon, 20

276

Mill Fork, 20
Miller, Ruben G., 107
Miller's Flat, 20, 23
Millsite Reservoir, 26
Moab, Utah, 32
Moapa Indians, 84
Moccasin, Arizona, 202
Moccasin Springs, 58, 60, 192
Mohave County, Arizona, 182, 198
Mohrland, 230, 233
Mojave Desert, 34
Monroe, Utah, 64, 247
Monroe Canyon, 70
Monroe Peak, 64
Monument Valley, 151
Moran, Peter, 209
Moran, Thomas, 252
Morgan, Dale L., 29
Mormon Battalion, 40
Mormon Corridor, 36, 38, 39–56, 62, 89, 110
Moroni, Utah, 12
Mountain dairies, 19–20, 49
Mountain Meadows, 34, 35, 180; Mountain Meadows Massacre, 43–44, 57, 177
Mount Baldy, 42
Mount Belnap, 42, 45
Mount Carmel, 59, 60
Mount Delano, 42, 45
Mount Dutton, 64
Mount Ellen, 149, 250
Mount Hilgard, 82, 83
Mount Logan, 191, 192
Mount Marvine, 82, 83
Mount Nebo, 10, 28, 29, 39, 40, 99
Mount Pennel, 149
Mount Pleasant, Utah, 12, 15, 17, 88, 99, 131
Mount Pleasant Rambouillet Farm, 15
Mount Pleasant United Order, 14
Mount Terrel, 82
Mount Trumbull, 181, 191, 192, 201
Mud Creek, 212, 213, 223
Muddy Creek, 26, 38, 106, 205
Muddy River, 84, 87, 162
Mukuntuweap, 55
Muley Twist Canyon, 149
Murdock Academy, 44
Museum of the San Rafael, 7
Musinea Peak, 27, 71
Mutual, 230

Naegle, John C., 194

Nail Canyon, 185, 186, 187
National, 230, 236
National Miners Union, 234, 235
Nauvoo Legion, 102–3
Navajo Indians, 93, 98, 101, 151, 153, 154, 178, 188, 191
Navajo Lake, 50
Navajo Mountain, 151, 157
Naylor, James, 218
Neilsen, Lauritz, 16–17
Nelson, John, 209
Nelson, Lowry, 26, 160, 162, 166–68, 169–70, 176, 204
Nelson Mountain, 20
Nephi, Utah, 39, 41, 238
New Harmony, Utah, 52
Nichols, John, 153, 155
Nielson, John, 5
Nine Mile Canyon, 136, 193
Nixon Spring, 201
Northern Shoshoni (Snake) Indians, 86, 89, 93, 94
North Tent Peak, 25
Nutter, Preston, 192–94

Oak Creek (Garfield County), 149
Oak Creek (Sanpete County), 22, 24, 25
Oak Spring Bench, 242
Ogden, Utah, 210, 221
Old Folks Flat, 20
Old Spanish Trail, 32, 33–36, 37, 38, 45, 63, 74, 87–88, 162, 205, 250
Orangeville, Utah, 17, 106–7, 131, 250, 251
Orderville, Utah, 59–62; Orderville United Order, 59–62, 192, 194, 202
Orton, 63
Osiris, 79
Otter Creek, 78, 82
Otter Creek Reservoir, 78
Otteson, Christian, 10, 245–49, 252, 254
Otteson, Joseph, 247
Otteson, Sarah, 247–49
Owens, James T., 187, 188

Pace, Josephine, 67–68
Pace, William B., 101
Packard, Milan, 209–10
Packer, Alferd, 193
Paguits Indians, 84
Pahvant Indians, 37, 84, 86, 89, 92, 94, 102, 104
Pahvant Plateau, 28, 31, 40, 42, 70

Pahvant Valley, 36, 40–41
Paiute Indians, 49, 84–104, 188, 191–92
Paiute Trail, 45
Pakoon, 181
Palmer, William Jackson, 210
Palmer, William Rees, 74, 93
Panguitch, Utah, 29, 63, 145, 160, 241
Panguitch Hayfield, 64
Panguitch Lake, 49–50, 51, 84
Papanikolas, Helen Z., 227–29, 243–44
Paragonah, Utah, 34, 46, 159
Paria Plateau, 181, 197
Paria River, 29, 79, 177, 178, 196
Paria Valley, 80–81, 140, 146, 155, 161
Parker, Robert LeRoy ("Butch Cassidy"),
    64, 238
Parker Mountain, 78
Parkman, Samuel, 29
Parmley, David, 235
Parmley, T. J., 219
Paroosits Indians, 84
Parowan, Utah, 38, 42, 46–48, 88, 102
Parunuweap, 55
Paunsagunt Plateau, 2, 28, 57, 58, 62, 64,
    78–81, 114, 141, 145, 177
Payson, Utah, 101
Peerless, 206, 230, 233
Pessetto, Caterina, 225
Pessetto, Paul, 225
Petersen, Elizabeth, 99
Peterson, Canute, 125
Peterson, Sarah Ann, 125–26
Phelps, W. W., 91
Philadelphia Flat, 27
Pigeon Creek, 39
Pine Creek (Garfield County), 140, 143
Pine Creek (Sanpete County), 110
Pine Valley Mountain, 50, 52
Pines, The, 157
Pink Cliffs, 50, 57, 64, 80–81, 146, 152
Pintura, 36, 52
Pioche, Nevada, 40, 44
Pipe Spring, 1, 192, 194–95, 202
Piute County, Utah, 64, 66
Pleasant Creek, 149
Pleasant Valley, 11, 21, 22, 30, 31,
    209–23, 239
Pleasant Valley Coal Company, 209–23
Plummer, A. Perry, 19
Point Lookout, 146
Pole Canyon, 20
Potato Valley, 160, 161, 162
Potter, Albert, 18

Potter's Canyon, 24
Powell, John Wesley, 14, 49, 57, 58, 80,
    90–91, 97, 109–10, 111, 140, 161,
    178, 181, 186, 191
Powerhouse Ridge, 20
Pratt, Addison, 41
Pratt, Anna Mead, 241
Pratt, Parley P., 36, 41, 109, 241
Pratt, Sarah Ewell, 241–42
Pratt, Teancum, 241–42
Pratt brothers, 1
Prattville, 241
Price, John, 208
Price, Utah, 5, 31, 38, 67, 203–6, 223,
    226–27, 228, 229, 230, 234, 237, 239,
    240–41, 254
Price Canyon, 21, 31, 206, 210, 223, 230,
    239
Price River, 17, 25, 26, 30, 37, 204–5,
    225, 241
Probert, William, 101
Proctor, 163
Provo, Utah, 221, 230
Provo River, 105
Puffer Lake, 45
Pugh, Thomas, 219
Pyle, Howard, 198

Rabbit Valley, 38, 78, 81–83, 139, 141
Rainbow Bridge, 151, 157
Rains, 206, 230
Red Canyon, 145
Red Creek, 34, 46
Red Gate, 82
Reeder Canyon, 24
Rees, John, 208
Revenue Gulch, 65
Reynolds, "Killarney," 243
Reynolds, R. V. R., 17
Richfield, Utah, 67, 71, 72–74, 78, 142,
    241
Richins, Lucile, 231–32
Rider, Rowland W., 1, 182, 195, 197
Rilda Canyon, 19
Robbers Roost, 136
Rock Canyon, 31
Rockville, Utah, 54, 55
Roger Peak, 143
Rolapp (Royal), 206, 222, 230, 237, 239
Rolfson Canyon, 24
Roosevelt, Theodore, 17, 188
Roundy, Napoleon Bonaparte, 167
Roundy, William, 118–20

Rowley Flats, 254
Ruess, Everett, 150–55, 157, 159, 165, 172
Ruess, Waldo, 151, 153
Rusho, W. L., 153
Ruskin, John, 252

Saddle Canyon, 189
Saint George, Utah, 40, 44, 47, 53–54, 58, 80, 124; Militia, 115, 140, 146, 160, 162, 191, 192, 198, 200, 201
Salina, Utah, 17, 21, 40, 74, 75, 78, 100, 238
Salina Creek, 11, 27, 32, 33, 74
Salina Pass, 27, 31, 32, 37, 38, 99, 210
Salt Creek Canyon, 39
Salt Lake City, Utah, 6, 20, 40, 42, 62, 88, 197, 210, 221, 227, 241, 242
Salt Lake Hardware Company, 70
Salt Lake Valley, 14, 29, 36, 94, 105, 109, 223
Sampson, Arthur W., 19
Sandbergs Hill, 254
Sand Creek, 143
San Francisco Mountains, 43
San Juan River, 162
Sanpete County, Utah, 7, 14, 16–17, 24, 96, 123–35, 247; dialect stories, 127–29; nicknames, 126–27
Sanpete Valley, 12–13, 14–15, 17, 18, 21, 23, 25, 36, 39, 88, 94–96, 102, 110, 113, 115, 123, 141, 175, 208, 209, 224, 250
Sanpitch Indians, 84, 86–87, 94–96, 104
Sanpitch River, 11, 12, 22
San Rafael River, 14, 25, 38
San Rafael Swell, 26, 31, 32, 37, 38, 114, 148, 204, 207, 210, 249–50, 254
Santa Clara, Utah, 196
Santa Clara River, 84, 87, 191
Santaquin, Utah, 241
Saunders, B. F., 197
Savage, C. R., 95
Sawmill Canyon, 20
Scad Valley, 23
Scanlon, Lawrence, 221
Scanlon's Ferry, 193
Schow, James, 166
Schow, Mike, 163
Scipio, Utah, 40, 41, 102; Scipio raid, 100–101, 159
Scofield, C. U., 210
Scofield, Utah, 205, 211–12, 214, 218, 221, 222, 223, 225, 238, 242

Scofield Reservoir, 22, 24, 212
Seegmiller, Dan, 118–20
Seeley Creek, 20
Seely, Hanna Olsson, 131–32
Seely, John H., 15
Seely, Montell, 107, 251
Seely, Orange, 13–14, 131
Seely, Justus Wellington, Jr., 13–14, 251
Seely Creek, 23
Seely family, 14
Seignerouch (Arropine), 95–96
Sevenmile Valley, 82
Sevier County, Utah, 66, 114
Sevier Fault, 64
Sevier Plateau, 28, 63–65, 69, 70, 77–79, 140, 141, 145
Sevier River, 11, 12, 29, 37, 38, 40, 50, 58, 62, 63, 65, 70, 100, 101, 121, 133; East Fork, 34, 64, 78–80, 139, 157
Sevier Stake Tabernacle, 71, 72–74
Sevier Valley, 13, 21, 27, 34, 36, 70–74, 85, 142, 247
Sheep Flat, 20
Sherman, Alfred, 164–65
Shingle Creek, 20
Shivwits Indians, 84, 90–91, 95, 191–92
Shivwits Plateau, 181, 191
Short Creek, Arizona, 58, 192, 197–200
Short Creek Towers, 199
Sigurd, Utah, 70, 78
Silver Creek, 22
Silver Reef, 49, 61
Simpers, Tom, 13
Singleton Creek, 20
Skliris, Leonidas G., 227
Skougaard, Charles, 67
Skougaard, Niels M., 72
Skutumpah, 58, 140, 177, 196
Skyline Drive, 22–27
Slab Pile Spring, 20
Smith, George A., 53, 65, 150
Smith, Gibbs, 153
Smith, Jedediah S., 29–32, 33, 38, 86–87
Smith, John Henry, 107
Smith, "Pegleg," 34
Smithsonian Butte, 55
Smithsonian Institution, 7, 247
Smoot, Reed, 103
Snake Range, 24
Snow, Lorenzo, 73
Snow College, 240
Soda Gulch, 151, 163
Soldier Creek, 11, 21, 22, 30, 209

Soldier Summit, 21, 29, 30, 74, 205, 210, 242
Sorensen, Virginia, 115–20, 129–31, 253
Sorenson, Jens, 99
Sorenson, Soren, 99
Southern Utah Equitable, 63
Southern Utah Wilderness Alliance, 171
South Tent Peak, 25
Southern Exploring Expedition, 36
Southern Utah University, 47
Sowiette, 94
Spanish Fork Canyon, 11, 21, 28, 29, 209
Spanish Valley, 177
Spencer, Carling, 197, 198
Spring Canyon, 206, 230, 234, 237, 238, 239, 242
Spring City, Utah, 12, 25, 88, 107, 131, 133
Springdale, Utah, 54
Spring Glen, Utah, 206, 241
Spring Lake, 102, 241
Springville, Utah, 93, 110, 209, 210, 230
Staker Canyon, 24
Standardville, 206, 230, 232
Star Point, 20; Star Point sandstone, 207–8
Starr Ditch, 106
Steamboat Mountain, 206
Steep Creek, 146
Stegner, Wallace, 8, 28, 49, 60–62, 114–15, 153, 185, 197, 198, 253
Storrs, 206, 230
Straight Cliffs, 151, 157
Strawberry River, 103
Strawberry Valley, 28
Stump Flat, 20
Sulphurdale, 43
Sunnyside, Utah, 206, 219, 223, 224, 225, 230, 231, 233, 237, 238
Surprise Gulch, 65
Swasey family, 13
Swasey Ridge, 20
Sweat Canyon, 20
Sweets, 206, 230, 236–37
Sweetwater Canyon, 157

Tabby, 94, 208
Table Cliff, 81, 139, 140, 146, 150, 155, 157, 161
Tavaputs Plateau, 20, 21, 23, 193, 204, 229
Taylor, Abram, 209
Taylor, Maria, 102

Teasdale, Utah, 82
Terrace Plateaus, 57, 181
Thistle, Utah, 17, 21
Thistle Creek, 11, 21, 22
Thistle landslide, 21
Thistle Valley, 96, 99, 123
Thompson, Almon H., 140–41, 142, 146, 160
Thompson, James, 68
Thompson Springs, 193
Thomson, Woodruff, 127–29
Thoreau, Henry David, 154
Thorny Pasture, 161
Thousand Lake Plateau, 2, 28, 81, 82–83, 139, 148
Tie Fork, 20
Tilton, Ed, 67
Tilton, Fred, 67, 70
Tintic Valley, 15
Tonoquints Indians, 84
Tooele, Utah, 120–21
Tooth, James, 98
Toquerville, Utah, 194
Toroweap, 181
Torrey, Utah, 82, 145
Trail Canyon, 20
Tropic, Utah, 80, 146, 152, 154, 155
Trough Springs Ridge, 22, 209
Tucker, 21–22, 30, 209, 210–11
Tumpanawach Indians, 84, 86, 87, 89, 94
Tushar Plateau, 27, 28, 31, 42–43, 45, 63–70, 140, 141
Twelve Mile Canyon, 26, 27
Twelve Mile Creek, 96, 99
Twin Creek Canyon, 24
Twin Peaks, 25
Twin Trees, 157

Uinkaret Plateau, 181, 191
Uinkarets Indians, 84, 90–91, 191, 192
Uinta Basin, 28, 103–4
Uintah Indians, 103–4
Uintah Reservation, 101, 102, 103–4
Uinta Range, 207
U.M. Valley, 82
Uncompahgre Indians, 103
Ungerman, Henning Olsen, 133
Ungerman, Leon, 237
Ungerman, Minnie Acord, 133–34
Ungerman, Ole Louis, 133
Union Pacific Railroad, 47, 189, 209, 210
United Effort Plan, 198, 200

United Mine Workers of America, 225–27, 234
United Order, 59–62, 241
United States Biological Survey, 189–90
United States Bureau of Land Management, 5, 175
United States Department of Agriculture, 12–13
United States Farm Security Administration, 79, 235
United States Forest Service, 5, 16, 183
United States Fuel Company, 232
United States General Land Office, 15
United States Works Progress Administration, 169
University of Utah, 7
Unkakaniguts Indians, 191, 192
Upper Valley, 146, 150, 155
Utah and Pleasant Valley Railroad, 22, 209–10
Utah Fish and Game Commission, 50
Utah Fuel Company, 214, 223
Utah Industrial League, 233
Utah Lake, 11, 36, 84
Utah Museum of Natural History, 7
Utah National Guard, 225, 235
Utah Parks Company, 47
Utah Southern Railroad, 209
Utah State Archaeological Society, Castle Valley Chapter, 6
Utah State Industrial Commission, 232
Utah Valley, 28, 29, 88, 101, 102, 209, 241
Utah War, 40
Ute Ford, 177
Ute Indians, 84–104

Van Nostrand, James, 12
Veater, Clark, 163
Vermillion, Utah, 78
Vermillion Cliffs, 54–55, 57, 58, 60, 181, 183, 191, 192, 202
Virgin, Utah, 54
Virgin River, 29, 32, 35, 50, 58, 59, 62, 106, 115
Virgin River Valley, 33, 35, 36, 51, 53–56, 60, 84, 115, 124, 192
Vuksinick, Louis, 233
Vuksinick, Zelpha, 233

Wagstaff, Isaac, 63
Wahweap, 157
Wakara ("Chief Walker"), 34, 42–43, 87–89, 94–95, 125

Wales, Utah, 12, 247
Walker War, 42–43, 88
Ward, Barney, 99
Wasatch Front, 14, 20, 25, 94, 101, 103, 208, 209
Wasatch Line, 28
Wasatch Plateau, 5–27, 28, 30, 31, 32, 71, 74, 98, 99, 101, 131, 132, 148, 203–44, 245, 247, 249, 252, 253–54
Wasatch Range, 10, 23, 28, 109
Washboard Flat, 205
Washington, Utah, 54, 60
Waterpocket Fold, 2, 83, 139, 146–49, 157
Wattis, 206, 230, 237
Watts, A. C., 215–16
Wayne Stake Tabernacle, 82
Weber College, 240
Weber River, 105
Weeminuche Indians, 93
Wellington, Utah, 38
Wells, Daniel H., 42
West Desert, 40, 47
Whipple, Maurine, 115, 124, 201–2
White Cliffs, 57
White River, 30
White River Indians, 103
Whitman, Walt, 154
Whitmore, James M., 192
Whitmore family, 13
Whitmore Ranch, 225
Wide Hollow, 143, 146
Widtsoe, John A., 79
Widtsoe, Utah, 78, 79, 157
Wilcock, Edward, 164
Wilcox, Hyrum, 226
Wild Cattle Hollow, 20
Wild Horse Ridge, 20
Williams, Bill, 34
Williams, David, 17, 213
Willow Creek, 238
Wilson, A. G., 99
Wilson, John, 61, 218
Winkler, Albert, 100
Winsor, Anson P., 192
Winsor Cattle Co., 1
Winter Quarters, Utah, 209–10, 212–22, 224, 225, 242; mine disaster, 217–22
Winter Quarters Ridge, 20
Wolfskill, William, 32–33, 85–86, 90
Woodruff, Wilford, 42, 109, 129
Woodward, Nuck, Canyon, 19
Woolley, E. D., 1

Woolley, Franklin B., 140, 146–47
Woolsey, Nethella Griffin, 66, 162, 163, 164, 167, 169

Yogo Creek, 33
Young, Brigham, 12, 36, 41, 42–43, 48, 77, 88–89, 92–93, 94, 96, 97, 101, 192, 208, 250

Young, John W., 1
Young, Joseph A., 72
Young, Sheldon, 41
Yount, George C., 32–33, 85–86
Yuba Reservoir, 29, 40

Zion National Park, 2, 28, 47, 52, 54–56, 151